Floating

Floating

A LIFE REGAINED

Joe Minihane

Overlook Duckworth
New York • London

First published in hardcover in the United States and the
United Kingdom by Overlook Duckworth in 2017

LONDON
30 Calvin Street, London E1 6NW
T: 020 7490 7300
E: info@duckworth-publishers.co.uk
www.ducknet.co.uk
For bulk and special sales please contact sales@duckworth-publishers.co.uk

NEW YORK
141 Wooster Street
New York, NY 10012
www.overlookpress.com
For bulk and special sales please contact sales@overlookny.com

Cataloguing-in-Publication Data is available from the Library of Congress

A catalogue record for this book is available from the British Library

Text design and typesetting by Tetragon, London

Manufactured in the United States of America

US ISBN: 978-1-4683-1492-2
UK ISBN: 978-0-7156-5180-3

1 3 5 7 9 10 8 6 4 2

For Keeley

PROLOGUE

The blinds were not doing their job. A shaft of sunlight breached the wooden slats as I stirred and fumbled around on the bedside table for my watch: 4.12 a.m. I lifted myself onto my left elbow, took a swig of stale water from the glass I'd left out the previous evening, and sighed.

Keeley, my wife, was sound asleep next to me. Her breath caught in her throat with a rhythmic click, her arms raised above her head the way she always slept. Her dark brown hair spread out across the pillow.

I moved carefully so as not to wake her, pushed my pillows back onto the headrest and sat upright. Through the break in the blinds I could see a bright blue sky emerging. It was midsummer, almost a year since I had quit my job as a journalist to go freelance, and my mind was full to bursting with worry.

Thoughts zipped across my brain like plane contrails. Every time I tried to follow one I would lose it as another hove into view. I would chase that one and then the next one. My mind could not settle. I had been awake all of five minutes and already I could not stop this swell of anxiety from lifting me up and taking me out into the depths with it.

Work was what made me most anxious. What was I really doing? In the past month I had written 'news' articles about the chipset of an unreleased smartphone and covered the launch of a new Bluetooth speaker. To my mind, everything I had set out to do when I had decided to become a journalist at the age of nineteen was gone. I had failed to amount to anything as a music writer, made a fool of myself while trying to learn to drive when working for a major motoring magazine and wound up presenting corporate videos from big brands to pay the bills.

Where was the glamour, the excitement, the buzz I had always wanted from working in London? What had happened to my dreams? I was struggling to equate the need to make money with what I was doing in order to get it. I felt as if I needed to grow up and be more mature, but just thinking about it brought me down.

To compound it all, the regular writing I had been doing on the latest technology trends for a friend's website had ended. Budgets had been slashed. I looked down at Keeley. She always believed in me and told me how well I was doing. But despite the fact that I loved her, I couldn't agree. I had never wanted to write about technology. But it had always paid OK, and now I worked for myself I had to find cash somehow. I had learnt on short work placements, and then over a series of full-time roles, that I hated the confines of the office. The rules. The politics. The clock-watching. But with this regular source of income gone, would I have to go back? How would I cover the rent otherwise? Would I have enough money to still go out, to go on holiday? How could we ever save to buy a house or have enough money to bring up kids in the future? Were these things I could even give her?

Keeley worked full time as a journalist. We would be OK. But I felt a strong sense of responsibility towards her to make everything right. To be in control. To show her I could provide. To make life predictable. That way, I believed, worry would stop and life would begin.

She had never asked this of me. But I worried all of the time about it. I wanted to make sure that everything was easy for her, for us. She was loving, warm, caring, supportive, and had always been there since we had got together at the end of our time together at journalism college.

I knew I was being overly harsh on myself, that my thoughts were needlessly cruel, but still I chased them, one after another, after another. Why was I not as successful as the people I used to work with? Success to me was working for big publications, going on glamorous assignments, interviewing my favourite bands; not having to churn out copy about phones, games consoles and speakers, or doing 'advertorials' to make ends meet. I believed, misguidedly it turned out, that 'successful' people didn't need to indulge in the everyday, the things that help pay the bills.

Why had I not done what I always said I would do and become a travel writer, follow in the footsteps of my literary heroes like Paul Theroux, seeing new places, meeting new people, learning new things and writing about them for a voracious readership? Could I ever do this? Surely not. I felt I had become trapped in a professional rut – failed to live up to the lofty expectations that I had set for myself.

I could never tell anyone this. It felt easier to lie in the dawn light and allow my mind to crank through the gears. I wasn't sure if Keeley would understand, but I didn't know why I felt like that. She was the best thing that had ever happened to me. A vivacious, life-affirming presence whose calm assurance and beautiful, glittering blue eyes made my stomach flip whenever I thought about her.

I felt guilty for not telling her how anxious I was and how, when she went to work every day, I felt an enormous sense of guilt for having all of this time on my hands to chase editors, to come up with killer story ideas, to be the person I always thought I could be, when instead all I would do was sit on the sofa and feel low. I felt ashamed of the whole sorry mess.

I knew where this guilt and shame came from. My parents had never made me feel like this, but fourteen years of being taught at Catholic schools had instilled in me the sense that I should feel bad whenever I wasn't doing something constructive or productive with my time. That to me meant working, or pushing towards a goal. Leisure and downtime were to be frowned upon as a waste of precious minutes, hours, days. This feeling had proved useful when I had first gone freelance, pushing me on to work harder for longer. But now I just felt guilty for feeling that I hadn't done a good enough job of striking out on my own. My work felt meaningless, and because I had made work my biggest focus, it felt like life had lost meaning too. I was realising, slowly, that all this worrying had made me depressed.

But most of all I felt that this anxiety, this burgeoning depression, was nothing but narcissism. I needed to simply buck up my ideas and knuckle down, I thought. People like me don't feel like this, I told myself. Not people who've had a happy childhood with loving parents. Not people who have strong, loving relationships. That thought played over and over in my mind like a mantra. It made me feel like more of a failure, yes, but I thought that by repeating it, I would remind myself of all the good things in my life, which would make me feel better. It didn't. I knew, deep down, I needed to tell Keeley how low I felt, but I didn't want to disappoint her. I was too embarrassed. I was aware that she knew that something wasn't right, but I knew she didn't know the full extent of my despair.

I looked over at her. She was still sound asleep. I rolled back over and looked at my watch: 5.03 a.m. I closed my eyes, followed the contrails of my mind and tried to get some sleep. I needed help, but I wasn't sure how to ask for it or what it would even look like if I did.

A tadpole dashed over my feet as I lowered them gingerly into the water. The first step of the metal ladder was cold, the green murk of Hampstead mixed pond below. I stood stock still and held on to the railings, staring out to the far-off boundary rope and the causeway beyond. Shaggy dogs shook themselves dry, while coots and moorhens scuffled in the undergrowth. Far below, I imagined a pike hiding in the depths, waiting for its moment to strike.

I looked down. There was now a swarm of tadpoles crowding around my toes. I stifled a nervous giggle and dropped my feet lower, one step at a time, before they were groping for metal and I could go no further. With that, I pushed off and felt the cold wrap itself around my chest, my arms, my legs.

I fell in love with wild swimming over one glorious summer in 2010. I swapped the strictures of the indoor pool for open water on a sticky

London weekend, the kind where the city forgets how to behave itself and people wander around as if every street corner is a beach. At her suggestion, Keeley and I took an overheated Tube north to Belsize Park and spilled out onto Hampstead Heath with the rest of the hordes who had come to cool off in its ponds' deep waters. We had always wanted to come here, and with the weather as it was, it seemed like the ideal way to spend the day.

This was my first time swimming outside in anything other than the sea, and as I swam from the steps towards the nearest tethered life ring, I felt buoyed up by the green water, any concerns about what swam beneath lost in a summer reverie. Teenagers screamed and shouted from the grass verge where they lay stretched out on towels, sunbathing and preening as if their lives depended on it.

I felt the cold keenly but kicked on to the far rope, eighty metres away from the safety of the concrete jetty, grasping hold and letting my legs sink and take a rest. I was gripped by an endorphin rush as I closed my eyes, yellows and reds throbbing as the sun's rays hit my eyelids. As I swam back, my strong stroke fast becoming something akin to a doggy paddle, I realised that this was something I wanted to do again and again. Swimming in the local pool had helped me get fit, but outdoor swimming could offer something more – a mental and emotional buzz to match the sweet ache of limbs.

In the weeks that followed, as summer stretched into autumn, I returned to Hampstead regularly. I came on wet days as well as dry, nosing through the flotsam and shrugging off the brush of dead leaves and errant weeds while the rain popped off the surface.

I would swim a serviceable if basic breaststroke, my head out and my neck snapped back so that I could see what was happening around me. This was partly through fear of what lay beneath in the deep green murk of the pond, and partly out of necessity – as my front crawl wasn't really up to much.

Having your head up and out has its advantages, though, even if it can leave you with a sharp neck ache. It gives you time to enjoy what's around you – the wildlife, the shouts of the people on the banks, the scorching rays of late summer sun – and for me it adds to the meditative aspect of wild swimming: it strips everything back to its essence and allows me to just be in the water at that moment, like a duck pottering along the surface. Everything else melts away and becomes irrelevant.

I swam further and for longer every time, relishing the fact that I could lose myself in the moment, my body forced to focus on simply staying alive, my mind going quiet.

More than that: the simplicity of it all eased the anxiety which was causing me to wake at night, following the contrails of my mind as I turned over worries about my work, money and life. The water soothed this worry like nothing else.

When I first allowed Hampstead's waters to envelop me, I was the lowest I had been in my life. It was not long after that sleepless early dawn, and things felt difficult and at times hopeless. I felt ashamed that I felt like this and kept things bottled up. I didn't tell Keeley. I didn't tell family. I didn't tell my friends.

Days would pass without my getting further than the newsagent, trawling the same web pages and social networks over and over for a sense of purpose. I was lost, lonely and in desperate need of help. Getting into the water, giving myself up to the pond's buoyant green depths, pushed these feelings away. When I was in the water, there was no worry. My only concerns lay in keeping my arms moving and my legs kicking. There was a sense of boundless possibility, a lightening and easing of myself which I no longer felt on dry land. I wasn't in sole control of my situation, the water was, and I found such thoughts immensely satisfying.

I could date the swell of anxiety I was struggling with almost to the day. When I was a postgraduate student, studying journalism and readying myself for the brave, terrifying world of career and adult life I made a pact with myself. By the time I was twenty-seven, I would be a freelance journalist. I would be my own boss, I would answer only to myself and my life would be perfect.

I achieved my goal six months after my twenty-seventh birthday, after five years of writing for magazines and websites about topics as diverse as poker, cars and technology, none of which held any particular appeal for me. On my first day working for myself I started work at ten in the morning and was in the pub by two. I thought that I had gamed the system, cheated my way out of a day-to-day existence of which I had grown weary. I looked at myself as a happy retiree, forty years ahead of schedule.

What I soon discovered was that I derived all my self-worth and my self-esteem from my work. I didn't like the work I had to do to get paid. At first, hacking out news stories and writing puff pieces about everything from car adverts to an Asian tech company's latest 3D telly didn't matter, because I was my own boss and had time to do something new and exciting, whatever that was. But rather than seizing the opportunity to do something for myself, to take my career and my life in new and interesting directions, I froze. The boundaries between work and home had blurred to the point where I couldn't separate them any more. I wanted to work for myself, but I didn't know what I wanted to do beyond journalism. I'd never given it any thought.

My anxiety manifested itself as inertia. And inertia came through comparison. Comparison with peers, comparison with journalists, editors and writers that I believed I could never hope to be as good as. Social media is both your best friend and your worst enemy when you work from home and spend most of your time alone. I began to trawl news feeds and read articles I wished I had written and look at people I knew professionally on Facebook and Twitter with an endless sense of envy, coupled with the feeling that I could never, ever measure up.

I tried to fall back on an old mantra from Jack Kerouac's *The Dharma Bums*, my favourite book as a teenager. 'Comparisons are odious,' was Japhy Ryder's wise line whenever Ray Smith, *The Dharma Bums'* Kerouac conduit, cast an envious eye over someone else's life. I played that line over and over in my head while I read another article and dreamt of another life where I was 'a success', where I had a more 'glamorous' job, wrote about things like travel and music rather than smartphones and games consoles. Yet still I allowed jealousy and worry to frighten me away from making my life better. I became depressed and fearful.

Soon this professional inertia spread to my day-to-day life. I would rise early and see Keeley off to work, before quickly completing the regular daily writing jobs I had taken to cover the rent and pay the bills. News about smartphone tariffs. List features about mobile apps. I told myself that, if I wanted to be a serious journalist it was time to read, develop ideas and write. To start something. Instead, I sat on the sofa and stared out at London stretching in front of me from the fifth-floor window of our flat, afraid to go outside in case I got caught bunking off – by whom I wasn't sure. I had made myself anxious thinking about what others thought of me, as if they were judging me for making my own schedule and working to my own beat. I knew it was preposterous to think like that, but I did it anyway. Worrying, I believed, made things better.

I developed a strong line in self-loathing. I would beat myself up for not casting around for work, for failing to come up with good ideas, for not living the freelance life I had always dreamt of. I stopped leaving the flat on weekdays, except for quick local errands. It just felt easier to stay in and hide away and succumb to that deep sense of guilt about wasting time, about not making enough of the gift I had somehow been granted.

Working alone was proving to be dangerous. It drove me to retreat into myself and becoming lost in a dark world where I felt useless, incapable and, worst of all, embarrassed to tell anyone how I felt. Seeking professional help felt, at that time, pointless to me. To my mind, this was all in my head. I was the only person who had ever felt like this and I was making it all up.

Ultimately, I came to realise that my anxiety was related to my inability to deal with events and emotions that were fleeting. I placed obsessive emphasis on the smallest details. I could work myself into a state of extreme worry about everything from making a phone call to paying the gas bill to whether I'd offended someone by asking them to pay me on time for work I had completed months previously.

I had somehow taught myself to believe that I could worry things right. A deep fug settled over me that would not lift. It felt like living with a permanent, low-level hangover.

Life continued along these similar lines for a couple of years. The feelings came in waves, and there were times when my self-worth and my self-belief came back briefly, buoyed by an interesting commission or long days spent with Keeley, walking around the commons of south-west London or lolling on the benches around Tooting Bec Lido.

Without her, I often wonder what would have happened to me, whether I would have even discovered swimming in the way that I did on that sunny afternoon at Hampstead. I felt enormous guilt for feeling continually anxious and hateful towards myself when this woman was only ever supportive, encouraging and full of love. She was the one who had joined me on my first swim, who had suggested we go to Hampstead to break the torpor of a too-hot summer's day, and I felt I owed it to her as much as myself to try and make myself feel better again.

I had lost all the confidence I had built up in my early twenties. My natural extrovert state was undermined by a growing willingness to go into myself. I felt drained of enthusiasm for anything. I knew this upset Keeley as much it upset me. She could see how low I was, even if it took me a long time to be honest about my anxiety and depression. Her solicitude for me at my lowest moments knew no bounds, but I had to find a way to fix myself. I did not believe that it was fair to ask her to do that for me.

In swimming, I found the only thing that truly broke me out of my anxious cycle for longer than a few moments. There was a long, deep burn of satisfaction and calm that followed in the wake of my bow wave. So I swam to fix myself, to cure myself and to make myself a better person in my own eyes. In the water there was nothing. My mind was empty and I floated without thinking. I could just be, without perceived judgement.

That first swimming summer was beginning to taper off, but my willingness to paddle on until the cloak of winter wrapped itself over London led me to investigate more about wild swimming and its benefits.

I began buying guidebooks and scouring the web for information on heated pools, hidden river swims and like-minded swimmers.

It was on one such search that I discovered the name of Roger Deakin. Deakin's *Waterlog* kept cropping up again and again, mentioned as a hallowed text for those looking to eschew the echo chamber of the indoor pool for something more visceral. I tracked down a copy and devoured it in a two-day session, imagining myself swimming in all of the far-off destinations he visited: the sweeping bays of the Isles of Scilly; the roaring of the Gulf of Corryvreckan; and the moat (really two ponds) which ran along the back and front of Walnut Tree Farm, his Elizabethan farmhouse in Suffolk.

Deakin, it seemed, was the archetypal English eccentric. He appeared to care little for what others thought of him and ploughed a singular furrow, swimming in lakes, rivers, streams and canals which he saw as representing a Britain that was fast disappearing in the late 1990s. He was a zoologist, a natural historian educated at Cambridge and a man with a deep and intimate knowledge of the British countryside.

This much I garnered from the 330 pages of *Waterlog*. But as much as Roger's evocative writing about place, I found his musings on how swimming could affect life profound and helpful.

'You see and experience things when you're swimming in a way that is completely different from any other,' he wrote. 'You are *in* nature, part and parcel of it, in a far more complete and intense way than on dry land, and your sense of the present is overwhelming.'

This was the same survival instinct I had felt deeply in Hampstead mixed pond.

But more than that, it was Roger's insistence that 'water has always held the magical power to cure. ... I can dive in with a long face and what feels like a terminal case of depression, and come out a whistling idiot', that hit me hardest. It was as if those lines were written directly for my benefit, almost twenty years after they had first been written in Roger's creaking home. If I had been interested before, I was obsessed now. I took up the concept of wild swimming with a religious zeal.

I read and reread Roger's book until my copy of *Waterlog* became tattered, its pages falling out. I carried it with me on the swims I'd take across London, reading it whenever I found myself anxious and unable to put on my swimming shorts and take a quick dip. Roger's words acted as a quick fix whenever I found myself feeling low.

It was on a midweek jaunt at Hampstead mixed pond, while swimming along the boundary rope and lying on my back to catch the sun as it peeped through bubbling cloud, that I first thought of retracing Roger's footsteps on a grand journey across the UK. I loved swimming at Hampstead, but the shouts of kids diving in off the jetty was puncturing the mood somewhat. A swim in Roger's footsteps would give me the opportunity to see the Britain he had discovered and also the chance to see how much, if at all, it had changed in the intervening twenty years. Wild swimming was booming, thanks in no small part to Roger's work, and I wanted to see if attitudes towards it had changed too.

Swimming outdoors had become a mainstream activity since Roger undertook his journey in the mid-1990s. The subject of countless broadsheet articles and glossy magazine spreads, wild swimming now had its own guidebooks. It was no longer a niche activity for borderline eccentrics. The mixed pond's popularity surely proved it.

As my journey began to gain momentum and take over my life in a way I could not have foreseen, I visited countless lidos and river-swimming spots where dozens of swimmers ploughed up and down or simply lolled in the shallows. Lido culture, so long something suppressed – pools filled with concrete and art deco gems left to rot and return to nature – was booming. London wasn't shutting outdoor pools any more, as it was in Roger's time, but opening them. In the years it took me to retrace Roger's breaststrokes, the capital gained a fabulous new unchlorinated pool on a building site in King's Cross, while swimming campaigners raised funds for a bath on the South Bank of the Thames. Saltdean Lido near Brighton was set to reopen and millions of pounds were raised to restore Penzance's spectacular triangular pool after it was destroyed by storms lashing in from the Atlantic. There seemed to be a willingness to accept that chucking yourself into cold water was not something bizarre, but rather something to be embraced, a bracing way to see our landscape anew. I appeared to have come to wild swimming at just the right time.

But beyond the notion of investigating our nation's new-found love affair with cold water, I believed that tackling Roger's nationwide pilgrimage would be a way to fix my anxiety once and for all, to make that post-swim high last forever. I fast developed a strong faith in the power of water to cure, taking Roger's words as gospel; Britain's rivers, beaches, lakes and lidos offering the chance of a regular baptism to protect me against the worries I battled daily. If a weekly swim at Hampstead allowed me to come back to myself for a few hours, what could a huge, all-encompassing journey do?

At that point I believed that swimming across the country could be the panacea for all my anxieties. That if I swam everywhere Roger had, I would be cured and could live a life without the scourge of constant worry. One which didn't mean days on end beating myself up over trivial details and feeling guilty for doing as I pleased.

While it certainly started that way, I quickly learnt that I'd need things other than swimming to make myself better. I was to discover that the physical and mental journeys I had undertaken, while closely related, were not quite the same. Swimming administered first aid, but it was an unexpected event that occurred during my adventure which would finally help me to arrive where I am now, capable of recognising my anxiety and coping with it. Finding that essential cure went beyond just soaking myself in cold water. But without undertaking the trip and immersing myself in his journey, I am convinced that I would not have made it at all.

Beyond the need to get out of my own head and break away from my obsessions and anxieties, I thought such a long trip could be a great way to learn more about Britain's waterways and their place in nature too. Unlike Roger, I am not a naturalist. I've got a second-class history degree and come from a new town in Essex, and although I love the outdoors, my knowledge of birdlife and Britain's flora and fauna is cursory at best. This would be a great way to learn. Spending time with the coots of Hampstead Heath had made me hungry to know more about their cohorts, both on and under the water, and swimming seemed like the perfect opportunity way do so. It was, as Roger said, all about being *in* the scene.

There would be obstacles. My inability to drive was definitely one of them, making the hardest-to-reach places all but impossible to get to. (Or so I believed on that day in Hampstead mixed pond. In fact, my failure to as much as learn how to release a handbrake would turn out to be an advantage in fixing the longstanding loneliness I felt keenly during my working days in London, when I went into my shell and worried myself senseless.)

There was also the fact I could swim little more than a kilometre without my arms feeling as if they were going to fall off. My swimming skills were hardly Olympic standard, and while I knew that wasn't what was required, I knew that tackling some of Roger's more challenging swims would need a level of stamina and skill which I lacked. Some time in lido fast lanes would be required.

And, of course, there was Roger's absence. Roger died after a short illness in 2006 and, in my own, self-inflated way, I felt this would be a fitting tribute to him. A way to thank him for pointing out a way to make myself better and lighten the worries about work, status and responsibility I had loaded myself with.

My mind was buzzing with possibility when I first resolved to swim in Roger's wake. In the afterglow of the initial decision, it all seemed so easy. I had no real plan, no concept of it taking any longer than the nine months it had taken Roger to complete, and an overwhelming sense of excitement. I had no idea at the time that this would be a trip that would become more obsessive than my love for the book on which it was based and change me in ways I could not imagine possible. It was time to go swimming.

PART ONE

Jumping in, Feet First

'When you enter the water, something like metamorphosis happens. Leaving behind the land, you go through the looking-glass surface and enter a new world, in which survival, not ambition or desire, is the dominant aim.'

ROGER DEAKIN, *WATERLOG*

CHAPTER ONE

August

~~~

Tooting Bec Lido, London – Highgate Men's
Pond, London – River Granta, Cambridgeshire

The dog days of summer were already here when I left my flat and cycled across south London to Tooting Bec Lido. I was starting my mission late in the year, I knew, but still I moved tentatively, despite the fact that were weren't many warm weeks left in the year for wild swimming. No swing down to the Scillies for me, where Roger had started; rather a leisurely stroll to a swimming hole I knew well, and which was one of the last Roger visited in *Waterlog*. It was a metaphorical toe in the water.

Tooting Bec Lido remains a well-loved south London institution. The 'Rastafarian doors' to the cubicles which lined the sides of the pool, which my predecessor spoke of warmly, were still there, but with an added dash of blue to complement the green, yellow and red of Zion.

A wedding cake fountain sprayed icy water outside the café, which sold tea in styrofoam cups for a quid and two slices of toast for 50p. It was a happy antidote to the expensive coffee and cake culture sweeping this corner of the capital.

I got changed in a cubicle on the far side, with sloppy wet footprints on the concrete where a previous swimmer had pulled himself free of clinging swim shorts. I left my bag on a bench underneath a framed newspaper article which ran with the headline 'Come on in, the Water's Freezing'.

I had visited Tooting numerous times over the previous couple of summers, but despite this, I still found its waters unaccountably cold, even on a searing hot day. The school holidays were well under way, but for some reason it wasn't too crowded, so I had a clear, straight route to the distant shallows. At a hundred yards, it remains one of Europe's largest outdoor pools, and the prospect of swimming lengths was daunting.

I stood looking down into the bright blue of the deep end, leaf mulch stuck fast to the off-white bottom. I readied myself to jump, counted to three and found myself still standing there.

A nervousness washed over me and suddenly I was back at the local pool in Bishops Stortford, aged eleven, on my first ever PE lesson at secondary school. Six fellow swimmers from the bottom ability group looked up at me from the water, three metres deep, each one in a silicone cap, nose clips giving their shouts of encouragement a deep, nasal quality which age had yet to truly gift them. I stared back at them before turning to the swimming tutor in fear.

'I can't do it,' I told her.

'You can,' she said. Standing above the deep end of Tooting Bec Lido, I swear I had the memory of her hand firmly on the small of my back, ready to give me some physical impetus. I was almost certainly projecting that little detail.

The thing was, I couldn't. In front of six classmates and now an entire pool of other students from different groups turning to watch, I was having a very public meltdown. I suppose you could call it a panic attack. Because even at that age, I was a hopeless worrier. If there was something to fret about, I would fret about it. Homework, offending my friends, trying to be popular with new classmates. It seemed normal and everyday then in the way it felt debilitating and tedious now.

Inevitably, the tears came. As they did, I was walked back down the pool and helped to jump in at five-metre intervals, until, finally, I was back at the three-metre mark.

I flopped myself in and an ironic cheer went up. I broke out my best doggy paddle to the nearest steps and climbed out.

I felt a sense of pride along with a deep sense of shame for showing my emotions so openly to a group of merciless peers who at that point I hardly knew. Packing my swimming kit into a plastic Dennis the Menace bag afterwards, one of them articulated what I believed to be the entire year's feelings towards me:

'Why are you such a wuss?'

My mind refocused on the icy water of Tooting in front of me and tried to push that resurgent memory back to wherever it had come from. I could hear Morrissey singing loud and clear in my head. About smiling now, but being mortified at the time.

I took a deep breath, began counting to three and chucked myself in at two. The lido's water completed the necessary ablutions of my anxious mind.

As I surfaced, I looked at my fellow swimmers. Some wore large goggles and wetsuits, swimming stealthy lengths, practising tumble turns, the recent London Olympics clearly imbuing the regulars with a sense of athletic purpose.

Head out, I began my long paddle towards the café and the blessed chance of putting my feet down on the bottom. I wouldn't be doing the seventeen lengths required for a mile today – a distance which my predecessor wouldn't have given a second's thought to completing. My emulation of Roger's feats would have to wait. Instead I let the water soothe my mind of work troubles and help it stay in a single place without wandering. I was lost in the moment when I was reminded where I was by a huge slap of water in the face. The wind had whipped up across the lido's vast surface, creating the kind of chop you'd expect on a south coast beach or a wide expanse of water in the Lake District. I found it amusing that someone would build a pool so big it could emulate properly wild conditions.

I continued regardless, taking the occasional mouthful and eventually dipping my head, surfacing with my hair slick across my forehead, the sting of hair product and chlorine in my eyes. I wiped my face and swam on with my eyes and nose peering out of the water like a periscope. I managed a measly three lengths before the shivers came on. The backs of my arms pricked with goosebumps as I clambered out at the shallow end, pulling myself up over the side – soaked, happy and no longer aware of my school-age hopelessness when it came to taking the plunge.

In the spirit of keeping up with Roger's approach to London swimming, his dips all completed in one short burst, I decided to stick within the M25. I wanted to stay on safe ground, without the need to check OS maps out of the library. My toe-dipping continued at Marshall Street Baths in Soho.

Much had changed here since Roger visited and played a game of water polo with the locals. It had closed in 1997, not long after that match, and did not reopen until 2010, as part of a private leisure centre which charged hefty fees for members and non-members alike.

On a late August afternoon, a cold shower presaging the onset of autumn, I forked out £5.65 and made my way through the beautifully refurbished changing rooms and into the stunning space in which the bath, first built in 1850, was housed. The barrel-vaulted ceiling created a great echo as swimmers chatted on the narrow sides, where once there had been bleachers for excitable spectators to cheer on gala participants.

The rebuild had ensured that these had gone, along with the training pool out the back. The whole thing was now run by Better Leisure, a company operated as part of the GLL social enterprise, and while the Friends of Marshall Street Baths had succeeded in getting this beautiful building reopened, it had come at a cost. This was not the council-run, community-minded centre it once was.

The decimation of affordable facilities for local people got to me. I believed strongly that such places should be open to all, regardless of wealth. It felt to me that this was indicative of London as a whole, a marvellous pulsating city which had been repackaged and sold back to those who could afford it with scant regard for those on the margins.

Social cleansing is a strong term, but it felt as if this was what was happening here.

The pool could no longer be seen from the narrow footpath which ran along Marshall Street, and it was office workers and media types who came here, not local residents. Paying almost £6 for a swim, just a few pence less than the minimum wage, was surely not what was intended when the baths opened more than a hundred and fifty years ago as a place for the public to swim, wash, relax and clean their clothes.

The whole place felt like a commodity. Something for 'consumers' rather than somewhere with society's well-being at its heart. While GLL said it reinvested any surplus it made back into its service, loftily dubbing its own work 'fair trade leisure provision', it felt as if the poorer residents of Westminster were being squeezed out.

But I was here and wanted a swim badly. I plopped in and slowly began to breaststroke my way to a kilometre. I followed the neatly tiled black line along the bottom, my arms aching as the metres passed by.

Marshall Street was stunning. But I couldn't help but feel that its rebirth had been handled incorrectly. That those who had written to MPs to complain of its continued closure in 2001 had been cheated out of the baths which they so clearly loved. I left frustrated, ready to find a swim that was less restricted by the ways leisure centre managers seem to think we should exercise these days.

Across town at Highgate men's pond the crowds were sparse, despite it clearly being one of the last warm days of summer. Perhaps it was because it was midweek. I loved swimming at the mixed pond across the other side of Hampstead Heath, but I was determined to stick to *Waterlog* dips only. Roger's decision to opt for the single-sex pool, coupled with the fact that the mixed was now shut for the season, had forced my hand.

An older gent towelled off in the corner of the metal changing shed as my friend Joe and I nudged open the wooden door and got ourselves ready for a cooling immersion. Joe was a good friend, former colleague and fellow freelancer, not to mention a highly skilled, barrel-chested swimmer. He was always willing to leave his desk behind for some kind of adventure. Previously that had meant the two of us going to the pub, but he didn't need much convincing that we should maybe take a bit of exercise before guzzling a few indulgent pints. After a few solo swims, I was glad of some company.

I had told Joe about my plans to retrace *Waterlog*, but I hadn't told him why. I made out that it was just a project on the side, a small something, a hobby to provide light relief from the regular work that I had come to resent. Sharing my anxiety, even with my closest friends, was not something I felt ready to do.

Scrawled in chalk on the blackboard was 19°C, next to the arrow pointing to the 'Nude Sunbathing' area. Not feeling brave enough to bare all, we both emerged from the changing hut out onto the long concrete jetty. The water temperature hadn't dropped sufficiently for the lifeguards to bring the ropes in close, as they had been when Roger came on a cold November afternoon. There was no coconut matting to warm our feet either, the ground sharp and rough on the soft balls of my feet.

We reached the cold metal steps which descended into the green-brown water. There was only one other swimmer, dragging himself along the far perimeter rope. Joe lowered himself in first, screwing his face up as his balls hit the surface. I felt like going back to my bag, wrapping up and heading straight to the warmth of the nearest saloon bar.

Geeing myself up, I followed Joe in. I had little idea of how to gauge temperatures, but there was no way this was 19°C. It felt far colder, especially as low scudding clouds now obscured the sun. I had read Roger's description of Highgate that morning and remembered his advice: swim fast between buoys. I set off in my smartest breaststroke, my goggles steaming up within seconds. I managed a single, long loop of the lake, before draping myself across a roped life ring. After a short breather, I headed off again.

This time I looped my goggles around my wrist and swam head up. I was joined by a great crested grebe, its shock of Mohawk feathers standing brightly against the greying sky and murky water. Pootling along together, it made me realise why I loved wild swimming. It wasn't just about finding a cure for the anxiety which dogged my mind, but steeping myself in nature and the outdoors.

I'm no naturalist. What knowledge I have of birds comes from the RSPB's online bird identifier and an ability to bullshit around those who don't know as much as me. But I wanted to learn more and spend more time with these creatures, to get to know them intimately, developing some true knowledge in the process. Plus there was no way you were ever likely to swim with wildfowl in a Fitness First training pool. The grebe took one last look at me before spinning itself around, swimming off and taking a dive after some unseen prey. His disappearing act made me wonder just what else I might be sharing the pond with.

There is a silky quality to the water at Highgate and at the Hampstead mixed pond, which makes these two unlike any other swimming hole in the capital. The large lidos are all shot through with chlorine, meaning there's always the whiff of schoolday swims, a stench you can't flush from your nostrils. The ponds on Hampstead Heath lack the serious feel of the Serpentine too, where triathletes and competitive swimmers go to train for long-distance swimming assignments. Delightful as the fresh water of that Hyde Park lake is, swimming in water that is often overlooked by pedaloes laden with gawping tourists is not quite as relaxing as spending some quality time with some of Britain's most beautiful waterfowl in London's finest park.

Joe and I climbed out of the men's pond after an ample twenty-minute dip, a slight shiver juddering through both of us as we made our way back along the jetty. Joe was desperate for a hot shower and wondered aloud if the basic cubicles here might have one on offer. The lifeguard nodded with a smile and waited to hear Joe's yelp as he stood under the inevitably icy blast. Joe blinked in shock as he emerged.

'It's good for you!' said the lifeguard, returning to his small hut with a chuckle.

By now Joe's shivers had reached shuddering point and we dried ourselves quickly, repairing to the pub to plot swims outside the city.

I felt happy in the moment, my anxiety temporarily alleviated, swimming my only concern.

Following Roger's footsteps in the rest of the UK was going to prove challenging. And not just because of the extreme nature of some of the swims (descending into Hell Gill in the Yorkshire Dales and negotiating the Fowey estuary in Cornwall were just two dips I planned on leaving until the very last opportunity). My lack of a driving licence was clearly going to be an issue in getting to the most remote locations of Roger's journey and I knew from the start that I was going to be reliant on the kindness of fellow wild-swimming acolytes, of whom at this point there seemed to be very few.

I could, of course, learn to drive. But my urge to swim *Waterlog* was too great and learning would take up precious time. I just knew that getting behind the wheel was going to prove tortuous. I hadn't done so for six years, since I spectacularly failed an intensive driving course while working for a well-known car magazine, my first proper job in journalism. I could still hear the intense road rage of the instructor, belted out heartily to fellow drivers in a broad Norfolk accent in exasperation at their lack of patience.

His hectoring of other drivers only served to turn me into a nervous wreck, wildly stomping on the clutch thinking it was the brake, swerving through traffic or stalling on roundabouts. He would smoke roll-ups as soon as we were out of sight of his office, wafting his inexpertly assembled creations in front of my face in the tiny car. I didn't have the heart to tell him to stub it out.

After almost crashing into a parked car, he broke the inevitable news that I wasn't up to taking my test that week. I let him drive us back to the centre and never saw him again. The thought of turning to one of the activities that made me most anxious of all in order to complete a quest to beat my anxiety seemed absurd.

Anyway, my inability to perform this most basic of tasks also made my *Waterlog* challenge that bit more interesting and a lot more social.

I decided it was an obstacle to revel in rather than rectify. Working alone from home and with many of my oldest friends not living in London, part of me hoped this would be a way to rekindle friendships and enjoy the simple social buzz of old times, when we'd skip lectures and hang out. Everyone had responsibilities now, but swimming together would be a way to subvert them, for a few hours at least.

However, for my first non-London swim, I decided that rather than find a willing driver I would choose somewhere close to a train station that wasn't going to require an overnight stay. Cambridge, and Grantchester in particular, seemed like the perfect place to start.

It was a hot and sweaty day as Joe and I made our way from Cambridge station towards the Granta. The meadows on the outskirts were dotted with grazing cattle and a keen breeze whipped up as we reached the river's towpath and walked out of town, the rumble of the M11 growing in the distance. Coming here for my first non-London swim felt right for all kinds of reasons. It was the place where Roger pored over old maps at the university library, laying plans for his huge sweep across the UK. It was the river of Rupert Brooke and Lord Byron, a wild-swimming spot steeped in literary history, where I imagined people whiled away their days and forgot their troubles. And, most importantly, it was close to the renowned Orchard Tea Rooms, where I fully intended to eat a gut-busting lunch and guzzle tea in a deckchair once the swimming was done.

This was my first river swim and I wasn't really sure how to go about my it. I did know for certain that I wouldn't be following Brooke's example and getting in naked. The poor cows of Grantchester Meadows didn't need to see that.

Roger had ploughed happily up and down this stretch, where the Cam and the Granta merge. His predilection for lengthy river swims, leaving his bag tucked in beds of nettles, seemed idyllic if a tad impractical. My anxiety about having to walk back to Cambridge in a pair of wet shorts and nothing else, begging a free train ticket for the ride home to King's Cross, was far too great for me to stray too far from my precious, warming clobber.

Instead of a long, downstream paddle, Joe and I opted to duck in under the shelter of an overhanging willow, the tentacles of its roots swaying with the current. I thought of pike and a chill went through me. My toes being nipped was my primary concern, although a whack from a punt pole or oar was a close second in my thoughts as I dropped my feet onto the muddy lower banks and felt the water lap at my toes.

Christ, it felt cold. Far cooler than Highgate just a few days before. I waded in waist high and was all set to glide into the billowing reeds as a noisy flotilla appeared around the river's bend. A pair of canoeists were quickly followed by a punt. Each one of the occupants, decked out in buoyancy aids, made idle chatter and passed comment on the increasingly large goosebumps on my arms. I tried to stop shivering as the last of them went by, waving a goodbye and wishing us luck. Joe remained on the bank, donning a pair of brash, luminous board shorts and peering into the dark brown drink.

With nothing but my own inner voice to stop me, I launched forward and swam with the current. I banished all thoughts of errant pike nibbling at the flash of my pale feet and called out to Joe to come and join me. I disappeared around the corner and heard Joe's 'hnnng', followed by a splash as he dived under the surface. This was followed by much swearing about just how cold the Granta was.

The current moved deceptively fast and I let it take me, my timid, head-out breaststroke transformed into a great big gliding flight down the central channel of this pretty, narrow river. Joe was far off when I decided to turn myself around and see how he was getting on. The going was much tougher heading upstream. From up on the bank the Granta had looked as if it was moving at a leisurely pace, but now its pull felt strong beneath me. If I was going to master river swimming and conquer the Medway, Fowey and the myriad others Roger had bathed in, I was going to have to get used to swimming against the current and teach myself to read water better.

Joe was swimming a proper, head-under breaststroke, creating huge waves which thwacked against the deep muddy banks and came back to slap me on the face. I left him to it, rounding the corner just as a flash of orange and blue darted above me and shot into the far bank, close to fenced-off farmers' fields. My first kingfisher. I'd caught the briefest of glimpses, but it was unmistakably that most colourful of birds. I felt elated as I swam back, braced and ready to dry off in the brief glimmer of sun on offer.

Despite succumbing to extreme shivers, I was on a soaring high as we walked the winding banks of the Granta to the sanctuary of the tea rooms. It was blissful. Perhaps it was the kingfisher. Or maybe just the fact that I'd spent too many minutes in the cold river. But I had a huge swell of hope about this project. That it wasn't foolhardy. And that swimming in rivers was going to be even more fun than leaping into more benign waters.

After demolishing a huge scone and vast bowls of jam and cream in the company of a scruffy robin, hungry for crumbs, Joe and I left the Granta behind and returned to normality. Cambridge proved a huge shock to the system after a day spent splashing in its watery meadows. The station felt too crowded, the train cramped, its toilets broken and reeking. But I was ready now for anything Roger could throw at me.

CHAPTER TWO

September

~~~

Burton Bradstock, Dorset –
The Oasis, Covent Garden

After my Granta swim I had let my thoughts drift from my wider *Waterlog* pilgrimage, taking myself off to Hampstead with Joe and making the occasional trip up the road from my flat in Camberwell, where I had recently moved, to Brockwell Lido. Summer was passing me by. An old friend from university sent me a message on Facebook, saying how much she loved the idea.

'There's just one thing,' she wrote. 'Haven't you started this a bit late? The weather's bound to be shit soon.'

She wasn't wrong. The first taste of autumn proper came not long after my train arrived back in London from Cambridge. There was a noticeable dip in the air temperature, accompanied by the need to wear a jacket even on smash-and-grab trips to the local corner shop. Every time I picked up *Waterlog*, read another passage and found another swim I was going to need to do, I looked out of the window at the small corner of grey sky visible from my office window with a growing sense of dread. This was going to take far longer than I had anticipated.

The worry of such a lengthy trip led me to start making lists of swims. Lists soon begat spreadsheets which in turn begat arbitrary deadlines.

Colour-coded documents told me which swims I had done (green), which swims I had to do (white) and which swims were no longer possible (red), due to lidos either being closed for good or damaged by extreme weather. Rather than setting a deadline for each one, I began telling everyone that I'd be done with the entire project by the end of the following summer. If Roger could do it quickly, so could I. I couldn't see it at the time but I was already taking the joy out of things.

Setting unnecessary deadlines, holding myself to them and then beating myself up when I 'fail' to meet them was one of the professional pitfalls that had made me so miserable in the years prior to my trip. And here I was turning what was supposed to be fun into work, therefore tying up all my self-worth with the project. It wasn't exactly a healthy state of affairs so early in the undertaking.

Poring over my plans after Grantchester, I managed to push away thoughts of rushing to get things done for long enough to realise that I could get in a *Waterlog* swim while on a short holiday Keeley and I had planned in late September in Lyme Regis with my best friend Tom and his girlfriend Emily. Tom and I met in our first year of university, bonding over a mutual love of mawkish Americana songs and doing shit impressions of each other.

Tom didn't need much convincing when I told him about my idea of driving around the coast to Burton Bradstock for a swim and maybe eating some locally-caught fish at the excellent Hive Beach Café afterwards. Tom loves outdoor swimming. Indeed, this is a man who once pulled his jeans on over wet swimming shorts after a brief dip in the Thames near his home in Oxford. On that occasion we sat in the pub for an hour drinking, his cream-coloured trousers staining an ever-darker shade of brown around the crotch. The reason? He hadn't wanted to get changed in a grotty public loo in Wolvercote. Tom doesn't care what others think, even if it involves sitting in warm river water while having a beer.

And so, here we were, on a bright blue day on the English Channel, ready to swim off Chesil beach. Keeley and Emily parked themselves high up the beach, calling out encouragement as we walked over the stones and into the water.

Tom hopped and gasped on the large, sharp-sided pebbles. I stood and looked up at him towering above me, enjoying his pain as we stripped off in a sharp wind, the crash of the waves behind us. Tom's thatch of light brown hair ruffled in the breeze, all peaks to match the tips of the waves out to sea.

One step, two steps and I was out of my depth. This was my first *Waterlog* sea swim and I could see why Roger had been so wary of these waters, even when they were glassy flat. The pull beneath was incredible, with the waves coming in perpendicular, The waves here are so powerful that the pebbles are graded from 'small' at Chesil Beach's north-west end to 'large' where it meets Portland Bill. If the water could do that to rocks, then what could it do to me?

Roger talked of swimming far out to the horizon here, but Tom and I opted to swim in big circles, pushing out against the current and letting the waves guide us back to shore. Despite the water temperature being little higher than 15°C, it didn't feel cold. Battling the elements, being 'in nature' as my predecessor put it, had sent me into a giddy mood. I couldn't have been happier as I looked back to shore, waving at the girls while Tom and I babbled about this being the best day of the year.

By now the sun was really up and we trod water for a time, indulging in what Emily called a 'water conference'. The four of us had enjoyed one in the more sheltered environs of Lyme Regis just that morning. I told Tom about my worries that I may have cornered myself into a rather lengthy project with my decision to follow Roger around the UK. Guiltily, I left out my true reasons for undertaking the trip.

'Look at how much fun you're having,' Tom said reassuringly. 'It doesn't matter how long it takes.'

We swam towards the shore. A huge wave propelled me forward and I clattered back onto the beach on all fours, my hands and knees reddening with the scrape of the shingle. Up went Tom's yelps of pain again as he padded over to his clothes. Keeley greeted me with a towel, wrapping it round my shoulders and scrabbling me dry.

She had a knack of making everything feel better, even when I was buzzing with a post-swim dopamine high. While she worked in London, I had set off on this wild trip around the British Isles. Our relationship was such that I had never asked whether she minded when I first set out, but in recent weeks I had asked again and again when I went swimming whether she did. She didn't. She told me how she could see how much happier swimming, following Roger's trail, was making me. Her only worries were that I stay safe and not go throwing myself into any particularly dangerous stretches of water. That I stay warm. That I relax and allow myself to enjoy it.

My toes were still caked with small stones as I yanked on my boots and made my way to the warmth of the café. It was pleasing to look around and see people enjoying the same 'simple pleasures' which Roger encountered here. A spot of fishing. Reading in a deckchair, togged up against the wind. A walk along the clifftops in search of fossil fragments and coastal views.

A pair of swimmers screamed with joy as they waded into the white breakers as we walked back up the beach. It was good to know we weren't alone in ignoring the whip of the breeze and going in regardless.

Back in London, I turned Burton Bradstock green on my spreadsheet and cast a worried eye over the dozens of dips left to do. Thankfully, the fear was not enough to stop me continuing my *Waterlog* mission with fervour. There were more dips to do inside the M25, and none as easy as the Oasis Sports Centre in Covent Garden. This inner-city pool is where Roger came towards the end of his journey, on a cold November afternoon.

When I arrived it seemed the weather had decided to give one final burst of summer before turning the taps on and reminding us what living in northern Europe was really all about. It was a gloriously warm day, and Joe and I arrived by bike, locking up on High Holborn and entering into a pleasantly calm courtyard where a few swimmers were working their way through languid lengths. The office blocks and high-rise flats around the pool truly make it an oasis, deflecting the noise of the city and giving it an air of escape that can normally only be found in the most secluded of swimming holes.

The price of admission had unsurprisingly gone up since Roger's time, just shy of a fiver for use of the outdoor and indoor pools. Changed and ready, we marched over that foot-shredding hard plastic that all municipal pools seem to lay down for fear of swimmers slipping over.

The heated water made it feel like high summer, the only suggestion of autumn coming when I wheeled my arms out during a front crawl and felt the freshness of the breeze on my hands. My crawl had slowly developed from a huffing breath-every-stroke kind of deal to something approaching respectability, with a quick swivel of the hips, a flick of the head skywards and a gulp of air every few metres. I liked the fact that the measured breathing gave me something to meditate on when I swam in a pool or lido, where I could see the bottom and the chances of enjoying the gabble of coots and swoops of kingfishers was non-existent, in contrast to some of the wilder spots I'd got used to swimming in. I was now reserving my preferred head-out breaststroke for ponds, rivers and bays, places where I wanted to observe nature and feel part of the scene.

We swam forty lengths each, just over a kilometre thanks to the pool being 27.5 metres long, and retired to a pub across the road for a pint. There I wittered on at Joe about how many swims I was going to have to do, about how I was going to swim through the winter. I also blasted him with details about my next trip.

This was to be to Roger's favourite river, the Waveney. I was heading there with an old friend and swimming addict who wanted in on the action. When Joe heard I was going in mid-October he offered to lend me his wetsuit. I took him up on the rubbery offer. I cycled back through London, thinking of distant Suffolk fields, river water on my skin, thoughts of water keeping me calm as the traffic swelled around me.

CHAPTER THREE

October

~

River Waveney, Suffolk/Norfolk border

Yanny was waiting in his green Vauxhall people carrier in the car park at Beccles station.

'Awright, Min,' he said, grinning as he pulled himself free from the driver's side and opened the boot. Used straw and a dull whiff of manure greeted me as I popped my head in and wrestled my backpack into the small amount of free space.

'Sorry mate, Albie's taken over a bit.' Albie was a horse belonging to Yanny and his wife, Suz. They'd bought him for a cut price from some local travellers.

It was clear just how much Albie had taken over when I got in. It was more like the back of a horse box than a car. There was straw everywhere. I pulled some from my jumper and threw it through the open window. Yanny took a swig from a can of Monster energy drink and looked in the rear-view mirror, where Amy, who had joined us for the day, had slid in next to a pile of riding gear.

'Ain't see either of you in ages,' he said as we pulled off, heading for the Waveney.

Before my swim in the Granta, Yanny and I had got talking on Facebook after I'd posted word about my latest swims on my personal page. The reaction had been positive and reaffirming, with many people sending me good wishes for the challenge ahead. Social media, that double-edged sword which often made me feel so lonely and useless, appeared to be helping my cause.

Yanny told me he was keen to take me to Roger's favourite places. He did, after all, live in the same part of Suffolk where Roger had lived for most of his life. As we exchanged public messages, we were joined by Amy. Amy is an old friend of a friend. We met when we were both wide-eyed young journalists, scribbling about average bands for crap money, looking for our big break in London. I hadn't seen her for the best part of ten years.

When Amy found out about my *Waterlog* plans she said she was keen to come along and would be down in England in mid-October, visiting friends and taking a break from her home in Orkney.

It seemed like the perfect opportunity, not just to swim with others, but also get a guided tour from a bona fide local. Yanny and I had met at the University of East Anglia in 2000. A mature student, he had spiky, bleached hair, wore a padlock round his neck and performed poetry to big audiences. He was everything I wasn't in those gawky early student days, but he was then, and is now, one of the most kind-hearted people I have ever met.

These days he cultivated an air of Toad of Toad Hall. Not the smug manner, rather the tweed clobber, half-rim specs, the sense of a man at home in the country. He threw the car fast around corners, clearly with a good knowledge of the roads, regaling Amy and me with stories about the loaded landowners in these parts, interspersed with asides about the grinding rural poverty in this beautiful valley.

We turned off and bumped along an unsealed road towards the Geldeston Locks Inn. It was here that Yanny and Suz had got married the previous summer and, handily, where Roger had launched off downstream for a radio documentary called 'Cigarette on the Waveney'. The track was a mess of rocks and ruts, Yanny's car not really cut out for the rough and tumble of this off-road adventure. He explained there was no point in sealing it. The track and surrounding fields flooded every winter.

We parked the car and grabbed our things. It was a cool day, not yet into single figures, but definitely not warm enough to linger on the bank. Amy spotted the wetsuit in my bag and looked at it in surprise. Swimming in the sea in Orkney had hardened her to cold water. And besides, it was positively tropical here in eastern England compared to the islands she called home. But I was not to be deterred when it came to donning that neoprene. I wanted a swim that would last longer than thirty seconds.

We walked through the beer garden, crossing a bridge over a riverside pool bound by nettles, passing through a kissing gate and on to the Waveney proper. A high bridge crosses the river here and we walked to the centre to get a better view of the marshlands that make up the Norfolk/Suffolk border. A row of poplars guarding the far bank hissed lightly in the autumn breeze. The river curved away to my right, while to my left the *Big Dog* ferry sat moored for the winter, having taken its last passengers from this isolated spot into Beccles a few weeks back.

I told Yanny about Roger spotting an otter on his swim through this stretch of the Waveney in *Waterlog*. He said he knew of a holt – an otter's nest – nearby, but grew coy when I asked if we could swim to it from here.

'Another time,' he said, as we ditched our bags. 'It's a secret.'

Amy already had her swimsuit on under her clothes and was out of them quickly and into the water. On the journey up from London she had told me about her escapades with the Orkney Polar Bears, a wild-swimming club that took to the water every day of the year, no matter the weather. It made my dips in Highgate pond sound as tame as a splash in a puddle. Clearly these daily dips had given her the kind of imperviousness to water that the hidden Waveney otters enjoyed. Tall and graceful, she settled into a fast stroke, head above water, and swam back towards the locks, unfazed by the cold, her white blond hair conspicuous against the black of the autumnal river.

Meanwhile I struggled awkwardly into the wetsuit Joe had lent me for the day. Yanny stood by, impressed by my James Bond-like get-up, still togged up in his winter coat. He wasn't joining us today, his arthritis stranding him on dry land. His jute bag wasn't laden with swimming stuff as I'd first thought, but spare towels and a flask of sweet instant coffee.

I had no protection for my hands and feet, which whitened into numbness the minute I worked my way down the steep bank into the river. I was desperate to see an otter, but our splashing and noisy chat would surely have scared off this most elusive of creatures, even if it had been there in the first place. Instead, I had to make do with the icy water sliding over the top of my wetsuit and down my neck. I stifled a yelp as it reached my lumbar and thought of Roger sliding through these waters a mile at a time, a water creature in all but body, unencumbered by neoprene on a hot summer's day.

The poplars now bowing to the brisker wind, Yanny began to regale me from the bank with tales of the Waveney in summer. The dart of kingfishers as he and our old uni friends sat drinking cider on a nearby bench. The otter he'd seen while riding the *Big Dog* a few months ago. He told me how much he wanted to help me make my *Waterlog* trip happen and talked of other nearby spots we should visit once the weather was better: Benacre Broad, the River Bure near Aylsham, the sweeping sands of Holkham Bay. He said an old group of friends in Norwich, some of whom I hadn't seen in years, were keen to join us. A wild-swimming gang was being formed on my behalf. I was elated.

While we chatted, Yanny high up on the bridge as I floated on my back, Amy heaved herself clear on the far bank. Where boats and barges would normally moor for the day, she had managed to push herself up and straddle a leg onto the top of a corrugated metal retaining wall. This kind of feat would have left me breathless, but Amy smiled and glowed red as the blood rushed back to her limbs after ten minutes in the Waveney. She made her way back to our bench, drying and changing quickly, not a sign of a shiver as she wrapped a large scarf around her shoulders.

I followed suit, albeit in more ungainly fashion. I opted to get out where I'd got in. The bank, though, seemed far steeper than before. I stood on tip toes, my feet like solid blocks of ice on the muddy riverbed, and tried to swing my left leg up. No joy. A huge bed of stinging nettles impeded me to the right.

Instead, I leant forward to grab two clumps of grass. Nibbled to near nothingness by cattle and withered by the onset of autumn, they barely took my weight. My palms stained green as I slipped back into the river. Roger hardly ever mentioned getting out. Where was the romance and poetry in falling backwards, arms whirring for balance, into a stretch of water you'd just communed with?

I stood up and assessed my options. I stretched out my arms and tried to pull myself clear, feeling Amy's hand take one arm and Yanny take the other. Anyone walking across the bridge from the Locks would have seen a man clad in black neoprene lying prone on the riverbank as if he'd just been on a failed police dive, two strangers pulling him clear.

My hands were caked in slick mud, the front of the wetsuit streaked with wet grass, its knees a shitty brown as I got unsteadily to my feet. Wild swimming can be many things, but glamorous is certainly not one of them.

I unzipped and opened the tight suit, my chest pimpled but dry, the only sensation of cold coming from the light breeze off the marshes. I sat drinking Yanny's coffee as I proceeded to make a meal of getting my legs free, the wetsuit glued around my ankles. Yanny offered to pull me out. But I had visions of him falling and going for a dip that he hadn't planned on. With great difficulty I freed myself and stuffed the rolled-up, smelly mass of neoprene into a plastic recycling bag. I needed a pint and something hearty to restore my pride after spending more time getting out and getting dry than actually swimming in Roger's favourite river. We decamped to the warmth of the bar, hot soup already waiting, a local ale being poured as I collapsed onto a bench. This had been just the type of mildly hapless and enjoyable adventure I'd hoped for when I decided to follow in Roger's footsteps.

Later that afternoon, as an autumn shower settled over the Waveney Valley, Yanny and Amy dropped me back at Beccles station. The greyness of the day cut through me and the last of my post-swim high dissipated as I gave them a final wave from the chugging, two-carriage train. A tattered copy of that morning's *Metro* lay on the seat next to me, decrying Obama's performances in the recent presidential debates. The future of the Western world was on a knife edge.

I had swum in Roger's favourite river, but a nagging sense of failure crept into my mind as I stared out over ploughed fields, rooks picking over the final, churned-up treats of autumn before retreating to branches barely visible in the fading light. I had thought I would do more than this, have seen more of Roger's world than this, before the weather turned and made swimming outdoors less of a joy and more of a chore.

I realised that this would likely be my last swim of the year. I had no others planned and the days were drawing in. And with that I had to face up to the idea of not having the water as my crutch, my Band-Aid, the thing I needed to make myself better. I was facing a long wait until I could soak my skin without a wetsuit, feel the soaring high of a dopamine rush and the long happy burn I felt after a lengthy dip.

I castigated myself for being so pathetic as I got off the train at Liverpool Street, trying to remember the flow of the Waveney at my back.

CHAPTER FOUR

February

~~~

River Windrush, Oxfordshire

Winter came on raw, and with the cold my willingness to swim diminished. I struggled to imagine days when I'd be able to take multiple swims and fulfil my *Waterlog* wish.

Instead, I sat in and reread Roger's words about places far from south London. His trip to Jura was foremost in my mind. I dreamt of days when the sun rose at four and set after eleven, of camping to the sound of deer groaning among the rough, hilly grass. I knew I wanted to make a trip to that Scottish island the culmination of the coming summer's swims, perhaps of my journey as a whole.

For now though, Scotland would have to wait. The shortest days of the year came and went and I realised how much I missed swimming in Roger's wake, the possibilities it opened up, the curative properties, the fact it had offered respite from feeling down on myself. I realised too that I took some small joy from the planning of it all too. Once again I had spent winter working alone in the flat, worrying and feeling constantly het up.

Opening my spreadsheet, looking at the plans I'd scribbled down and pinned to my office wall, offered me a way out of that low, a chance to imagine being outside and basking in nature. The plans didn't stress me out at that point, but spoke to me of a year of swimming my way towards a state of calm. Such thoughts urged me on and gave me a renewed impetus even as winter's grey skies failed to relent.

I missed the sociability that I had enjoyed so much on the Waveney with Yanny and Amy. Working from home, alone, meant I often only socialised once a week. I felt guilty, too, for burdening Keeley with all the thoughts that whirred around my head during the day when she got in from a long day in the office.

As the swims had become more regular and my *Waterlog* project took off, I had explained to Keeley why I was doing it. Not just to swim in Roger's wake, but to ease my anxiety. I had told her about how I could never stop worrying: about work, about feeling responsible for her happiness as well as mine, about my perceived failure to live up to the expectations I had set for myself.

It made me feel better, talking to her, opening up. It felt better than any swim. She hugged me tight and said she would always be there. That we were a team and that our love for each other was all that mattered. Her encouragement gave me the nudge I needed to get back out on the road, weather be damned. She said that if swimming helped in any way, then that's what I should be doing.

With that in mind, I splashed out on my own wetsuit and called Joe to see if he wanted to join me on a short trip out of London.

Around the same time, I ran into Jools, an old work colleague. Six foot four with the frame of a cruiserweight, Jools's love of extreme sports was legendary. He had completed an Ironman triathlon and had once run a half marathon by mistake. He asked after my wild-swimming trips, which he'd read about in a couple of blogs I'd written, and said he was keen to come along.

Two weeks later Jools met us at Twickenham station, folded up uncomfortably in the Volkswagen Polo he'd borrowed from his mum for the day. The small boot was stuffed with kit: a wetsuit, neoprene boots, swimming gloves and a GoPro action camera. I had a feeling this swim was going to be a little more hectic than mine and Joe's quiet glide along the Granta.

We were heading for the River Windrush in Oxfordshire. More specifically, we were aiming for an oxbow bend, a sweeping curve in the river, the finest Roger had ever seen. While making plans for the day, I'd told Joe and Jools about Roger swimming round the bend again and again, indulging in what he called 'boomerang swims'. It sounded like the perfect way to start the wild-swimming year, a natural washing machine to clean away my winter blues.

Of course, Roger had visited the small Thames tributary in August, whereas we were going in mid-February. He may have written about the sky being gloomy, but as far as I could tell this was the only thing the weather had in common with that summer's day fifteen years ago. It was positively Baltic as we drove onto the M40, the car's dashboard thermometer reading 5°C.

We parked up in the Cotswold village of Burford and walked past stone cottages towards the Windrush's towpath. Within five minutes the heavens opened, our hands scrambling round our necks for hoods, reaching into bags for brollies. A swim in icy rain was not what we had signed up for.

The rain wasn't the only problem. It had been particularly wet over the previous weeks, the relentless winter downpours inescapable. And from where I was now standing, by a dead tree in the middle of a muddy field, it seemed almost all of that rainwater had wound up in the Windrush. Its banks were a marshy mess, dull grass poking through the murky brown river. As the water swung left into Roger's beloved oxbow bend, it raged, eddying on the surface as the river narrowed sharply. If we tried a boomerang swim we'd certainly be swept merrily on our way to the other side, but it was doubtful there'd be much swimming involved. Rather, we'd have trouble staying above the surface.

There were other obstacles too. A brand-new wooden fence had been erected across the base of the deep river bend, cutting off the peninsula. Despite a public footpath running from Burford out onto the banks of the Windrush, the owner of these fields clearly didn't want anyone hopping in and out of the water, whatever the time of year. Our fears were compounded by the distant ring of shotgun fire.

About a hundred metres downstream, two other, more pressing problems arose. A pair of mute swans. If the current and speed of the river, mixed with the crack of gunfire, had made me wary about following exactly in Roger's footsteps, the idea of encroaching on the territory of a pair of angry waterfowl made my mind up for me. We'd stay close to the banks and swim against the current as best we could, upstream from the fence, minimising any fears of being shot or fending off the jab from a swan's beak.

We dropped our bags on the sodden ground and started getting changed. It was at this point that I realised that a wetsuit and silicone swimming cap were not going to be adequate protection for the task ahead. I placed my bare foot on the muddy ground and it instantly grew cold, going numb in a matter of seconds. Meanwhile, Jools tugged on his thick-soled neoprene boots and strapped the GoPro to his head, grinning.

We walked to the water's edge, where a calm pool above what would usually have been the bank made for a relatively easy entry point. Jools went first. Chest high and a couple of metres into the channel, you could see that even he was struggling. Joe followed and looked winded by the push of the water against him. I was up next.

Roger talked of a sparkling stream and a clear gravel bed, but I could only just make out my hands as I swam as strongly as possible behind Jools. At one point, feeling the current tug me towards the centre, I found myself reaching for his huge mitts, which heaved me back towards safer water.

Yet for all this, and the fact that my hands and feet felt as if they'd been given a particularly strong local anaesthetic, it was hard not to find joy in it all. As Jools smashed out an absurdly powerful front crawl, actually managing to swim upstream, I lay on my back in the shallows. I could feel the winter's gloom lifting from me. If I wasn't an atheist or lapsed Catholic, I'd have called it a spiritual experience. Everything was about that moment and that moment only. I felt as if I had transcended the everyday. Being in the water made me feel reborn. I felt a great urge to get going, to revisit more of Roger's swims, to emulate his feat and use nature as the cure for my anxieties.

I looked downstream, at the swans' necks raised like periscopes, as cars passed on the nearby road. They were a few hundred metres away, but I swear I could see a look of mystification and horror on the drivers' faces as three grown men dressed for a Channel swim frolicked in a Thames tributary in deep midwinter. The subversiveness of it all added to my sense of elation. There was happiness in being the other, the outsider, something I was sure my predecessor would have revelled in.

By now the sky was a heavy, gunmetal grey, with more rain beginning to sweep down the valley. I hauled myself out as Jools stayed suspended in midstream, his arms a windmilling blur against the colourless winter backdrop. Joe was not far behind. We stood by a pollard willow and began the tortuous task of disrobing. If it had been difficult on the Waveney, the frozen waters of the Windrush made this all but impossible. Joe sat on the grass shivering, his suit seemingly clamped to his ankles as he attempted to wrestle himself free.

With Jools now out of the water and reviewing his action cam footage with pride, we dressed quickly. Despite wearing thick socks and walking boots, my feet remained frozen. We tramped back to the car, my body giving the tiniest hint of an endorphin rush under the countless layers of winter clothing. We decamped to a local pub and demolished a pie and a pint, before I nodded off in the back seat on the drive home, the first swim of the year done. I dreamt of longer, lazier days, when wetsuits weren't needed and swims could be done in twos and threes. It would only get warmer from here on in, surely?

CHAPTER FIVE

April

~~

Benacre Broad and Covehithe Beach, Suffolk

Snow and rain continued to fall throughout March and I stayed trapped at home. A swim in this weather, dressed up to the nines in expensive water sports kit, just wasn't going to do it for me, despite the happiness and sense of freedom I had found on the Windrush. I wanted something more languid. Essentially, I wanted a summer swim. And with the weather finally starting to perk up at the start of April, I made my move.

Yanny had talked often over the winter of swimming at Benacre Broad, not far from his Beccles home or, indeed, Roger's moat at Mellis. So, with the early spring sun burning off the clouds, I hopped on a train to East Anglia for what would turn out to be the first of many trips with a bigger group of friends in an area I'd once called home.

I lived in Norwich for four years. Three as a student at the University of East Anglia, one more staving off the inevitability of career and adulthood. They were some of the happiest times of my life and I was glad to be going back after a few years away. Many of my old university friends had returned there after moving away, and getting off the clunky old InterCity 125 at Norwich station, it felt like a homecoming. I walked through the cathedral grounds, staring at its high steeple to try and catch a glimpse of the peregrine falcons which had made their home on the city's highest vantage point. I reminisced about old times and thought about recapturing the youthful spirit of those days on my swimmer's journey. There was a simplicity to them, a romanticism which had grown rose-tinted down the years, of long days spent drinking in old pubs, talking about music and books, of late nights and house parties and the belief that anything was possible. This all played directly into the easiness and possibility I felt when I was in or around water.

I passed through town, tottering over the cobbles of Elm Hill, past the arts centre where I'd embarrassed myself as a first year student at an open mic poetry night, and out onto the Dereham Road.

Molly was parked up in the Jet garage, face lit blue by the glow of her smartphone. I rapped on the passenger window.

Molly was a friend of friends. Close with Yanny, she had moved to Norwich to study on the creative writing MA at UEA a few years after I had left. We'd met on the odd occasion, exchanging hellos at mutual friends' birthday drinks. Beyond that, we hardly knew each other.

Yanny had told me she'd be up for a swim when I'd joined him on the Waveney. Molly is from Cornwall and has a long history of throwing herself into cold water. She'd once swum across Falmouth Harbour as part of a school P.E. lesson. I thought back to my inability to jump in the deep end at Bishops Stortford's grotty Grange Paddocks municipal pool, trying to repress the memory and shake off twenty years of residual embarrassment.

It was what you did as a kid in Cornwall, Molly told me as we drove out of town, through narrow country lanes towards the Suffolk border. Our chat about swimming holes, Roger Deakin and how my journey was coming along was occasionally interrupted by brief bouts of road rage, Molly switching between shouts of 'Fuck' and flicking Vs at errant drivers. The window was wound down, causing the breeze to blow her red hair across her face, and I could see the glee in her eyes behind her oversized sunglasses. It made the drive oddly compelling.

Yanny and his wife Suz were waiting for us at Covehithe church, which stands high on the cliffs about a mile south of Benacre Broad. Every year, the sea edges ever closer to this ecclesiastical ruin. The road towards the water was blocked by a metal gate, a huge sign proclaiming 'No Access to the Beach' and warning of a steep drop towards the sea. The coast erodes here faster than anywhere else in the UK. Five hundred metres disappeared between the 1830s and 2001. The path where Roger walked to Benacre Broad is now shifting sand under the heavy longshore drift.

I was particularly excited about this swim. We were going to double-dip. First we'd tackle Benacre Broad itself, in what Roger called 'water liked cooled tea', before striding across the shingle beach and into the galumphing, grey waves of the North Sea. It was a windy day, so the idea of a swim in calmer waters before being buffeted by the ocean was hugely appealing.

Ignoring the warning signs about landslides on the old path, we set out for the broad. We wandered along the edge of the cliffs, through a fallow field and then past a pig farm, the snuffling of sows reaching us on the spring wind. We clambered over a heavy wooden fence, Benacre Broad opening out in front of us. The water here was salty now, seeping through the beach and ending its time as a freshwater lagoon, as it had been in Roger's day. But it wasn't this that bothered me.

Once again, a fence was hampering my progress. Strung all around the water's edge, back inland and along the rear of the beach, this electric barrier was here for good reason: to protect the ground-nesting birds. Reeds grew tall in the shallows, so even if we braved a sharp jolt from the fence, we'd still face a huge natural obstacle. We repaired to a convenient bird hide, resting on stilts, to survey our options. From this vantage point, it was abundantly clear that stealing a swim here was going to be nigh on impossible. Roger's August excursion would have been less strenuous, and despite my experience in the Windrush, I'd yet to catch the insouciant trespassing bug in which my predecessor seemed to revel.

Instead, we made for the beach. By now, the wind was really whipping in. It is never still on the east coast, but the gale was making it hard to stand up straight, let alone pull off my clothes and get changed into my swimming shorts. I made brief mention of the fact that I'd packed my wetsuit. Molly, by now in a bikini despite the chill, gave me a withering look.

'Don't be a dickhead.'

I could tell right away that Molly was going to be just the person to help me get into the water when feelings of uncertainty or fear swelled up. The idea of 'don't think, just do' appealed to me and had cropped up on countless anxiety advice blogs I'd read in lieu of seeking out professional help for my problems. It was the kind of helpful advice Keeley had given me too. And out here on the exposed east coast, it was just what I needed to hear.

It wasn't just about conquering fears. If I was going to swim all through the year and complete my *Waterlog* mission in short order, I needed to build up my stamina. I changed awkwardly into my swimming shorts and Molly and I entered the water together, Yanny and Suz watching, sweet coffee and starchy towels out and ready for our exit. The beach shelved steeply, and as my feet cooled in the roiling waves, I dived under, all the air pushed from my lungs as I surfaced and gasped. I knew this wasn't going to be a lengthy swim, but I wanted to take a good look at my surroundings. I rolled onto my back, the huge dome of Suffolk sky wheeling above me as I tried to stay as still as possible while remaining afloat.

Back on the beach, two dead trees poked their spindly limbs through the shingle. These were once part of the bluebell wood through which Roger had walked, the remnants of which we had cut through on our walk down to the beach from Covehithe church. Sandblasted and bright white, their trunks were buried deep, branches sprouting just a few inches above the beach's surface. From my sea-bound vantage point, they swayed on the horizon. I imagined their brittle branches snapping if I dared try to clamber over them once I was dried off.

The relentless tide had changed much here since my predecessor had made the short journey from his home. The salty broad, the bluebell wood 'blindly marching into the sea'. It felt good to be in a place where I could report changes, rather than just idly wonder about the small tweaks in landscape which Roger would notice. Even since his death, just seven years previously, Covehithe and Benacre Broad had inched further into the grey pull of the rollers. Nothing, not even concerned locals, could stand in the way of the power of the sea.

I rode one of those rollers back to shore, Suz holding a towel wide to welcome me to dry land, her glasses covered in sea spray. Despite the chill breeze I realised that I wasn't feeling the cold too badly and dutifully posed for a photo in a salty pool under the cliffs, my wet shorts clinging to my thighs, my feet covered in heavy sand and pebbles. I revelled in the same feeling of possibility and freedom I had enjoyed on my Oxfordshire dip, except that this time, without the wetsuit to dull my senses, it was something approaching a chemical high. It coursed along my arms and legs and turned my pasty white body bright red. It felt magical. While I luxuriated in this soaring rush, Molly, whose scorn for the wetsuit I had to thank for this growing high, headed off to the bird hide, using it as a convenient changing room on this otherwise exposed stretch of coastline. At that moment nothing mattered and I had no worries.

With spring here Yanny's enthusiasm for my *Waterlog* project was blossoming. He spoke effusively about how he could drive me all over Suffolk to his favourite swimming haunts. We decided Bungay beach, that elusive spot on the Waveney just off Outney Common, would be our next calling point. Molly wanted in too, work depending. It was like the old days were back again, but with swimming and nature taking the place of cheap booze and student house parties.

We strode off back to the car, Molly and Suz cooing over the pigs as Yanny shouted out warnings to me to stay away from the crumbling cliff edge. The waves here had me energised and I could feel them pushing me on into a summer and a world where wild swimming, and following in Roger's footsteps, would be my only thoughts.

CHAPTER SIX

May

~~

Parliament Hill Lido, London –
Ironmonger Row Baths, London

Summer was beginning to come on strong, so I pulled the dusty tarp off my bike and cycled the eight miles through central London from Camberwell up to Hampstead Heath. Instead of my usual dip in the green-brown waters of the ponds, I was heading for Parliament Hill Lido. This art deco gem had just reopened for the season and I wanted to try its waters before the weather got searing hot and the crowds began to swell.

The previous week Joe and I had immersed ourselves for twenty minutes at Highgate, the water a barely believable 8°C. We emerged delirious, incapable of speech, giddy laughter giving way to terrifying shivers. I had ridden my bike the short distance from the pond to the Parliament Hill café in wobbly fashion, my teaspoon clinking violently against the china cup as I tried desperately to warm up. It had been funny for a brief few minutes until we realised we were on the edge of hypothermia. I had got cocky after Covehithe and the ruddy warmth I'd experienced on the beach. Today I wasn't going to be so cavalier, even if the desperation to feel what I'd felt after my Suffolk swim burned deep inside me.

The blackboard as I emerged from the changing rooms read 15°C. I pinged on a pair of scratched goggles I'd been forced to borrow from reception, having left my own at home, and stepped into the shallow end. Parliament Hill Lido had had a spruce-up since Roger's visit, the main tank replaced in 2005 and now absurdly shallow at one end. The water barely kissed my knees as I leant down and splashed my head to get a feel for the cold. I was the only one in the water, a few fellow swimmers sitting along the sides, splashing their feet, and the odd sunbather getting to work on their tan in the first of the summer sun. I worked myself into a freestyle stroke, literally crawling along the bottom for ten metres before the water buoyed me up and on towards the deep end.

With no one else in the pool, I settled quickly into a Zen-like state. Roger was lucky enough to experience the same solo joy as me. 'The absence of wavelets, or other bathers, means you can move in perfect rhythm, so the music takes over,' he wrote. 'Mind and body go off somewhere together in unselfconscious bliss, and the lengths seem to swim themselves. The blood sings, the water yields; you are in a state of grace, and every breath gets deeper and more satisfying.'

I was fully blissed out by the time I turned and pushed off back towards the shallows. Even the disappearance of the sun behind a huge grey cloud and the swift drop in air temperature couldn't deter me. I could only liken it to yoga – something I'd dabbled in while on holiday in Thailand and enjoyed immensely, though never followed up – where breathing is the only permanent thing. There was a rhythm to this swim that I had never experienced before, and I swam on and on, my muscles crying out for relief after one particularly speedy lap. That state of grace Roger talked about? This was it. It was harder to find when battling waves on a North Sea beach or trying to ignore the attentions of mute swans on a Cotswold river. But in an empty lido at the start of summer it was a feeling that could be easily accessed as long as you swam hard and let your breathing take up the slack.

Stepping out and onto the cold concrete, I dried myself off frantically, desperate to prevent a repeat of the previous week's chattering after our icy Highgate experience. It worked up to a point, aided by the indulgence of a warm shower in the ramshackle changing block. I was still utterly dazed by my experience when I eased my bike through the car park and out past Gospel Oak station. I was so high that I was unfit to be riding through busy north London streets. The rhythm of my pedals mirrored the whirling of my arms in the water and soon I was zipping down Haverstock Hill at lightning pace, letting out a hoot of joy at the sheer brilliance of the day.

The sun was going to my head and I was almost manic as I cycled past Regent's Park and on towards the centre of town. I'd become an obsessive outdoor swimmer. Cold water had replenished me, and with the heat rising, I was finding the momentum to get this journey moving quicker. Work, deadlines, that need to feel responsible for everything: all of these things were falling by the wayside now I knew there were countless stretches of cold water to throw myself into. Excitement was replacing anxiety, and my swimming journey, which felt as if it had taken forever to get going, was finally in full swing and doing what it was supposed to do. It was curing my worries, giving me a sense of lightness I had rarely enjoyed. Perhaps it wasn't a sticking plaster after all.

A few days later the early summer sun had gone and a chill returned to London. I fancied a trip to Brockwell, but Keeley wasn't so keen on the cold water of a lido on a cold spring day. So instead we settled on a trip to Ironmonger Row Baths. These facilities are one of east London's finest examples of Victorian benevolence: a place to cleanse body, soul and clothes for the working people of the city.

The idea of a 'steam up' was definitely appealing as low clouds broke and began spitting rain on us as we made the short walk from Old Street Tube to the baths. Roger's talk of off-duty cabbies sharing stories in misty steam rooms deep below the streets had me excited for an old-style London experience. The Porchester Spa in Bayswater has this untouched ambience: plastic recliners, a deep pool and tatty magazines for reading after being scorched in the sauna. I fancied this would be a similar deal.

Rounding the corner it became clear that things had changed at Ironmonger Row. Significantly. The facade had been spruced up and inside was a swanky leisure centre. This once proud local space was now very fancy and run by the same people behind the revamped Marshall Street Baths. We enquired about the spa and were sent downstairs into a wood-panelled waiting room reminiscent of the worst kind of soulless relaxation area in a fancy hotel basement.

'Have you booked?' asked a rather bolshy attendant, chewing gum and looking into the middle distance somewhere over our shoulders.

'Er, no.'

'You need to book online. There ain't no places left this weekend.'

We exchanged a glance and headed back out into the cold. We hadn't even managed a swim in the baths' smart new pool to at least make us feel like we'd earned a heavy evening meal.

Back at home, we fired up the baths' website. And there it was, the price writ large across the home page: £25 per person, £18.75 for members. If the atmosphere had suggested that things had changed at the baths and spa built to serve local workers, then this confirmed it.

There was no doubt in my then furious mind that this was a clear attempt at attracting tired office workers from the Square Mile's skyscrapers, as well as the affluent young things who patrolled the streets of east London, while shutting out those who'd lived nearby for generations. Those from the estate north of Ironmonger Row were clearly not welcome in the underground spa. Twenty-five pounds is a huge sum if you're struggling to make ends meet. It seemed a spa was an indulgence that no normal working person should be afforded.

I grabbed my copy of *Waterlog* from the shelf as Keeley filled in our bank details and booked a session for a week's time. I remembered Roger writing about the people he could just make out through the steam. One passage in particular had struck me:

'Most of the people who come to Ironmonger Row do so regularly, simply because, for a few pounds, the experience gives them an enormous amount of pleasure,' he wrote. 'They are what Josie in *Steaming* [a play by Nell Dunn inspired by Ironmonger Row] calls "the ordinary men and women who have been coming to these baths all their lives, for a swim or a laundry'".

Defining 'a few pounds' in early twenty-first century Britain, and London in particular, isn't easy. To me, a few quid was what you pay for a pint. Perhaps for those who worked in the City, that's what £25 represented. My anger swelled and I grew increasingly cynical about what Ironmonger Row had become. All this, of course, without actually stripping down to my shorts and going deep into the bowels of the spa itself.

That £25 hole in our bank account niggled me all week. It wasn't as if I couldn't afford it, but the principle of the matter led me to question who was profiting from these enterprises. Why does it cost more than £6 to swim at Tooting Lido? And a fiver at Parliament Hill? Is it because as wild swimming, swimming outdoors – whatever you want to call it – grows in popularity, it becomes an obvious target for those looking to cash in? Maybe.

Certainly that was what had happened to leisure centres across the UK. The sense of social cleansing, of keeping out the great unwashed, was there at every turn in places run on behalf of or instead of local councils. High prices and monthly membership fees abounded. It felt like another example of how our country has become a profit-making tool for a small elite.

I raged about this at Keeley as the following Saturday came around and once again we walked through damp, drizzly streets to Ironmonger Row. She nodded, but being a person who'll take any opportunity to be steamed and scoured, she was happy to wear the £25 cost. She knew that the equivalent, fancier joints in the centre of town cost four or five times as much, something which I'd failed to factor in as I grumbled.

Presented with a robe and slippers, we were ushered into separate changing areas, where I struggled with a magnetic key for the lockers, requiring the help of two members of staff to stash my belongings. I emerged into the communal area beyond feeling harried, ready to spend some time lying down and doing not much at all while the steam worked its magic. I was missing the simple joy of throwing myself into a pond, lake or lido. This all seemed a little too fussy to me compared with the basic joys of a wild swim.

The first thing that greeted me was a distinct whiff of effluent as a cleaner opened a hidden door and shoved away a broom. Hardly the ideal start. I tried to get past this initial disappointment and found Keeley lolling on a lounger reading a fashion magazine. Her short brown hair was tied in a small ponytail. Her blue eyes sparkled with excitement.

'Ready?' she asked, before bustling purposefully past a group of refuseniks in the plunge pool and into the closest steam room. I could just make out the shape of one man in the corner, curled up with his forearm covering his eyes, sweating as if he'd just completed a marathon. There was a burble of conversation, but I kept myself to a quiet corner and tried to empty my mind of all thoughts.

My cynicism subsided and I fell into a reverie, quietly contemplating the cold swims of recent weeks and the contrast with this skin-puckering room. I lasted about five minutes before I lunged for the door and forced myself into the iciness of the plunge. A group of women squealed as they immersed themselves. Highgate's cooling waters had prepared me for this moment and I offered up a simple 'hnnng' as I dropped my head and shoulders right in.

My skin seethed as Keeley led us to the ice chips, spat out from a specially designed tap. I scratched some across my face and chest and retired to read in the relaxation room, all dark panelling and slippery, marble floors. I slept and went back for another steam.

Dried off and with the complexion of a prune, I emerged into the spa's foyer a hopeless convert, Keeley's glowing face a picture of post-spa happiness. I felt amazing. The feeling was wholly different to the endorphin rush I'd enjoyed on my most recent dips. Movements were slowed, my body didn't shiver and my mood was blissful rather than ebullient. For a brief moment as we returned to the Tube, I wondered if I ought to make my journey one that visited Britain's best high-end spas and leave Roger's swims alone. At that moment, the cost was immaterial.

But my disaffection crept back in the days after. I spoke about it with an old journalist friend. He had lived in Shoreditch, before it had been rid of its character and turned into a theme park for those who thought it was a place the world's hipsters still bothered with, and told me about trips to Ironmonger Row with fellow hacks. It seems it had become something of a haunt for those after an authentic taste of the East End.

'It always had the feeling of something about to kick off,' he said. 'You got proper characters in there. Cabbies, old Turkish guys on the staff to rub you down, low-level gangsters. There could be a funny vibe, but it was mostly welcoming.'

When I told him how much it now cost, he was gobsmacked.

'It was eight quid last time I went. That was before it got tarted up, though.'

I felt cheated. For all my elation, it felt like Ironmonger Row was just another place that had lost its soul in this part of town. The revamp had cost £16.5 million between 2010 and 2012. That's a lot of money to spend on something that looks great but has no heart. Yes, there was still an old-style laundry for the locals, but it felt like the smallest of concessions. Like nearby Spitalfields Market, Ironmonger Row had turned into a parody of its original concept, somewhere for most visitors to go once and forget about, rather than being a cornerstone of a community to always return to. This was an area of East London that was changing rapidly: council houses being sold off, luxury homes being built, people who had lived here for years being forced out. And having gone just that one time, I felt like I was part of the problem.

CHAPTER SEVEN

June

∼

Holkham, Norfolk – River Waveney, Suffolk

With the mixed feelings after my trip to Ironmonger Row still fresh in my mind, I decided to get out of London again and head back up to East Anglia. I wanted to sling myself into cold water and come up dazed and giddy, the regrettable changes at Ironmonger Row blitzed away by the iciness of a slow-moving river.

Yanny and I had plotted another trip to the Waveney, this time to the quiet stretch near Mendham Mill. Summer was here and I was ready for my pasty arms and chest to sear red after a day of swimming and idling.

I had invited my old university friend Tim to come and join us. Tim was a writer also, based in Norwich. We had been firm friends back in the day and I was looking forward to catching up with him and sharing the water with someone new. I enjoyed the fact that as my journey wore on I was surrounding myself with a growing band of willing cohorts. It was proving to be a chance to rekindle old relationships at an age when, it seemed to me, it grew increasingly harder to maintain the friendships of earlier years.

As the knackered train creaked and clattered into Manningtree, past mudflats pockmarked with oyster catchers and derelict factory buildings smashed to smithereens, my phone buzzed. Yanny. He'd had a flare-up of his arthritis and wasn't going to be able to make it. His guidance at Mendham was essential, my own failure to bring along a map of any kind compounding the problem. Until now I had been solely reliant on Roger's words and a blind faith in the power of Google Maps. I was going to have to start preparing better.

With no other guide to hand, I dug out *Waterlog* and scoured the passages dotted throughout the book that dealt with this part of England, Roger's home. There was his moat at Mellis, but without seeking prior permission we couldn't swim there. Or John's Water on the River Bure. But, again, without a map we'd be driving blind along single-track country lanes. And then it appeared on the page, its huge skies and empty sands calling out to me. Holkham Bay.

I broke the news of our change of plans to Tim as we drove out of the car park at Norwich train station. Having only just passed his test a week earlier, Tim wasn't too concerned about where we were going, just that it was straightforward and that neither of us would die getting there. His licence made him another handy cab driver for my nationwide wild-swimming exploits. I didn't mention this new role to him as we caught up, but I knew then that we would be seeing a lot more of each other over the coming summer months.

By now it was getting properly warm. We wound down the windows and followed the long road north out of the 'fine city' and away to the coast. As the fields flatten here, the skies appear to grow and grow. If Covehithe's great dome was vast and impressive, this was a whole new level. The only thing blocking the sun were the tall hedgerows lining the dusty roads.

Parking up at Holkham Hall, in the shade of the swaying poplars on the avenue which leads to the beach, Tim was buzzing about our impending dip. Tim's excitability was legendary among our friends. His capacity to do and try new things had seen him always toe a fine line between the impressive and the idiotic. On the one hand, Tim had become a crack clay pigeon shot, learning the ins and outs of vintage firearms to ensure a key passage in the novel he was writing was accurate in every detail.

On the other hand, I had witnessed him order the hottest curry available on the menu of the greasy tandoori establishment we frequented as students. The reason? Just to prove that he could do it. Sweat poured from his forehead as he mixed more and more rice into the sauce in the hope of cooling it down. This youthful braggadocio had thankfully found an outlet in extreme research for his writing projects.

As we sorted through our swimming kit and locked up the car, Tim told me about a recent sea swim at nearby Waxham, where his wife Lisa had looked on in horror as he'd bounded in, through the high rollers and out into the bob and sway of the North Sea. The water there had made him a convert to the joys of sea swimming, hence he'd got in touch to see if he could tag along next time I was up near Norwich.

Roger's long walk along this stretch of coastline heralded a day of endless dips in shallow pools left by the retreating tide. Walking out over the sandy boardwalk, I was hoping for the same, and as we crested the last high dune, I was not disappointed. A light breeze ruffled my hair, the odd grain of sand catching in my untrimmed beard. As Roger said, the tide line here was 'only a distant, whispering line of white.'

The huge tidal range at Holkham makes the sand hard as rock the closer you get to the beach. I could feel the thick ridges through the soles of my shoes as we made brisk headway towards the churned-up water, Tim's carrier bag stuffed with swimming kit cracking in the wind. By contrast, my kit was neatly folded in a large rucksack which sat heavy on my back.

That distant line of white we'd seen half a mile back was now a high, roiling squiggle. The North Sea was swirling in the wind, hissing in the brief moments when the breakers stopped to draw breath. Rather than go in together, we agreed to take a one after the other approach, keeping an eye on the bags. In reality, there was no need for such caution. Our only company was a pair of horse riders splashing in the surf back towards Wells. Only our shared levels of anxiety were to blame for such nervousness. Tim didn't know that I was on a mission to cure my worries, but I knew that he too suffered. He'd written about it extensively, his book on the subject making for essential reading whenever I caught myself in a fret or panic.

Tim gamely struggled out of his trousers and into his red swimming shorts. He bolted towards the water and shouted bloody murder as the waves took him. His mop of dark curls and his broad shoulders disappeared immediately, the sheer height of the waves making it impossible to spot him. I panicked. What would I tell Lisa? How would I get his car home? Where would his bloated body wash up?

Ten seconds – which felt like ten minutes – passed, and then there he was, soaked and pumping his arms as if he'd just struck a ninetieth-minute winner in the World Cup final. He disappeared again, and again my anxiety swelled, only to be allayed when I saw him jumping wave after wave after wave.

A quarter of an hour later he ran back, belting out the *Baywatch* theme tune at the top of his voice.

The only thing missing was an orange buoyancy aid and a tenuous mission to protect the coastline from a nuclear leak out at sea.

I was on the edge of tears with laughter, Tim's loud cackle catching on the wind and sounding out across the empty beach. I felt ten years younger, delirious and happy.

'Ah man, it's fucking amazing in there. It's not even cold,' he said, his face fixing itself into the kind of grin only a hefty amount of time swimming outdoors can provoke.

I only half believed him. It was June, after all, and this was the first proper hint of what you'd call summer. Surely it hadn't heated up that much.

I stepped out of my jeans, my swimming shorts already on, and made a run for it. Tim was right. This was like lukewarm, salty bathwater, albeit wilder. Everything around me was white. The bleeding edge of the sky and the sea, the bubbling water which was now up to my waist. I dived under and felt its force, surfacing just as another wave came in and slapped me backwards, causing me to fall and graze my knees on the sandy bottom.

I stood up and waded in further. A small break in the waves allowed me to swim a few strokes before the swell lifted me and sent me further out. I lost sight of the beach. I could have been miles out to sea, treading water off the side of a yacht rather than twenty metres from Tim and a pile of clothes.

A huge wave appeared on the horizon. I quickly spun around, swimming front crawl furiously in an attempt to ride its crest back to the shallows. Knees grazed again and mood rising, I turned and did it again. And again. And again. This cycle went on for ten minutes or so, until I was so worn out that my body cried out for respite. I dunked my head under, rubbed the salty water into my beard and made my way back to my towel.

Dried off and exuberant, we began to walk back over the beach. The lagoons Roger spoke of weren't deep enough for a dip, so we contented ourselves by crunching our way over razor clams, their shells emitting a fizzing sound as the wind flung sand across them. I had forgotten all about the Waveney and our plans for Mendham. I was too lost in a seaside dream.

In Wells, I bought fudge for Keeley and ate fish and chips by the harbour. By now the sun was gone and grey cloud was billowing in from the north, a final reminder that summer wasn't quite underway. It didn't matter. We folded ourselves into the car, buzzed by the day's restorative dip and drove back to the city along winding roads under high cloud.

A week on, I enlisted Tim's driving skills and we set off east out of Norwich towards Bungay. We left the car by the town's pretty church and set off across Outney Common to begin our search for Bungay beach or 'the Sandy' as some locals call it.

This elusive spot on the Waveney runs along the top end of the common, where an oxbow bends the river until its deep meander almost bites its tail. With rope swings and a sandy spot for laying towels, it sounded like the ideal place to cool off on what was fast becoming the hottest day of the year so far. The underwater roots hiding hungry pike from view didn't seem too alluring, though. I decided I would swim well away from their reaches.

Once again, I had failed on the map front. If I was going to do this journey seriously, I was going to have to start collecting OS maps. The empty green space on Google Maps was never going to cut it and I was a fool to think it would. I scrolled over the dead space on the map until I caught sight of the blue Waveney, a squiggle on the screen of my iPhone. We tramped on through long grass and nettles towards the water, increasingly losing hope of finding the beach and having a lengthy session by the water.

Teetering over a rotten wooden bridge which crossed an old ditch clogged with brambles, we emerged onto the banks of the Waveney. Cries of 'fore' from the golf club which swallows up part of the common receded as we tracked along the water's edge, looking for a convenient spot to slip in. Weed billowed beneath the current, green and abundant, lush in the summer sun. It looked like the perfect place for a pike to hide, readying itself for a nibble on a flashing toe.

Staring down into the depths from the high bank, I remembered the only time I'd ever caught one of these beasts as a teenager, my line tautening and reel screaming as it shot off down the River Stort. Pulling its huge body from the water, I recalled teasing out the hooks through its gills so I didn't lose any fingers. It thrashed and thrashed before it tired itself out and I let it slip away out of the net and back to a better hiding spot, where it wouldn't be so easily tempted by the quick, garish blur of an old spinner.

I mentioned this to Tim and he began regaling me with a passage from *Swallows and Amazons* about the dissection of a pike and the discovery of smaller fish deep within its guts. By now he was really getting into the subject, discussing strategies on how to get such a huge, angry, voracious fish off various bodily appendages. Nothing was left to the imagination, Tim's instincts as a writer taking over. The thought of taking a swim here, so appealing as we walked over the common, was quickly receding.

We walked slowly, realising our hopes of finding 'the Sandy' were slim to non-existent. A muddy cutaway led quickly down from the bank to the water – not quite a beach, but good enough for wading in and out. I slung my towel around my waist and yanked on my swimming shorts. Unlike at Holkham, Tim was more than happy for me to go in first.

Despite the rising temperature, a long wet spring meant the river water was still bitingly cold. The sweatiness of the walk was quickly gone and I turned to beckon Tim in.

Last week he'd bounded in, but now I could see he was stepping with extra caution, sinking into the muddy riverbed and grunting as his waist edged towards the surface. He dived in face first and emerged shouting at the top of his voice.

'Oh my fucking God. Oh my fucking God, it's cold!'

Tim is prone to melodrama. This is a man who once thought he'd fractured his kneecap jumping off the front platform of a double-decker bus. And while I rolled my eyes at the show he put on for the bored cows on the far side of the Waveney, I did have some sympathy.

This was Tim's first ever river swim. He had told me this in the car on the way to Bungay and explained how he'd mentioned our adventure on the phone to his nan that morning. There had been dark portents about Weil's disease and the need for a hot shower the minute he got home.

I recalled my first time. The sliminess of the Granta's bed and the slight pull of the slow current. The fresh whiff of the water which clung to my beard and didn't leave me all day. I remembered not showering until the following morning, wanting to keep that natural scent about me as long as possible. I realised now, as I swam along the Waveney, just how grim that must have been for anyone who'd come into close contact with me that day.

Staying warm was doubtless Tim's top priority as we each settled into our own pace and peered up at the Suffolk sky, streaked with vapour trails.

We shambled out together after twenty minutes of perfect summer bathing. By now it was scorching and neither of us was in a particular hurry to get back to the car. We passed an amiable half an hour nattering and snoozing on the bank, sussing out swimming spots nearby and deciding when we'd hit Roger's trail together again. The cool water and pike talk hadn't deterred Tim. If anything, he was already more of an evangelist for jumping into rivers than I was. Being around him had left me energised and enthused about what was beginning to look like an epic trip around the British Isles.

CHAPTER EIGHT

July

~~

Mendham Mill, Suffolk – Geldeston Locks,
Suffolk – Hampstead Mixed Pond, London –
River Itchen, Hampshire – Little Ouse, Norfolk –
River Avon, Fladbury, Worcestershire

A month passed, and as the heat soared I really should have been out swimming my way through *Waterlog*, heading deeper into the maze, as Roger put it. But a holiday in New York to see friends, followed by the need to crack on with work to cover the costs of my transatlantic sojourn and my recent dips, meant it was over a month before I made my way out of London for a dip. It was a beautiful July day when I met my friend Joe at Liverpool Street and we boarded the Norwich train, chatting about Andy Murray's recent Wimbledon win and how Joe's beloved Swansea City were shaping up for the new football season. Joe is a writer of some renown, an old friend and one who's never been afraid of doing anything which involves more than a modicum of mild peril. I've heard tales of him climbing cliffs in South Wales in howling gales while mutual friends looked up from the beach in horror.

He was also the subject of one of my favourite swimming mishaps, thankfully one with a happy ending. After a particularly heavy night at the Port Eliot literary festival, Joe decided to join a group of hardy fellow festivalgoers for a brief dip in the nearby estuary. At least, he thought it was going to be a brief dip.

After two hours' sleep, he woke up and joined a bunch of swimmers who issued him with a number and a swimming cap, before ushering him into a minibus and driving him a mile to the start point. Everyone waded in through gloopy mud, setting a mean pace with the tide. Joe, usually a man capable of holding his own in physical challenges, battled gamely on to the end, only to emerge blue and in need of a long lie down.

I had been regaled with this story by Molly, who had witnessed it first hand and swum strongly that day, somewhat delighting in Joe's misery as he brought up the rear. We were on our way to meet her, as well as Tim, Yanny and another friend, Luke, for a swim at Mendham Mill. Having failed to get here in June, I was desperate to have another crack and swim in yet another section of the Waveney.

The mill pond here is where the painter Alfred Munnings, an official artist at the Western Front, learnt the basics of the breaststroke, according to Roger, and it was outside the pub named after him in Mendham village that we congregated, shading ourselves while Yanny headed off in search of a convenient place to enter the water.

It wasn't looking promising. It seemed Roger had stolen a swim here. The mill is private and the grass cutters were in, the river filling with cuttings billowing from the lawns. We walked slowly back through the village, peering over the bridge which crosses the Waveney as it widens. Open to the road and in view of houses, it was hardly an idyllic summer swimming spot.

Yanny assumed the role of my wild-swimming Sancho Panza, tilting at watery windmills, desperate to don his Victorian gentleman's swimming costume and submerge himself in Roger's favourite river. He said he knew of a spot further downstream, and so we piled back into our respective cars and took the short drive to Shotford Bridge. Despite running close to the road, the Waveney here was well hidden down a steep bank, a convenient landing stage for fishermen, and perfect for changing out of sweaty clothes and into swimming shorts.

After sharing swims with just one or two people, this was the first time I'd had what could be described as a swimming party. The July weather lent the whole morning an end-of-school-year vibe and we each plopped into the shallow waters shouting and jostling. Yanny disappeared away upstream, wading off in his striped swimming costume. Molly and Luke went belly-sliding downstream, the Waveney here shallow enough for underwater exploration as long as we shared the two pairs of goggles Joe and I had remembered to bring.

Tim and I swam out of our depth and splashed out fast circles while Joe disappeared back up towards the road, emerging at the top of a high, metal-clad retaining wall, readying himself to jump. He fired imaginary pistols above his head like a cowboy, his long blond hair and pale frame striking against the deep greens of the trees. The water was far too shallow for jumping, but he did it anyway, legs wheeling, his face gurning into a comedic grin as he looked towards me, crashing into the river. We sent up a cheer as he emerged unscathed, scaled the bank and did it all again.

Each of us slowly drifted off into our own river trance. I put on my goggles and breaststroked up and down as far as this short stretch would allow. Small chub swam nonchalantly back towards the dark, rooty spaces beneath a willow tree as I floated face down, the light refracting on green and gold pebbles just inches from my nose. Shade from the high branches and swaying nettle beds made the river cool and calm, a blessed respite from the scorching heat of the open road.

Luke, Tim and I took it in turns to sit on the landing stage, warming up for a few minutes before going off exploring again. As I finally dried off, I looked up to see Molly on point, leading a band of wild swimmers upstream through the centre of the river, each one picking out an awkward path over the slippery stones. Luke was still wearing his Wayfarer sunglasses, his hair slicked back, somehow managing to retain a level of cool. The woozy opening bars of 'The End' by The Doors looped in my head as I watched my friends in their own strange *Apocalypse Now* here in the East Anglian countryside. It wasn't quite the long swim up to the mill pond which Roger had indulged in, but my faith in river swimming as an inherently social experience, something to be embraced rather than feared, was reaffirmed. Sharing this sometimes illicit activity with a big group added to the warm glow of my already strong endorphin buzz. It soothed my anxiety, it made my depression feel less all-encompassing.

Suitably geed up after our excursion at Mendham, we formed a convoy and drove to Geldeston and the locks, where I had swum with Yanny and Amy back in the gloomy onset of autumn. Down by the water a smattering of schoolkids were lounging, drinking cans of cheap cider and holding cigarettes daintily between thumb and forefinger. Occasionally, one of the boys would execute an impressive dive from high up on the concrete bridge, watched by the girls who cooed further up the bank.

It was great to return here on a steamy day and see the river taken over by swimmers and idlers. No one from the pub complained about people jumping into the water. In fact, they seemed to positively encourage it, bar staff occasionally popping up and waving encouragement to those down on the banks.

Most of all I was excited to be back without my wetsuit and wasted no time yanking on my wet shorts and sinking in. The water here felt deep and luxurious compared to the shallow, riffling white stuff near Shotford Bridge earlier in the day. Not ones to be outdone by younger revellers, Luke and Joe set about showing off to the assembled crowd.

Being a stand-up poet, Luke's predilection for public boasting is a source of professional pride. His wild hair, each strand usually styled just so, was a browny-blond mess now that it had begun to dry out in the summer sun. He strutted over the bridge as if he was walking on stage at the Edinburgh Fringe, threw a long leg over the high fence and then carefully balanced himself, ready to jump, enjoying the encouragement of onlookers.

After milking the attention, Luke threw himself ten feet below into the weed-packed water, an ungainly whirl of limbs disappearing into the Waveney's depths. The young lads didn't even try to hide how impressed they were, even if Luke emerged gasping and spitting out the long draught of the river he'd accidentally taken on board.

Joe was up next. Ever competitive and always looking to one-up his pals when it comes to feats of derring-do, he picked his way through the kids' bags and errant limbs, flexing his toes over the retaining wall, opting for a shallow dive rather than a cannonball from the bridge. It was nigh on perfect – a small splash as his hands, head and then feet disappeared. The appreciative cheer sent Luke scurrying through the kissing gate and back to the bridge's crest for another go.

Molly, Tim and I eschewed the festivities for something more sedate and in keeping with the hot weather. The poplar trees on the far bank sang in the light breeze as I swam off against the sluggish current and let the cold take hold of me. The water was thick with weeds which wrapped themselves around my arms and legs. I swam on regardless. Once again, there was no chance of spotting otters. No matter. Three successive swims in this hallowed river had made my summer, and there was so much more to come. We crawled out one by one, sunk quick pints of Green Jack ale in the sunny beer garden and readied ourselves for more adventures, following wherever Roger pointed.

I returned to London thirsty for water. As the weather got warmer, every day without a dip – a *Waterlog* dip – was beginning to feel like a waste. But with work tying me to town for a few days, a longer trip wasn't immediately possible. Instead, I packed my swimming things and headed up to Hampstead and the mixed pond.

Roger's passing mention of this shared bathing spot meant it wasn't strictly on my list, but I had come to see it as my version of his moat. There was no chance of me digging my own in the small yard that passed for a garden at the back of my Camberwell flat, after all. The place held happy memories for me. It was, after all, the first place Keeley and I had swum wild, not to mention the perfect place for skipping out of writing up features on the latest expensive tech for the day. Phone reception here was non-existent, thanks to the bulk of Parliament Hill.

I had been coming here regularly in between my *Waterlog* adventures ever since it had opened at the end of May. Now it was late July, the last chance for a midweek dip before things got crazy and the place became a hormonal theatre, with demob-happy teenagers from across north London looking to impress each other on long, hazy summer afternoons.

On my recent visits I had found the place empty, muddy after a long series of downpours and free for me to roam around at leisure, strewing my clothes and bags over benches and flagstones, allowing me the chance to indulge myself in a slow lap of the rainy pond without distraction. It was a quick fix for anxious thoughts which welled up when I worried about why I didn't feel like a success with work and how long this *Waterlog* adventure was going to take. My spreadsheet was turning green at an alarmingly slow rate and it was beginning to sink in that it was going to take a lot longer than anticipated. I beat myself up about failing to follow through on my initial plan to be finished by the end of the summer, even though this whole trip was meant to stop me from doing just that. When I got to the pond, whatever the weather, these concerns were washed away in the murky water.

London was cloudless as I pushed through the old kissing gate at the pond's entrance. Spanish exchange students sunned themselves on the rammed banks, and I had to stuff my rucksack deep into some nettles, the only green space not covered in towels and lithe bodies.

Molly had joined me. It was her first time at the mixed and she was in need of a swim after a sweaty train trip down from Norwich.

We changed quickly and joined the long queue down the jetty towards the cold metal steps. Molly still had her sunglasses on to deflect the glare and had eschewed my high-factor sunscreen for something less protective. She wanted her light skin to tan quicker, she said. Swimmers trod water and waited their turn to climb out as we kicked our legs in preparation for the cool water. It was a refreshing 21°C. Cold enough to know about it, warm enough that you could stay in an age and not get the shivers.

As we swam, heads out and chatting like a pair of swimming retirees in a local pool, we talked about the joys of swimming when skiving. Molly told me about a particularly dull workshop she'd attended in Stratford which she left to go for a swim in the Avon. She'd even bought a single glass of wine from Marks & Spencer to toast her swimming success on the banks afterwards. I could only applaud such dedication to choosing this activity over anything else in life.

This is one of the joys of head-out breaststroke: the chance to swim and catch up at the same time, the social aspect of the experience at its fullest. This was my kind of swimming.

One of the best things about the mixed pond is that no matter how busy it gets, you can always find your bubble. Swim ten metres from where the kids are diving and you'll find your own space away from the crowds. Plough out the eighty metres to the rope and your nearest company will likely be a golden retriever swimming close to the causeway, a further twenty or so metres away. It's a place where solitude is an art, a rare thing in our capital city. You can go in harried by the world and emerge cocooned from its excesses.

Molly and I swam in sync, water boatmen darting across our surface-level field of vision. Back towards the jetty, a scream went up as a huge fish galumphed out of the water. Thanks to this interloper, the water cleared, giving us a clear route back to the steps and dry land.

Hampstead's water had thoroughly soaked my bones and partly allayed my anxieties about how well I was doing with my trip. It also steeled me for what I knew was going to be an awkward trip to Winchester and the fast-flowing Itchen. Roger had revelled in a dispute with the staff from the college in this ancient town, jumping fences and darting along the expensive trout stream, treating it like the wild-swimming paradise it so clearly should have been. When collared he fought his corner expertly, clearly enjoying battling the killjoys who wouldn't countenance sharing their expensive riparian pleasures.

He described his set-to with a dog-walking warden as 'first rate', but I was in no mood for any kind of confrontation. I'd never been bawled out for taking a swim and I didn't want to start now. My need to stay on the right side of authority, so heavily ingrained since childhood, swelled within me as I walked down the busy high street and onto College Walk.

The Itchen here was hidden from view, fences keeping the chalky path arrow-straight. After half a mile or so, the river swung into view and kissed a high wall. Rushes, weeds and darting fish hove into view. I could make out everything in perfect detail, the water gin-clear and crying out to be swum in. I weighed up picking my way over the barbed-wire fence and being done with it. But the shallow water and long drop meant this was no place to be hopping in.

Instead, I walked on and found the perfect place for a swim. Three benches overlooked a fine curve in the river, water rushing left to right and away out of town. On the far bank, a huge, officious sign had been drilled into the ground:

'PRIVATE FISHING. NO BATHING.'

I had been prepared for this proprietorial approach. Roger had spoken of this being an expensive place to fish. Today, twenty-four days of trout fishing on the Itchen starts at £2,415.

It was an obscene price to pay and I felt a sudden urge to do as my predecessor had done and stick it to the private members who had taken this river from public use. Rivers should be for everyone. As long as users show respect, there can be space for all.

I walked on. The signs began appearing with more frequency, even as the Itchen crept off into the trees and the path settled back into its straitened ways. I weighed up swimming in the long, man-made stream which ran to my right, but decided it wasn't deep enough. I stopped on a small bridge and tried to think what I was going to do. I had to swim, but where?

While I muttered to myself over my map, a yellow wagtail dropped to my side, bobbed its tail and flew off downstream. I had begun to formulate a plan and now I followed this natty bird's lead, convinced it was showing me the way.

A couple of hundred metres on, I found my spot. Where the path met the road and the Itchen turned left to meet the Itchen Navigation, an old wooden field gate hung open, a faded 'No Entry' sign stuck fast across its middle. I edged through and tramped across dry leaf mulch towards the water. There was no one around and I knew immediately that this was my place. The path I had walked on was just visible and I could hear voices, so I kept low, changing by the trunk of an oak tree. This was to be my homage to Roger's long, luxurious Hampshire swim.

I slid myself down the short drop into the Itchen. The long shadows of the trees meant it was brilliantly cold, even in late July. I nosed off, the only things visible the banks to either side, the water racing around me at impressive speed. The odd fish bobbed to the surface, air bubbles echoing outwards, each one doubtless wondering who this joker was and why he was taking a swim in their river.

It felt glorious to be in the scene here, actually part of this spectacular little river, renowned for its wildlife and oxygen-rich water. I ducked my head under and allowed myself a few more minutes before the cold finally got to me and I sprang out, skin raw, the sharp rub of starchy towel on skin bringing me back to reality. I had succeeded, even if it was a shorter swim than Roger had managed. This was becoming a pattern, but it didn't matter. I was seeing how this journey was turning into my own take on my predecessor's efforts. Still, I was finding time to enjoy some of the other, non-swimming delights Roger had revelled in here on the Itchen. The sense of stealing a swim, thumbing my nose at the college's unseen authority figures, felt fabulous and was something I wanted to experience again.

I'd never been one for breaking the rules. At school I'd taken great pleasure in boasting about never getting a detention and was always the first to run away from any kind of trouble. I was the archetypal goody two shoes, something which I had revelled in at the time, even if it made me wholly unpopular with my schoolmates.

This new-found taste for subversiveness, albeit discovered in the hardly daring act of a five-minute swim in a private trout stream, made me like myself more. It was a side of me I wanted to spend more time with. I was finding pleasure in wild swimming beyond the water itself, in the truth and beauty of the wildlife and countryside which I was experiencing now on a regular basis, whether it was accessible to all comers or not. My first illicit dip felt fantastic. I thought of Roger strolling through the long grass in the meadows here, arms swinging, whistling an aimless, happy tune. I know he would have approved of my antics.

I walked back towards Winchester grinning inanely. On the train home, though, a rumble of discontent welled up when I thought about all those prohibitive signs. The right to roam has been greatly extended since *Waterlog* was written, opening up land that had otherwise been lost to the wider public. But not here in Winchester. I wanted the same golden days, Roger had dreamed about when he came here. Days where the whole town decamped to the Itchen and enjoyed its embrace. There were times like that at lidos now all over the UK, more so than at any time since Roger's trip, but our rivers were made out to be cut off, unloved and 'dangerous' when it came to wild swimming. In fact, they were anything but. They were – they are – magical and waiting to be explored.

One river I'd been desperate to explore further was the Little Ouse in the sandy Brecklands in southern Norfolk, where it flowed through the village of Santon Downham. It sounded far away from everything, a wide trickle in a strange and fantastical place that would provide a neat counterpoint to the chalky dip I'd enjoyed down on the Itchen.

I criss-crossed my way back across the country, stopping in London long enough to cross off the Itchen on my *Waterlog* planner, spend some time wandering around Ruskin Park with Keeley and get some cursory work done before meeting Tim in Norwich. The weather had taken a muggy turn: warm enough for shorts, wet enough that you needed to sweat your way from car to riverbank in a rain jacket. Tim parked a few feet from the smart iron bridge which crosses the Little Ouse at Santon

Downham and we picked our way carefully through tall stinging nettles down to the water. The water looked inviting, and while Tim dallied on the side I got undressed, letting my feet be sucked into the sandy mud beneath the surface.

I could tell Tim wasn't feeling this spot. Normally he was the first to run headlong into the cold and scream and shout about it. Midges clouded the bank and nipped at my chest as I waded in deeper. A huge dragonfly hovered across my eye line for five seconds before zipping away upstream.

The Little Ouse here was barely thigh deep. Roger spoke of a long wade upstream, letting himself be pushed back towards the village with the current at his back. If it was good enough for him, it was good enough for me. While Tim farted around with his backpack, I went off on a long wander, the rain now falling steadily on my back and keeping me warm as my feet and ankles slowly, steadily lost all feeling in the cold river water. Water crowfoot ballooned around my legs, the occasional air bubble giving up the river's fishy secrets.

Being the height of summer, everything down the middle channel of this secret river looked green: the water beneath me; the shrubs falling to its edges; the dark, gloomy trees higher up on its banks. A verdant little oasis untroubled by angry signs, it was so unlike the Itchen, but equally as beautiful in its own way.

I finally dipped my shoulders under and belly-slid through the shallows, back towards Tim. With the rain teeming down, it felt great to be properly wet, not just given a cursory soaking while out on a walk.

I'm a passionate hater of the rain. But I had discovered that I loved it when it came down while I was in the water. I'd experienced the rising flotsam during a rain shower at Hampstead mixed pond in my first summer of swimming outdoors and was immediately hooked. It felt like the sky and the pond were at one.

I felt the same here on the Little Ouse, a summer downpour bolstering my mood as I peered out from just above the surface, my nose blowing bubbles as I went. Just as I decided that the cold was getting a bit too much, Tim followed me in, a quick shaft of sunlight greeting his descent into the shallows.

He plunged quickly and swam hard as I hopped back to my bags. As I turned I saw he was about to be trapped in a classic pincer movement by a flotilla of angry looking swans. A pair were sauntering upstream, a trio of cohorts quietly making their way in the opposite direction. I had been hissed at enough to know that angry swans are best avoided. As fast as Tim had got in he was out again, cursing their approach.

We drove through Grimes Graves, the site of a Neolithic flint mine, a prehistoric industrial hub in this rural corner of one of England's most cut-off counties. I wanted to find the River Wissey, that little hush of a stream which flowed out of MOD land and away to join the Great Ouse on its journey out to the North Sea via the Wash.

We parked up in the village of Ickburgh, by the beautiful stone church of St Peter's, and set off in completely the wrong direction. We worked our way through tall grass, across private land and over fences looking for this secret spot. Once again, my navigational smarts hadn't extended to a map. Roger would be appalled, I knew. I vowed that this would be the last time this happened. Surely a swimmer should have a decent map collection to fall back on? I skulked back to the car, angry at myself for getting so close but not doing my research properly. Rather than forgive myself this oversight, I brooded on it as Tim drove me back to Norwich and I boarded the train to London. I managed to convince myself that I wasn't living up to Roger's lofty expectations, whatever they were. I don't doubt that he would have laughed this off and suggested we go for a swim so I could clear my head. Roger had pored over maps in Cambridge University's library and, rather than beat myself up for failing to do some cartographical planning of my own, I just needed to make sure I did so in the future.

Where I was heading next maps were not required, because a local guide was on hand to direct me. Cropthorne Water Mill at Fladbury on the River Avon was a private affair, and I'd been invited to swim there by the owner, George, after I'd done some detective work, found his email address and written to him about my trip. His cousin Judith had asked Roger down in the 1990s having seen one of his newspaper articles on wild swimming.

The Environment Agency had seemingly wanted to go to war with Judith's family for having the temerity to paddle in these waters. A letter spoke of the 'considerable risks' of jumping into the Avon and the need to 'take children to a local swimming pool instead'. It clearly hadn't deterred them.

George and his son John, who had collected me from the train station at Evesham, led me down to the river from the road, ringing a bell and hailing the punt from the mill on the far bank. Attached to a pulley, it slid across the water, a huge group of fifteen swimmers awaiting our arrival on the other side.

It was everything I had hoped for. In my email to George I'd asked if I could possibly come down, snoop about and perhaps go on a long swim upstream. I had thought I'd be the only one taking to the water, pushing off and turning back for London within an hour or two. But already everyone had changed into their swimming kit, ready to join in. After the briefest of introductions to young cousins, grandparents and spouses, I was ushered into a back room of the mill to put on my shorts, before being led up into the living room on the first floor by John and his brother. I knew what was coming.

Roger mentions that swimmers here jumped out of the window into the Avon far below. But he doesn't say whether he did it. It seemed I had no choice in the matter. John ushered me forward to look out of the window. I had thought it was a sheer drop out into the river, but there was a four-foot wide path skirting the mill which needed to be cleared first. John clambered into the frame of the window, which stood a few inches from the floor, stretched his long tanned arms backwards and catapulted himself out into the open. A huge splash and the odd cheer told me he'd made it safely. His younger brother James was next. He was fourteen and just a few inches shy of six feet. Gangly but extremely confident, he disappeared and emerged soaked and smiling. I tried to remember being his age, memories of failing to flop into the deep end during school swimming lessons once again resurfacing. If these teenagers seemed fearless, it was because they were.

George watched behind me as I moved up to the window and looked out. By now, everyone downstairs was watching, eying me gleefully for any signs of weakness. At that moment I wanted nothing more than to walk back to the river bank, slip in and swim away as fast as possible on a solo exploration. I closed my eyes, the faces of my old classmates gawping and jeering at my eleven-year-old self haunting the darkness. I couldn't let my hosts down. I hung back in the frame, kept my eyes shut tight, began counting to three and jumped on two. I felt my legs wheeling and then disappeared into the green water.

I emerged gasping to a round of applause. John took my arm and helped pull me out, smiling. His long curly hair was slick across his face, his board shorts slung low.

'You made it by about four inches,' he said. 'Good effort.'

I imagined my heels cracking on the edge of the path, my body sliding forward helplessly into the water. What if I had been the person to end the halcyon days of wild swimming here in Fladbury? I imagined the paramedics arriving, shuttling across on the pulley ferry, strapping me to a stretcher. I pictured myself with metal pins through my legs and wearing protective boots on both feet for the next year, a short article on the BBC News website remarking on my idiocy. George and his family having to sell up because of my poor jumping skills, never returning to a place that had brought them so much happiness. Years of anxiety had made me an expert at making imaginary mountains out of non-existent molehills. 'What ifs?' were my forte.

Once I'd let my overactive imagination work through this implausible scenario, I realised I was actually in the grip of an intense adrenalin rush. It was a heady mix of the feeling I got after a long cold dip and the joy of abandon I'd felt after my stolen swim on the Itchen. I had found my rebellion in jumping out of mill house windows.

Dried off but still shaking, I took my seat around the large picnic table, listening to *Test Match Special* with George's friend Mark and his kids. England were in the process of demolishing the Aussies for the third home series in a row. Mark, a healthy-looking guy in his mid-fifties, had been coming here ever since he was young and told me how proud he was to see his children still able to enjoy the kind of daring activities he and George had indulged in. They were all excellent swimmers, happily practising dives and playfully pushing each other under, enjoying what I saw as a proper, old-style summer holiday.

I had thought my feat of derring-do was enough for the day. But George and Mark had different ideas, talking about erecting a high board on the punt. I had thought this idle chatter until I saw George disappear into the far corner of the garden and start dismantling a hitherto unseen platform usually used for decorating and DIY. Slowly it came down, before being re-erected, stage by stage, on the rickety little vessel. Balanced precariously on either side, George lay a final board about three metres up, and so began an impromptu diving contest.

One by one the cousins came forward, climbing high, the entire makeshift creation swaying violently as they stood, fingertips pointing to the sky before diving forward. John's efforts were spectacular, but Mark's eleven-year-old twin daughters were incredible, unafraid of toppling in and clearly loving the cold crash of the Avon around them. They went in turns, practising tumbles, tucks and somersaults, as if jumping from a creaking alloy tower was the most normal thing in the world. I had found myself in a watery paradise.

That was, until it was my turn. I scaled the makeshift construction slowly, again watched by the extended family, grins and shouts of encouragement abounding. They'd seen my near-disastrous window leap and they were ready for more light entertainment. I made no mention of the fact that I didn't particularly enjoy heights, particularly ones where it involved throwing myself off and into the unknown. I remembered the brief feeling of fearlessness I'd found in the window frame and let myself half jump, half flop into the river.

It was a pathetic effort, considering the rest of the talent on show. John filmed it all on his smartphone, and I cringed as I watched myself back, a 31-year-old man shown up by a bunch of kids who'd never known fear of the water.

Over lunch, I asked George about any recent travails with the Environment Agency. Apart from an attempt to string oil barrels across the adjacent weir to prevent anyone falling down it, everything had gone quiet. No one other than the family swam in this stretch of the Avon much, George said, and recent problems with flood defences, coupled with crippling government cuts, meant the Environment Agency had better things to do than hassle a few swimmers exercising their inalienable right to a dip.

Before being allowed to swim off upstream, George and the boys insisted I try out one of their coracles. It felt as if they wanted to show me everything this magical place had to offer, and I was powerless to resist. I could quite happily have hunkered down and spent the rest of my summer here – swimming, daydreaming and listening to England edge out the Aussies on the radio.

John pulled out a larger vessel and told me this was one of the easier coracles to pilot and impossible to fall out of, demonstrating the figure of eight movement needed to propel it forward. I plonked myself in and immediately started paddling backwards, spinning in circles before being taken away upstream by a gust of wind. Despite my best efforts, I found myself heading for the rush of a nearby lock gate. Shamefaced, I called for help. One of the cousins powered across in a kayak with a length of rope and towed me back to shore. If I did stay, I was going to need to practise this waterborne art at length.

By now I was ready for a long dip. I slipped in at the weir and swam slowly against the current towards a distant road bridge. 'Swimming is often enhanced by company, and sometimes by solitude,' Roger wrote of his visit. I had enjoyed some beautifully social swims in recent weeks, none more so than my morning spent here in the Vale of Evesham. It was wonderful to be surrounded by so many people who loved the water and didn't find swimming outside to be a subversive activity, but rather a wholly natural one. But I felt an overwhelming need to digest it all, take it in on my own and feel the sun scorch my back as I did so.

The Avon wasn't especially warm despite the late July heat, and I felt the cold touch my heart, reminding me of its presence with every stroke. At a cedar tree on the near bank I turned back and swam through a bunch of ducks, who quacked and fussed out of my path.

Beautifully manicured lawns fell away from stunning homes towards the Avon's banks, but none were so alluring as the majestic mill up ahead. The water surrounding it was alive with people. The kids were still on the diving board and coracles zipped back and forth around them as they fell in one by one. A kayak, piloted by Mark, disappeared over the weir to the distant sound of whoops and cheers. It was delightful to realise that whether I was here or not, these antics would carry on regardless. Swimming was essential to this family and I was overjoyed that in the intervening years between mine and Roger's trips, little had changed to spoil this perfect summer scene.

— PART TWO —

The Break

'I longed to swim the lochs and wild islands, and at last I
felt ready to cross over the sea to Jura.'

ROGER DEAKIN, *WATERLOG*

CHAPTER ONE

August

~~~

River Lark, Cambridgeshire – The Oasis,
Covent Garden – River Wissey, Norfolk

Lifted by the solitude of my swim along the Avon and the marvellous company in the hours beforehand, I decided to head out on a longer solo jaunt. I was off on a mission to baptise myself and be born again in the River Lark near Isleham.

The Lark had been known as a place where Baptists were totally immersed, what Roger called a kind of River Jordan in the heart of the Fens. On the map it looked like any other river in this flat landscape. This was a place where the map was devoid of cramped contour lines, where the eye stretched for miles over empty fields.

My mood turned grey thanks to the gunmetal clouds that hung low over London as my train trundled out of King's Cross towards Ely. I had brought my bike with me and resolved to cycle to my solo baptismal. I arrived in the cathedral city in a proper grump and saddled up for what I had hoped would be a pleasant change from the ceaseless fear of riding through central London. My trip from Camberwell to the train station that morning had involved being sandwiched between two swaying double-deckers on Waterloo Bridge and almost being driven off the road by an oblivious cabbie on the Strand.

I was disabused of any notion I'd had of bucolic calm when I was overtaken by three HGVs in quick succession, each one almost pulling me into its speedy slipstream. I finally turned off onto a quieter road only to witness someone overtake on a blind bend, leaving me pedalling into a bank of nettles for safety.

I reached the village of Prickwillow exhausted, my thighs screaming from the bumpy tarmac and woeful driving. I cursed the fact that, although we were supposed to be a nation of reborn cyclists, this activity was still seen as somehow subversive, for weirdos and eco-warriors who could be bullied by petrolheads with a taste for brinkmanship. It did nothing for my feelings of frustration at this whole *Waterlog* trip becoming an out of control adventure, one I'd seemingly never finish at my current rate. I had started it as an escape from work, and on days like this, with the weather bad and the water distant and hard to reach, it felt like it was nothing but a chore to be undertaken, a series of boxes to be ticked. I wondered if the whole thing was a pointless exercise, especially if I was just going to make myself angry and het up. Jumping out of mill windows and frolicking in coracles felt very distant as the August chill intensified.

I knew that the bike, and by extension those who'd nearly had me off the road, were to blame for these dark thoughts. But I allowed myself to brood on them nonetheless. What exactly was I hoping to achieve here? And was I even getting close to learning new things about the places I visited, beyond what Roger had done? I honestly had no idea, and this was starting to worry me. Was this whole thing nothing more than a vanity project, a way of escaping day-to-day reality? What would happen when the swims ended and I had no specific goal to keep me coming back, searching for that feeling of peace and escape which I always found in the water? My mind raced away with me as I began the final stretch of the ride to the Lark.

After a tedious pedal along flat, featureless roads, I finally turned off and headed down Soham Tunnel Drive to my chosen immersion spot. After passing a derelict hut I pushed my bike for the last hundred metres, over a grassy levee built up to protect the surrounding fields from flooding. I was suddenly overwhelmed by a huge sense of being alone. The solitude I had enjoyed on the Avon had been tempered by the fact that I could see my fellow swimming fanatics playing downstream. Here, my only company was a family of great crested grebes, who eyed me cautiously as they swam off into a pool to the side of the river. Only Keeley knew where I was. I felt a jolt of loneliness so deep that it frightened me.

If I stopped swimming in Roger's wake, would it matter? No one cared about me doing this, did they? I felt tired just thinking about how many more swims I had to do to complete my retracing of Roger's work. I wanted the simplicity and joy from these swims to alleviate my depression, but all I was doing was creating more work for myself. That meant I worried more – that I wasn't doing this journey properly, that I wasn't really a swimmer, that this was merely a pale imitation of Roger's efforts. As I lay my bike down and took in the river and the fields around me, I let these worries, this blossoming self-pity, nuzzle their way down into every part of my being. All this because of grey weather and an unpleasant bike ride. When I say my anxiety is a result of fixating on fleeting emotions, this is what I mean.

I looked around. Litter dotted the bank. Empty Burger King wrappers and crushed cans of cider were strewn around an old fence post, where someone had carved 'Back soon 2 tidy up'. I wondered if they'd bothered taking a dip. Further upstream the grass was flattened, otter spraint shat out at a convenient entry point. I decided I would keep my eyes peeled for more telltale signs of the elusive creature as I changed into my shorts.

Beyond my infuriating concerns about the trip as a whole, I was also worried about slick mud. Roger talked of having to pull himself through sharp reeds and black, tar-like stuff to free himself from the Lark. But as I put my foot over the bank and into the water, I found the bottom to be sandy and quite firm. I waded out a few feet before swimming off. It felt appropriate to slide my head under quickly and give myself a proper baptism. The wide river sits high here but you can't see over the banks and so I felt as if I was swimming across a vast aqueduct, the huge dome of the Fenland sky so impossibly high I felt I could fly up into it for days and never touch it. The sun was coming out now and it was starting to heat up.

Once again, pike also dominated my thoughts. I had googled the River Lark the previous evening, the first image I saw being of a champion angler wearing a head torch and clasping a slippery twenty-pound specimen near this very spot. I let my feet fall to the riverbed and search for something to stand on, but there was nothing.

Immediately I imagined this monster of the deep going for my toes. Two months on from my Bungay dip, when Tim and I had discussed pike dissection strategies, my fears had not been allayed. Perhaps I needed to heed Roger's advice and remember that pike only ever really attack in little pools where they've eaten everything in sight and pinkies are their only option. This was an open river teeming with young wildfowl and small roach: a veritable feast for a giant pike.

I swam on for a few more minutes, letting the sun warm my back as I kept an eye out for otters. No joy. Instead, I paddled slowly back to the bank and took my time drying off, serenaded by a just-visible reed warbler rustling in the rushes at ankle level. I ate my sandwiches and waved a hearty hello to two people who chugged past on a long barge. They asked after the water temperature – clearly they'd spotted me flailing about, although I hadn't noticed their approach.

I set off back towards Ely in far higher spirits, happily reborn, enjoying a brief respite from a mind that never seemed to stopped whirring with worries and pessimistic possibilities. I didn't realise that this would be my last proper swim for three months. My trip was about to be brought to an unceremonious halt, the need to fight years of anxiety and depression with more than just a swim thrown into sharp focus. The bike that had taken me through London and over the Fens to the Lark was about to lead me down a much more important, unexpected and ultimately more rewarding route.

*   *   *

It was a warm afternoon, so I decided to set aside the article I was working on about expensive headphones and take a ride into town for a swim at the Oasis pool. I'd already marked this central London spot green on my *Waterlog* spreadsheet, but with my next dip on Roger's trail over a week away, I fancied a paddle to work off the late summer sweat. I was feeling buoyant, the Lark's magic still giving me a buzz a couple of days on, keeping the black dogs at bay.

I settled into a steady rhythm as I cycled past the Oval and on towards Waterloo. It was a route I followed at least once a week into the city and I knew it well: the deep potholes in the bus lanes on Kennington Park Road, the off-kilter phasing on the traffic lights at Lambeth North station.

It happened there, at the lights, in slow motion. I felt the touch of the Range Rover's flank on my rear wheel, my bike wobbling dangerously beneath me. I shouted and turned to the driver, his face looming across at me from the passenger seat, contorted in rage.

We exchanged pleasantries. My hand was raised in a gesture usually reserved for gentlemen trying to put footballers off when taking corner kicks. Anger swelled inside me and I swore loudly, invective pouring from my mouth as the black SUV accelerated fast in front of me, cutting me up before its brake lights glowed scarlet, screeching to a halt across the bike lane, impeding my path.

I muttered a brief 'Oh fuck' and dropped my foot to the ground, my breathing laboured, as if I'd just emerged after jumping into Hampstead pond. I scooted my bike around the car, but the driver was on me in a flash, striding towards me, hurling abuse, fists raised.

I put my arms across my face, expecting a punch. The shove was unexpected and I dropped my hand to break my fall. I landed in a heap underneath my bike in the middle of the road and looked up at the driver. He loomed over me, stared down and spat a quick 'fuck off' as I tried to stand up. I mouthed the registration number repeatedly as he slammed his door and drove off, his tyres squealing in my ears.

I managed to stand. From the corner of my eye I could see a crowd looking on, but I saddled up and left the scene, mortified.

The adrenalin rush was incredible. It was every bit as visceral as the one I'd felt jumping from the window at Fladbury. My heart gave a deep thud as I pushed on. I was almost hyperventilating. It was the most intense high imaginable, coupled with the bizarre, disturbing realisation that I'd just been attacked in broad daylight.

I only noticed the dull throb of my wrist when I squeezed on the front brake. A sharp pain zipped up my forearm. I stopped, called the police to report what had happened, then carried on to the pool regardless.

I changed quietly and looked at the blue bruise from my fall. It seemed to grow with each length that I swam, the pain increasing every time I touched the wall and turned to push off on another lap. I was adamant that the swim could fix this. My mind worked the situation over and over, faster and faster. With each stroke came a new thought – wilder, more outlandish, more troubling.

I shouldn't have sworn at him.
This was my fault.
What if he followed me?
What if he's waiting for me?
It can't be broken. It can't be broken.

I swam forty lengths, my mind working at terrifying speed. Swimming hadn't worked its usual soothing magic. I changed, easing my right arm through my shirtsleeve carefully, gently. The pain was getting worse.

I unlocked my bike, swung my leg across and set off. There was no other way home. I cycled back slowly, past the spot where I'd been attacked, swerving around the potholes of Kennington Park Road, back to Camberwell. I found a bandage and wrapped up my wrist. I sat down and cried.

Keeley got home early. I was sitting on the sofa reading, and watched as she pushed her bike through the living room and out into the back garden. I followed her through the flat and asked about her day. Good, she said. Yours?

It all poured out. The accident, the attempt to swim through the pain, the ride home. I tried to claim my wrist was just a bit sore, but by now I could barely move it. Calmly, she convinced me of the need to get it looked at. We walked to the casualty department close to our house and I returned four hours later with my wrist in a temporary brace and an X-ray confirming what I'd known all along. My wrist was broken.

A broken wrist isn't debilitating. You can still sleep in relative comfort and wash yourself each morning. But it is a huge inconvenience if you make a living by typing out hundreds of words every day on a freelance basis. And when your hobby involves swimming to escape the constant worry and guilt that you're not doing enough work and aren't living up to the unrealistic expectations of success that you set yourself, it essentially renders you incapable of doing anything.

This is how it was for the first week after the attack. I felt useless. Not to mention the fact that when I recounted the incident – to the concerned police officers who came by to take a statement, or friends who noticed the brace on my arm – I felt ashamed, as if the whole thing was my fault.

As I had done while swimming at the Oasis, I allowed myself to extrapolate the situation into needless and unlikely directions. I blamed myself and beat myself up for reacting the way I had done, for failing to apologise for an indiscretion I hadn't committed, replaying the attack over and over in the futile hope that it would turn out differently, that my wrist would miraculously heal and that I would feel better.

I sat down at my desk and opened up the long list of *Waterlog* swims I had left. There were more than thirty, roughly half of what Roger had accomplished in just nine short months. With my brace set to be replaced by a cast, there was no chance I would be able to swim for another two months, maybe three, by which point winter would be nipping at the edges of autumn and I would be facing another year of chasing Roger's trail, of trying to fix myself and my anxieties using his tried and tested method of a cooling outdoor dip.

As I had done in the months before I took up my quest to follow Roger, I slid into a downward spiral of misery and spent days doing nothing but trawling social media, wasting hours on the internet, waiting for Keeley to get in, eating dinner and going to bed early. Without my swimming trip to help me, things felt hopeless. The lifebuoy I had been clinging to had been lost in the storm. I felt so low. I did not like myself very much. My self-loathing, from telling myself my broken wrist was my fault to claiming that I had failed in my career and by extension my life, scared me enough to realise that something needed to be done.

Speaking openly about anxiety and depression was not easy for me. It's hard not to believe that 'it's all in your head' because the simple fact is that that's the truth. For so long it felt much easier to bottle up these feelings of inadequacy and professional failure. In my mind, I had created these problems, therefore the onus was on me to fix them.

When I had suffered from bouts such as this in the past, such as the one that had convinced me to undertake my *Waterlog* odyssey in the first place, I had let it simmer and fester before eventually confessing my feelings to Keeley, ashamed that I had made myself this way. Her understanding, her willingness to listen, her gentle urgings to seek professional help to fix a problem she knew could be fixed with the right guidance, were always welcome and always helpful. They helped patch me up and change my perspective. They made me stop judging myself so harshly by the high standards I believed everyone must live up to. She made things easier and rounded my edges. I experienced a greater clarity, an unburdening. I didn't see the need to seek the help of a therapist or doctor.

But in truth, these conversations were like the swims I had enjoyed over the past twelve months. Always helpful, but never definitive in helping me discover what was wrong and how I could make it right once and for all. No amount of swimming or gentle, loving persuasion was going to make me seek out the help I needed. I needed to find that urge within myself.

I realised this as my wrist was carefully placed into a royal-blue plaster cast a week after the incident. Speaking up when things finally overwhelmed me was not enough. Neither, I saw, was using my *Waterlog* journey to make things better. I was going to have to find a proper cure, one which could teach me how to access that lightness, that sense of ease, which I had found in the times when I had told Keeley how low and anxious I felt or when I had pulled myself free from a cold river on a hot summer afternoon.

So it was that I finally found the courage to contact a therapist, someone who might be able to throw some light on my problems. I set an appointment and marked it in my online calendar, just a couple of days after the next swim I had slated, a dip in the secret River Wissey, the one Tim and I had failed to find after our jaunt down the Little Ouse in Santon Downham.

At the fracture clinic I had been told in no uncertain terms that I couldn't get my cast wet. I was issued with a plastic sleeve which slipped over my right hand, now the size of a heavyweight boxing glove, clamping fast over my upper arm. This was designed to stop things getting soggy when I took a shower. It looked like an ill-fitting condom.

The consultant flicked through my notes and got ready to send me on my way.

'So, I definitely can't go swimming?'

She shook her head and stood up, opening the door to her windowless office.

'You've broken your wrist,' she said. 'And that cover is only shower-proof anyway. I'd stay out of the water until it comes off, maybe longer.'

I knew that already. My Google search history had become a growing list of specious articles about how to swim with a plaster cast. None of them offered any proof that it could done, and plenty served up scare stories about bones not setting and casts having to be cut off.

Not only had I planned a swim in the Wissey, with half a dozen cohorts in tow, I had also booked a trip up to Jura, that magical island in the Inner Hebrides of which I'd dreamt as a teenager longing for adventure far from home. I couldn't swim in its bays, lochans and burns, but I couldn't cancel either. Train tickets had been bought, accommodation booked.

I felt downhearted. I told myself I had failed in my quest and wondered aloud to Keeley whether I should bother going on at all. Roger had already done it anyway, I said, and had made a better fist of it than me. I felt I had turned it into an exercise in trying to recreate Roger's experience, carefully shading my spreadsheet but not fully experiencing the water and the nature which surrounded it in my own way.

Gently, persuasively, she told me that wasn't the case, that I should think of the happiness I had found in and around the water, get on the train up to East Anglia and meet my friends. They'd be going anyway, she said, and all you'll do is think about them and feel sad about the fact that you haven't gone.

She was right. And so, wrist in plaster and my mind still fragile, I called Tim and Molly and told them about what had happened and that I'd be coming along anyway. I packed my shorts just in case and set off on a bright, late-summer morning which burned with promise.

I could feel my pulse beneath the cast, the sweet, rancid smell of unwashed skin emanating from beneath it. My hand was a burnished yellow colour, fading to black as I stared down the opening by my fingers.

The whizz of the frisbee and a shout of 'catch it' snapped me out my daydream and I ran across the makeshift grassy car park of St Peter's church to pick it up and attempt a throw with my weaker left arm.

Molly, Tim and I were waiting for Yanny, Suz and my cousin Megan to arrive. It was a scorching hot day, my skin clammy as I chased after each throw. I was hopeless at playing frisbee, but that was true when I had two fully functioning arms instead of one. It didn't matter. Being outside with good friends, enjoying the final blast of heat of a long summer, was a happy antidote to the past week of worries, the fug of depression lifting slightly as we chattered.

I realised, while we waited for our fellow swimmers, that these two friends had been with me on my favourite swims of the past year, from the galumphing rollers of Covehithe to the burble of the Waveney. I had spent so many years working for myself, spending time alone, but this project had helped make me more social and brought with it new and rekindled friendships. These people cared about me and I them. They knew that my wrist was in pain, but I knew there and then that I wanted to tell them more, to explain why I'd started swimming on Roger's trail in the first place, to explain the difficulties I'd been struggling with over the past few years. I knew they would understand about my constant struggles with anxiety and occasionally depression. For the first time ever, I did not feel embarrassed or ashamed by it.

With the others in tow, we set off down a dusty country lane towards the whispering Wissey, in the complete opposite direction to where Tim and I had gone a few months before. It was hot, but I stayed out of the shade, allowing my good arm to toast in the final searing rays of summer sun.

I fell into stride with Molly. She asked about my wrist, despite the fact that I'd already regaled her with the details of how it happened and how long I'd be in plaster in the car on the way here.

Instead I decided to lay it all on the line. I told her the incident had left me feeling low and anxious and that this was nothing new. I'd felt like this for a long time before I got taken out by an irate Range Rover driver. In fact I'd felt like this for the past few years, I told her. Swimming, I said, was the only way I thought I could snap myself out of it.

'Mate,' she said. 'Getting in the water helps me when I feel like that too. It's something we do to make ourselves better, to feel more human.'

I could feel my burden lighten as we talked through the finer points of my anxiety. The constant worrying about minor details and supposed transgressions, the need to have everything lined up just so, the desperation to find validation through work. How I'd looked to swimming to lighten the load and how I'd found that while it felt good for a moment, it didn't give me the lasting relief I needed. I told her I was going to see a therapist to help me navigate a course through it all.

'It's going to be great for you,' she said. 'Just think about how much better it could make you feel.'

As we spoke, I forgot the inconvenience of my wrist break. Just being around friends when I came on these trips to follow Roger was every bit as good as being in the water itself. They made me feel happy by showing their willingness to join me on my escapades, and now to listen to me talking about my feelings. There was no shame any more. At that point, it felt only like there was possibility.

As we skirted what Roger called 'the never-never land' of the MOD firing range in which the Wissey rose, I looked around to see people who were here to have fun, to forget work and daily life for a while. To be friends and to share an experience. It was a direct by-product of a journey I'd embarked on a year previously. I realised I had helped bring everyone together after years of intermittent meet-ups and social media interactions, and that made me feel better. The idea of carrying on my mission, with everyone around me, didn't seem so daunting any more.

The road swung west and, as we turned the corner, we came to a deep pool next to a road bridge, the water zipping beneath and emerging white and frothy as it spilled over a weir. A shingle beach slid into the pool, and on the far side a frayed rope swing dangled invitingly from a high willow branch. It was the most perfect of wild-swimming spots, the river scurrying off down a shady green tunnel, much like Roger would have seen on his visit here.

Everyone engaged in a frenzy of pulling off jumpers and trying to protect their modesty with not-quite-large-enough bath towels. I hung back and watched it all. Unabashed joy at my friends and I sharing such a bizarre passion was mixed with envy as one by one they dropped down to the water and slipped in and away with the current.

Meanwhile, I struggled into my shorts one-handed, trying not to flash my river-swimming pals while standing behind a sturdy oak. Togged up, I waded in as far as I could manage, water up to my waist, holding my right hand to the sky as if begging to be asked how I felt about not being able to get in properly. I could feel the cool lap of the Wissey around my shorts and knew that having flowed through the MOD range it would be clean and delicious to swim in, no fertilisers or pollutants running off into its glistening head waters. I peered beneath the arch of the bridge into the forbidden zone. Seen through that lens, the dark shadows threw everything into sharp focus. The trees and bushes looked more verdant, the flowers more vibrant. If my wrist hadn't been out of action I'd have crawled through and indulged the urge to trespass which I had felt so keenly on the Itchen back at the start of summer, that same feeling of abandon I'd enjoyed when jumping from the window at Fladbury.

While Tim hauled himself out and began swaying wildly on the old rope swing, daring himself to plunge into the deep, fast-flowing water where the Wissey kinked and meandered, I waded out and dried off.

I parked myself on a tree stump and looked around, oblivious to anxiety. I felt as if I was seeing everything with greater clarity and wider eyes after my chat with Molly and my wade in the water. And as I scanned the beach and the riverbanks, I noticed that this wasn't quite the quintessential bucolic English paradise that Roger made it out to be.

As with most hidden river holes I'd visited, this faraway pool was blighted with litter: burnt cans, empty cigarette packets, floating water bottles, discarded chocolate wrappers. This was something I had been happy to overlook until now, something that annoyed me but which I tried not to take notice of as I attempted to get into Roger's romantic mindset about the English countryside.

I began thinking about all this rubbish and whether it was a new thing, something that had happened since Roger's days of swimming all over Britain. I weighed up my recent trips, realising Molly had filled a bag with litter at Mendham and that I had failed to do the same on the Lark just a few weeks previously. It felt like rivers were more prone to this kind of thing, as if people, having finally understood that leaving all manner of tat on a beach was harmful to the environment, still thought doing so on a river bank was fair game.

As I looked around, unable to swim properly and instead keeping a keen eye on my surroundings, I realised that this was far from a modern phenomenon. I remembered the River Stort, near my parents' home in Essex, was always pockmarked with old litter when I was a kid. The Huddersfield Narrow Canal through Marsden in West Yorkshire, where my uncle had lived for twenty years, was the same.

Roger didn't seem to mention this problem at all. It seemed odd, this environmentally conscious man, a founder member of Friends of the Earth, not complaining more in *Waterlog* about morons thinking it was OK to toss rubbish where they saw fit. Did he not think it would fit with the Arcadian, dreamlike quality of his book? Or was he so caught up in the abundant nature he found in virtually every spot, that he simply forgot? This certainly had been my experience in the previous months. And forced to be an observer rather than a participant, I discovered that perhaps I had been romanticising the swimming process a bit too much. Far more needed to be done to clean rivers up and stop people treating them like the local tip.

I realised that having a slight detachment from the scene afforded me the chance to assess and see the water in a new light, through my own prism rather than that of *Waterlog*. Looking at nature and understanding it on my own terms could make the rest of the trip even more special and worthwhile.

Packed up, we set off back towards the church and the car park. Listening to Keeley's advice and choosing to go to the Wissey instead of feeling useless and lonely at home hadn't just allowed me to see my friends and forget about my wrist for a while. It had made me realise I wanted to share the whole reason for my trip with them and, just as importantly, it gave me the urge to carry on. I didn't have to get into the water to have a feel for it. After a year on Roger's trail and two dozen swims, I already carried it with me.

That night I got back to London late. It was wet as I slammed the door of the train shut at Stratford station. I felt melancholy after a day of fun and abandon. My wrist was sore and a surge of hopelessness flowed through me as I dipped my head to the rain, the optimism of earlier in the day ebbing away in the downpour.

Sitting on the Tube, waiting to set off for home, I took out my phone and checked my email. There was a message from Molly.

'Read this and thought of you'. It was a link to a poem, 'Where Water Comes Together with Other Water' by Raymond Carver. It is a striking piece of verse, about loneliness, recovery and water. Its final lines stayed with me as I put my phone away.

> *It pleases me, loving rivers.*
> *Loving them all the way back*
> *to their source.*
> *Loving everything that increases me.*

I smiled at the memory of my non-swim on the Wissey, forgetting the wet weather and the impending cold of autumn and winter. Any lingering doubts about wanting to continue on Roger's trail evaporated. I had to go on, finding the joy and humanity in every swim and not worrying about shading spreadsheets or ticking boxes. Swimming couldn't fix my anxiety on its own, but the water was part of me now. I would swim on and follow Roger, not because I wanted to emulate him, not because of any vain hope it might cure me, but because I loved it. As the doors beeped shut and the train pulled out of the station, I knew that it was a good enough reason by itself.

CHAPTER TWO

September

~

Jura, Scotland

The door to the flat was open. I hung my jacket on the coat rack and shouted a tentative hello as I stepped further inside. Mark's head appeared around a door at the end of the short corridor.

'Joe? Please come in.'

Mark's room, in the small clinic he worked out of in south London, had the air of a university professor's study. Wipe-clean carpets, a desk with an iMac, copies of Freud on the top shelf of the bookcase. It was mid-afternoon, and though the curtains were open, the lights were on, the windows opening onto bare brick walls which made it seem darker outside than it was.

'Please, take a seat.'

I parked myself in an armchair, a glass of water and box of tissues on the small table where I lay my bag. Mark shut the door and sat down opposite me, pushing strands of his white hair out of his eyes and slapping his thighs. I crossed my legs and sat deep into the chair. He offered an encouraging, toothy smile.

'So then...'

I couldn't help but feel as if I were in a job interview. I began by giving Mark a potted history of my post-university life. I had worked for five years as a full-time journalist for a variety of magazines and websites, I said, before fulfilling my dream to go freelance four years earlier.

I sighed and looked around and wondered why I was here, whether it was really worth it. I was telling my therapist, a concept which seemed ludicrous to me, nothing that any of my friends and family didn't know already. I could feel myself burning up. I took off my jumper and rolled up my shirtsleeves.

I took a few deep breaths, imagined I was jumping into a new stretch of unknown wild water, and went for it.

'The thing is,' I said, 'I think that's when things started to go wrong. I feel like it's all gone off half-cocked. I was supposed to be a world-beater, writing articles for big newspapers, travelling the globe, spending hours honing highly praised copy. Instead I feel like a nobody, an impostor, a fraud. I hate the work I do, I hate how it doesn't challenge me and I hate what I've become. I feel lonely all day. I get stressed and worried about the smallest things. Going for a walk or seeing a film should be easy, but I prevaricate about doing them because I don't believe they're productive, so I stay at home even though I've done all my work. I turn every small occurrence into a big deal, worrying myself with things that don't matter, whether it's a spilt drink or clothes being left out in the rain. I feel bad for dumping all my worries on my wife. I feel guilty about work not taking longer than I think it should, leaving me feeling as if I'm not up to scratch. I don't think I work hard enough, I don't think I'm good enough as a person and I believe that worrying makes things feel important and purposeful, even though deep down I'm well aware that's ridiculous.'

Mark gave a sage nod and, it seemed to me, a quick grin.

'What happened to your arm?'

I told him.

'What a twat,' he said.

'Worst of all,' I said. 'It means I can't do the one thing that made me feel better. I can't swim.'

Over the next fifty minutes, Mark listened as I talked. I told him about how I got het up about small things, felt guilty about taking time off or enjoying myself, and how I'd tried and failed to use swimming as the panacea for my problems. How I had embarked on my journey on Roger's trail and how I felt I'd turned it into an exercise in box-ticking, sometimes losing sight of the joy it was supposed to inspire. I told him how I tried to keep everything just so and wanted to make things perfect. How I liked to always be in control. And, most importantly, how I thought worrying could make that happen.

'You're trying to line your ducks up in a row,' he said. 'And the fact is that's just not possible. Because life isn't like that. Change is constant and things happen all the time. Just one thing – swimming, in this case – isn't going to make you better.

'Think of life as if you're floating, bobbing around with all the flotsam. It's essentially a Buddhist theory, but let's forget the religious aspect. You need to try and see what's going on around you as largely uncontrollable. In short, you need to step back and recognise whenever you feel yourself get stressed and anxious about situations you can't affect, take some deep breaths and learn to say "fuck it".'

'Fuck it,' I mouthed. 'Learn to say "fuck it".' I grinned and Mark let out a loud, 'Ha.'

Just saying it made me feel better.

'There's not an awful lot wrong with you,' Mark said. 'And I can definitely help you if you want. Let's have a few sessions and see how we go. Come in, talk, get it off your chest, and we can work out ways to make things better.'

Mark handed me a questionnaire asking about my feelings, as well as a document detailing how talking therapy worked. This was going to be as much about me talking my way through my problems as it was about him giving me concrete solutions. A safe space to be honest without judgement.

We settled on a six-week course. I left feeling lighter than I had even after I'd spoken with Keeley about my problems, better even than when

I had waded into the Wissey a few days before. For the first time I had a clear path through to the other side. It was a start. With that, the rest was inevitable, surely. I left the clinic and turned my mind to Jura. It didn't matter that I wouldn't be able to swim when I was there, I was going anyway. Fuck it.

Just the name Jura was magical to me. Even before I had devoured *Waterlog* I had wanted to come to this bleak, beautiful island and walk its raised beaches, camp on its tussocky hills and stare back to the mainland on a bright, clear day.

Like many, I had first heard of Jura through George Orwell. Roger details the circumstances of Eric Arthur Blair and his family's stay here in the 1940s: the hardship, the knackered motorbike, the swimming prowess of his brother-in-law, who had somehow managed to cross the lethal whirl of the Gulf of Corryvreckan. And, of course, the writing of *Nineteen Eighty-Four*.

I remember reading of Jura in the weeks after I had read *Nineteen Eighty-Four* as a wide-eyed eighteen-year-old readying myself for university. I spoke to my uncle Dave about it. An English teacher, he was obsessed with Orwell and told me about his own journey up the narrow road along the island's eastern side, to the little village of Ardlussa and Orwell's ramshackle home, when he visited Jura in the 1980s.

I dug out my parents' road atlas and found Jura, so close to Glasgow yet so far from anywhere. I stared at its long form, the way Loch Tarbert almost cut it into two Hebrides rather than one. I wanted to travel the long distance from my Essex home, use the long last school summer to do something amazing that I could use as something to brag about when university started. But my lack of a car, not to mention my lack of gumption, meant Jura soon faded from my mind. It would be another thirteen years before it began to dominate my thoughts again.

Of all my *Waterlog* trips so far, Jura was the one I had been most excited about and the one I had planned with the most care. The sleeper train to Fort William with my dad. The long drive south with my uncle

Dave and Jim, an old colleague of Dave's I'd known since I was a teenager, both of whom had been island-hopping from Rum to Eigg to Muck. The swims across Loch Tarbert and around West Jura were all lined up just so.

As it was, the first two parts were unchanged. But there was no chance of me getting a wetsuit over my arm, still less of me wading out and feeling the peaty swell hit my chest, the power of the Atlantic holding me up to the last of the summer sun. Like Mark had said, I had to accept that not everything in life can be controlled. I had packed the natty plastic cover I'd been given by the fracture clinic to use when showering just in case, though. It was almost a dare to myself to leave it in my rucksack if I fancied a dip. But I knew as the train clattered out of Euston and slowly north I was going to have to look on and use my imagination to swim these Scottish waters. I'd felt water seeping in when I used the cover when having a wash in the morning, the top of my cast starting to fray. The Atlantic and Jura's burns would doubtless render it useless and leave me returning, tail between my legs, to the same consultant who'd told me not to get in the water and admitting I'd ignored her advice. That deep feeling for water I had experienced on the Wissey, my realisation that I carried it with me wherever I went, was going to have to see me through and lessen the frustration of not being able to dive in.

It was dark and wet when we rolled off the 'wee ferry' from Islay to Jura, deer lit up in the headlights as we bumped along Jura's A road up to the village of Craighouse and the bungalow we'd rented for the next five days. Rain lashed at the passenger window. Just half an hour before, dusky clear skies had marked our arrival from the mainland on the CalMac ferry from Port Askaig, a minke whale trailing in our wake, a single gannet tracking out to sea. This fast-changing weather was a fact of life in Jura, the relentless winds blowing through storms clouds at a ceaseless pace.

I woke the next morning to a swimmer's dream view. Pulling back the curtains from the wide patio windows, a young stag stood just twenty feet away, obscuring a huge, watery view of the Sound of Jura. Despite the wind whipping around the eaves of the house, the sea looked calm from this high point. The Small Isles which dot the Sound looked so close I could imagine putting on my wetsuit and swimming all the way out to them. Smaller skerries burst from the surface, the perfect place for flopping out and drying off on a warm day.

We walked down to the village and got a closer look at the water. It did little more than lap here, slowed by floating seaweed, the boulder-strewn beaches offering plenty of escape routes into the sea for swimmers. As we walked out of the village, seals tracked our path, popping their heads up at intervals, their deep black eyes drinking us in before sinking away into their submarine world. Roger didn't swim in this spot, but I knew that if I'd been able to, I would have had no hesitation in flinging off my clothes and diving straight in. I wanted to feel the nettle-like sting of cold water on my skin and it hurt to know that the closest I could get was flicking the fingers of my left hand in to test its coolness. I could feel myself growing anxious, beating myself up for coming all this way and not getting in, worrying as I had in the past that I wasn't doing this trip 'the right way', Roger's way. I stopped as the others walked on. I slowed my breathing, a mindfulness trick I'd read up on after my first therapy session, and intoned Mark's mantra. 'Fuck it. Fuck it.'

It worked, and I walked on north out of the village, reaching a small stone jetty where we looked out across the bay as it swept east and then north towards the fearsome Corryvreckan whirlpool. My plaster cast did at least come with one blessing. It prevented me from even making a vain attempt at getting near this lethal phenomenon, the third largest of its kind in the world. I had read Roger's passages detailing his own fascination with this unnavigable gulf and was not keen in the slightest. At that point, I didn't care if I was letting my predecessor down. And anyway, he'd taken one hard look on a rainy summer afternoon and knew it was too dangerous even for him.

While I contemplated my convenient Corryvreckan escape, I saw a small splash next to a nearby skerry. Thinking it a seal, I wandered back towards the road, before Dave whipped out his binoculars and hushed us all to silence. An otter. After failing to see one on the Waveney on one of my earliest *Waterlog* jaunts or on the Lark just before my accident, here was that most secretive of mammals in the most majestic surroundings imaginable. Far enough away, and with the wind blowing slightly off course, it ignored the four of us as we gawked at it for what felt like hours.

It moved purposefully from one rock to another, diving once and emerging with a fish between its paws, tearing the flesh with abandon as it pulled itself out of the water. This was one of those rare occasions when being in the water would have been worse than being out of it. Swimming would have scared the creature away, and I'd have only been left with the briefest of glimpses. Instead, I stayed stock still and watched it devour its lunch, before it scurried around to the far side of its chosen rock and swam off to a place unknown.

The weather was on the turn now, but the sight of the otter and the fact I'd managed to allay my anxieties by using techniques I'd learnt in therapy made me feel content. It was similar to the happiness I usually experienced after a soothing swim in cold water, but with a much less intense edge. It felt good.

Despite not being able to get in and enjoy that dopamine rush, I still wanted to get up to Loch Tarbert and the boathouse from where Roger had set off on a long swim after hitching a ride from nearby Islay with Viscount Astor, the man who owns half of the island. Leaving Craighouse behind, we got in the car and bumped along the appalling A road, gravelly in parts and clearly unloved for many years, pulling up at the island's pinch point, where the loch almost completes its task of severing Jura.

The famous Paps were just about visible to the west, appearing every few seconds behind lashing rain clouds which scudded along the loch and dumped their hailstones on us. We pulled on full waterproofs, I shoved an old walking sock over my wrist for protection and we traipsed into the storm, a short stony walk down a wide path towards what would have been my second swimming spot.

Despite being early September, and nominally still summer, the Scottish weather was really putting on a show. Gusty winds whipped up white-tipped waves even in this most sheltered part of the loch, the water fully churned up and roiling as we looked further out to sea. Despite that, I could easily imagine why this would be the perfect place for a long, delicious swim after a day of walking over Jura's tussocky hills, ankles aching for buoyant relief. The beach was slippery and difficult to walk on in boots, let alone in the neoprene shoes I'd rather have been wearing.

Across the water, the sun cut through the grey cloud, its yellow streaks reflecting back off the fields of flowering heather in a glorious display, as if to remind us that for all the rain, this island could still lay claim to being one of the most beautiful places in the British Isles.

It was a short interlude, and I was back to nestling as deep as possible in my waterproof jacket as we set off west to explore. Deer watched from on high as Dad and I walked along the back of the beach, over wet grass and round to a wide inlet where a burn flowed off the Paps and into Loch Tarbert. The water here was deep enough that you'd get your feet properly wet if you waded over, but a makeshift set of stepping stones helped us on our way.

We followed the burn upstream, splitting up as its spidery course diverged uphill. After ten minutes or so I reached a sluggish spot where the stream turned sharply, its meander creating a deep pool, perfect for a short dip. My trunks were buried deep in the bottom of my bag in the unlikely event I decided to risk my plaster cast and take a swim, but I had no towel and was wary of the changing weather. I'd left the plastic cover for my cast back at the house, meaning the only thing protecting it was the soggy sock which sat floppily at the end of my arm.

I contented myself with sitting on my haunches and dipping my left hand in. The water was mild to the touch and beautifully soft, the peat below giving it a golden, whisky tinge. A convenient natural step made for the most perfect entry point.

As on the Wissey, I could sense the water without fully immersing myself and I could access its joys without having to get in. For now, looking at the scene was as good as being in it. I didn't feel disappointed about not being able to slide in. The weather was dreadful anyway and I knew I'd have been searching for excuses not to bother if I had had two working arms. But what made this place more special, more magical than the Wissey, was that Roger was so right about it. He had perhaps over-romanticised that spot in rural Norfolk, neglecting to mention its grubbiness. But here, looking back out at Loch Tarbet with my hand wet and my feelings less fragile than they had been, I knew he was right to make Jura seem like the most magical place he had visited on his own swimming journey.

'There will always be more to discover of its beauties and difficulties', he had written of the island. I was facing up to my own difficulties on this latest leg of my trip. But the natural obstacles this island offered up, the bad weather, the tussocks and hills, the shoddy road, made it seem all the more worthwhile to come here and try and clear the obstacles in my mind by tackling them. I rubbed my wet hand on my cagoule and took a long look around at the hills and across Loch Tarbet. Deer dotted the horizon as the rain came down in icy sheets. Just being here was enough to know that feeling of ease I'd enjoyed whenever I got into the water.

The following day dawned grey, but with our time on Jura limited we had to get out and explore. We drove south to the Sound of Islay and walked up past the Inver Estate office towards the raised beaches which had so beguiled Roger.

Once again we were togged up in full walking gear, but I had kept my swimming shorts in my rucksack just in case the urge to get in gripped me, the need to wait out the healing process outdone by my need to feel cold water on warm skin.

Dave stayed behind as Jim, Dad and I set off past Loch Chnuic Bhric, this small inland lake choppy and fenced off, cattle chewing the long grass on its banks. The Paps loomed over us to the east as we walked along a car-wide track made passable by the estate's Land Rovers. I didn't feel nearly as intrepid as Roger, who had camped and schlepped his way from Glenbatrick Bay, miles north of here, all the way around to Loch Tarbert and the boathouse where we'd visited the day before.

The muddy track gave way to a peaty path which soon became a sandy runnel, slipping its way down to the beach. Colonsay glimmered in the distance. We slid down on our backsides through gaps in the cliffs and out onto the most spectacular of isolated coves. The sea was pancake-flat and the sun was beginning to scorch the edges off the lowest cloud, making it perfect swimming weather. A pair of seals appeared as if to egg me on.

I cursed my tendency towards common sense over joyful recklessness. I know exactly what Roger would have done, but the most I allowed myself was a quick stalk off towards the water's edge, letting the lap of the water touch my new walking boots. I plunged my left hand in and found the water cold and bracing, far less inviting than the burn near Loch Tarbert. Perhaps my wrist was doing me a favour today. I told myself I'd have been shivering all the way back to the car anyway and looked up to see autumn rays catching the hills of Islay and the higher waves far out in the Sound. The views were just as good from dry land as they would have been with my head bobbing above the surface.

This stunning beach gave way to another, and another. Each one was reached by climbing through natural obstacles: perfectly formed arches, short sea stacks and huge, washed-up boulders marking the end of one bay and the beginning of another. As we reached the last one, we were forced to clamber back up onto the moor in order to get back down to the sand. From on high, the views over the sea to Islay and Colonsay were relentless, the fast-moving clouds opening and closing to allow a carnival of light on the water. At that point I wanted to be far out, swimming head-out breaststroke and ducking my head whenever I felt the urge, letting the Atlantic sweep through me and push me back to shore when I tired. Instead, I took deep, salty breaths and imagined myself into the scene, calmed by the thought of the swim, accessing something approaching a dopamine hit without having to dip my shoulders beneath icy wavelets.

We walked on and soon came to the first raised beach on this long coastline, the pebbles shelving hundreds of metres inland, neatly graded, like Chesil beach set at right angles. Three islands of tufty grass pockmarked the surface and we each took one, lying by turns on our backs and chests, taking in the long view. Jim reeled off pictures on his camera while I resolved to go for a quick paddle before having to make my way back to the car and the rude interruption of everyday life. As I began telling Dad of my watery plan, a storm blew in, gales and horizontal blasts of hailstones slamming into our waterproofs as, instead of swimming, we tramped out the final mile back towards the car.

It meant that my feet would not be numbed by Jura's water. I hadn't braved Corryvreckan. The burn near Loch Tarbert remained unswum. I had walked the raised beaches of the west coast, but would not leave a piles of clothes on the sand as I strode out towards the depths.

For all that, I had learnt more about how to feel the water without being getting into it. There was not a mark against me for not getting in and doing exactly as my predecessor had done. Those feelings of not doing Roger justice began to dissipate the longer I spent in Scotland. I finally saw this as my trip, not just a retracing of his. I felt Roger's presence here keenly and understood just why he had chosen this island over any other for the Scottish leg of his trip. Water was everywhere you looked. It fell from the sky, trickled slowly down mountain burns and helped make the whisky that I sipped from a hip flask as we headed back on the ferry towards the mainland.

I looked out of the window onto the red-brick wall, a smudgy London evening turning things dark and grey well before 6 p.m. Rain sloshed down the double glazing, which stopped the sound of splashes and spray from penetrating into the room. I'd spent the first half an hour of my session with Mark talking about Jura, about the sense of being able to feel the water without stripping down to my shorts and getting in. About how I felt able to float above it all and not hold myself accountable for not emulating Roger to the letter.

'It sounds to me like you turned this project into something like work,' said Mark. 'And you've been holding yourself up to the same impossible-to-attain standards that you set in your professional career. It's good that you've remembered that it's meant to be about fun.'

I couldn't deny that I had been applying the same religiously held beliefs about work, to my retracing of Roger's journey. What was supposed to be an escape had become a chore at times, but my trips to the Wissey and to Jura had helped me realise that I needed to hold on to some of that original impetus of water's life-giving promise of happiness and possibility in the face of anxiety, while remembering that it wasn't the be-all and end-all. It was just one part of a larger story that made up my life.

As the weeks passed, Mark steered me away from the water. We began touching on the reasons why I might be so anxious all the time. Why I held myself up to unrealistic assumptions about work. Why I never wanted to rock the boat either professionally or personally.

Time and again we would come back to my sensitivity to shame. I didn't like being told off as a kid and I hated it just as much as an adult. Over the years I'd built up this idea that being in the wrong and doing wrong, of breaking the rules, to be an inherently bad thing, something to be avoided at all costs. I wanted things to be perfect and I wanted to please everyone, all of the time. I would always apologise for things even if they weren't my fault. Somewhere along the line, I had begun attaching blame to everything. Stuff had to be someone's fault. It could never just be. This idea of wanting things to be just so made me a nervous wreck. I hated not having everything in its right place and lashed out or became anxious if I felt that it wasn't.

I told Mark about dropping a mug and accidentally smashing it while Keeley was cooking dinner. How I was to blame and had got hopelessly wound up about it when she told me it wasn't a big deal.

'Hold on,' he said. 'Blame? Can't something just be an accident, especially something as minor as that?'

'Er, I suppose so.'

Mark uncrossed his legs, pushed his white hair from out of his eyes and started scribbling on the whiteboard which was hung on the wall. Together, we worked out stages of a scenario. I would, for example, spill a glass of water, break a mug. I'd then blame myself and start apologising profusely for it. I wouldn't be able to let it go and got increasingly wound up and stressed, allowing myself to grow frustrated and angry. Then I'd go away and brood for a while and feel anxious, before feeling ashamed about how I'd behaved.

Seeing that written down made me feel ridiculous. And it also made me realise that I did it in plenty of other situations too. I'd get a piece of work and spend so much time worrying about how I was going to do it that I'd take days to actually sit down and get it done. I'd tell myself I wasn't good enough to work for this newspaper or that magazine, so wouldn't ever bother trying to see if I could. But when it came to actually having to do the work, it was never as hard or stressful as I made it out to be.

If I did something 'wrong', like file work late or tell a lie about why I couldn't meet a friend for a beer after work, I'd feel acutely sensitive to the shame and guilt attached to those actions. Always wanting to do the right thing was stultifying and frustrating, but I tried to do it anyway. I'd managed to subvert those feelings somewhat on my journey following *Waterlog*, jumping from that Fladbury window and dropping into the Itchen. I told Mark all of this with mild embarrassment.

'And did it matter that you did things? Of course not. There's nothing wrong with trying something and there's nothing wrong with making mistakes or doing something that leads to a minor blip or accident. That's what happens in life.'

As more and more sessions passed and I talked more to Mark about how I felt, I painted a picture of myself that often seemed ludicrous to me as I spoke, but felt honest and real at the same time. It was becoming ever clearer that I was a sensitive person, perhaps too much so, acutely attuned to feeling guilty about everything, even the most minor indiscretions. Catholic school had given me a solid moral grounding but had left me with a yearning never to do wrong and always be in the right.

This had come to the forefront when I went freelance. Setting my own agenda, I allowed myself to feel bad for ever having a good time or enjoying myself when I thought I should be doing something 'productive'. Swimming had become one of the things I beat myself up about and felt guilty for doing, because it meant I wasn't earning or living the freelance life I thought others, whoever they were, expected of me. It was why I had placed too much emphasis in finding meaning in it, hoping it wouldn't make me anxious any more, when in fact it was just something I loved and made me happy.

'A little bit of guilt is a good thing,' said Mark in our last session. 'But this much can leave you paralysed. You get to choose what you do and you need to take an objective look and see that what you're doing is just fine. In fact, it's better than fine. You just need to not put so much stock in any one thing at any one time.'

I considered my life at that point. A loving partner, a successful career in an industry everyone had been saying was dying for the past decade, a hobby which had reignited friendships and indulged my love of travel.

'It's like I said, it's all about learning to float. Bob along, recognise when things require a big response and when they don't. You're already doing it. I think you're going to be fine.'

I stood up and offered Mark my good hand and said a brief thank you. I knew he saw people in far worse predicaments than mine, but his willingness to listen, his sound advice and his calm and understanding made me feel I could go on without seeing him all of the time. I gained a sense of balance and calm from therapy that made me realise what was important in life: love, people, friendship, family.

Swimming was a part of that and helped bring those essential things closer to me. My cast was due to come off in the coming days and my attention turned to a last dip before the weather set in for the winter. I didn't feel downbeat about the cold putting a stop to my journey. It meant that I had another summer with Roger to look forward to.

CHAPTER THREE

October

~~

Walberswick, Suffolk

Y ou could track my path from the fracture clinic to my front door. A trail of dead human skin followed me on the short walk home, before tracing chaotic routes around the living room and kitchen as I held the phone in my newly liberated right hand and paced about while making some calls. First, I rang Keeley to tell her that my hand was free and somewhat flaky. I called my mum and did the same.

Then I dialled up Molly.

'Mate, when can you go for a swim?'

It was one of those unseasonably warm October days, a final blast of summer heat before the curtains are drawn and the heating goes on. I was desperate for the cold slap of the sea, something to deepen that sense of happiness I'd felt while staring at the water on my past two journeys. We settled on a trip to Walberswick on the Suffolk coast in a couple of days' time. I hung up and went to scrub my arm of dry skin and hopefully get rid of the sweet stench that had also been released along with my wrist.

On the train to meet Molly, my arm now thankfully less fragrant, I read over Roger's passages about Walberswick. He went there for the very last swim in *Waterlog*, the culmination of a swing from his moat in

Mellis and on through Eye and Heveningham, 'swimming into the quiet waves' to mark the end of an epic journey. I knew I wasn't quite halfway in following Roger, but it felt appropriate to be going there now and to be closing the first full year of my trip at the place where he had ended his.

As the train rattled along, clunking through Essex and north to Suffolk, I put *Waterlog* down and marvelled at just how Roger had completed his entire trip in the short space of nine months. I was amused that, back at the start, I thought I could do the same. Now I was pleased that I was getting some more time to delve deeper into these swims, to explore and to learn about what Roger had seen and found. I had given myself extra time to think about each dip, to plan them more carefully. It gave me time to earn a living so I could finance what was turning into a full-scale exploration of some of the British Isles' furthest-flung corners. There was no rush.

Molly sped up the hill from the main road and came to an abrupt stop where I stood outside Diss station. Her driving skills were still idiosyncratic, to say the least, but I enjoyed that. It was good to see her again. We set off for the coast, a high bank of grey cloud edging in from the North Sea and rubbing out the sun. The window I had wound down was quickly wound back up again, the temperature sliding the closer we got to the water.

In the warmth of the car, the cooler air outside didn't bother me anyway. I wanted my first post-fracture dip to get right to my core, to feel the cold thump of nature against my chest and re-emerge invigorated and ready to tackle each swim with more vim and wider eyes.

I told Molly about my therapy sessions, about how they had helped me see things from a new, calmer, perspective by talking out my concerns and seeing them objectively. How that had helped me on a path towards gaining greater perspective. How I was worrying less as a result.

'I'm really pleased for you, mate. I think this swim is going to make things even better.'

We parked up as close to the beach as possible, coats zipped high against the chill. We walked past a block of scruffy-looking public toilets and through the warren of beach huts that sit behind the dunes, emerging onto the beach via a neat boardwalk. The breeze was light, but still the sea crashed in, as it always does on the east coast. It's never calm on the water in Suffolk and that's why I love it. There was a slight drizzle in the air as we made our way to the centre of the bay and flung our kit on the floor.

The bravado I'd felt on the train and in the car quickly ebbed away as both of us stared out to sea. It was cold and damp, not dissimilar to the weather on Jura. For a fleeting moment I wished the cast was still on so I had a bona fide excuse for not getting in.

We began chatting about anything that came to mind: whether we'd ever been stung by a jellyfish (no) and how different this all was from the clear, blustery day up the coast at Covehithe just six months ago. We kicked at pebbles and began tittering at our inability to get out of our clothes and into the water. I even floated the idea of going back to the tea room in the village for some pre-swim sustenance.

Molly rightly baulked and peer-pressured me into pulling off my coat. I knew once one layer had gone that the rest would have to follow, so I yanked off jeans, jumper and T-shirt in ungainly fashion and left them to collect sand in an untidy heap.

With new-found purpose, I ran towards the sea. Long strides quickly became tentative steps as my toes felt the fizz of the ocean. I waded out to thigh depth, my body already heaving for breath, and pushed myself forward the way I'd seen Labradors enter the ponds on Hampstead Heath. It was an ugly sight, but, finally, I was swimming again.

In *Waterlog*, Roger speaks of how he would come here with his friend Lucy, who would set off towards the horizon at electric pace, allowing the swell to carry her off into the distance. This would have been in high summer, though, and it was far too cold for such antics. Molly and I settled for our now tried and tested tactic of swimming in small circles, huffing loudly before letting our breath fall into a steady rhythm with our stroke.

My right wrist felt sore and I twisted it this way and that. It was still stiff and couldn't move much after weeks of being stuck fast in one place, but now it was free I knew I could make it better if I exercised it more.

After a few minutes I settled my feet on the sea bed and stood with my shoulders out of the water enjoying the marvellous way in which the sea tilts and sways on this part of the English coast. Nowhere else does this happen in quite the same way. Boats lope at odd angles while the horizon bobs this way and that. As I stood there, the crashing wave of an endorphin rush settled over me. I felt hopelessly high and had to remind myself that this was fleeting, that I couldn't always feel like this, and that that was part of the pleasure of outdoor swimming. While it lasted, I let it fall over me and guide me back towards my clothes. Mark's advice about being able to stand outside the scene, recognise it, assess it and deal with it worked just as well in the water as it did when I was anxious and fretting at home about work. Like my arm, my mind had been freed but needed time to start functioning properly.

I waded out, shivering and happy. We dressed quickly, trying our best to shake off the wet sand that had clogged our things, and headed for a cup of tea and some soup. I gabbled about my plans for the next twelve months to Molly as the endorphins throbbed and the adrenalin flowed: where I would swim and how I was going to finish up my retracing of Roger's story. Perhaps breaking my wrist had been the catalyst I needed. Where before I had sometimes felt trepidation about the task at hand, now I felt only hope.

—PART THREE—

Surfacing

'... swims are like dreams, and have the same profound effect on the mind and spirit.'

ROGER DEAKIN, *WATERLOG*

CHAPTER ONE

January

~~~

River Test, Hampshire

I didn't worry about geeing myself up for winter swims. My wetsuit stayed dry for the rest of the year, tucked away next to a moth-eaten army coat in my wardrobe. I backed up my decision not to take more dips as the nights drew in with the fact that only a smattering of Roger's *Waterlog* swims took place in the cold months of autumn and winter.

New Year came and went. The days were getting marginally longer and the weather was hardly worse than when Molly and I had braved the North Sea three months earlier. Heavy rain swept over the south-west, but the downpours meant the temperature was touching double figures on most days, meaning swimming with the aid of neoprene was more than possible.

I looked at my spreadsheet, the one which had made the journey feel less exciting and more like hard work during the previous summer. This time, the non-shaded destinations felt like new places to love and explore, not cells to be blocked out. It wasn't even close to being spring but I could see the year opening out in front of me, the promise of warm weather surely not that distant a dream. Work was quiet, and rather than let that worry me, I took a few deep breaths, told myself 'fuck it' and decided to set off on Roger's trail again.

I took the train to Potters Bar with Joe and met our old work colleague Tom. Tom had managed to lay his hands on a top-of-the-range wetsuit via a magazine-writing gig which seemed to bestow him with all kinds of goodies and treats, and he was keen to get involved in a wild-swimming adventure. It lay prostrate in the large boot of his vintage Jaguar saloon next to bags stuffed full of winter swimwear. I was looking forward to seeing Tom trussed up. I thought his Captain Haddock beard would look all the better when in full swimming attire.

Joe and I were also packing 'condoms', so to speak, and we both fully intended to get rubbered up. The air temperature may have been nudging double figures, but the water where we were going was bound to be freezing. Spending time with Joe and Tom was always easy. They were relaxing company and around them I always felt my edges were smoothed, my anxieties lessened. They were the perfect people for attempting something less than Arcadian, especially as Joe had been with me on that freezing day on the Windrush a year earlier. I didn't feel bad about taking us on a cold dip after that particular experience. We all knew this wasn't going to be a casual frolic in a sun-soaked stream.

Our destination was Stockbridge, close to Winchester. Roger spoke of this place being alive with water, of being able to hear it before you saw it in the streams which bordered the town's wide main thoroughfare. These little waterways flowed out into the River Test, renowned for its trout fishing, much like the nearby Itchen. And as I'd found out the previous summer, those chalky waters were icy cold even in midsummer. There'd be no stealing a swim here, though – this was open water and all the better for it.

Tom opened up the Jag and we roared down the M25 listening to old opera tapes I'd picked up while volunteering at my local Oxfam. The unidentifiable arias of Verdi and Puccini, known only to me through the music round on University Challenge, gave our winter adventure an added air of grandeur, when in fact we all knew that we'd be wading in and screaming like toddlers once it came to the actual swimming.

We passed through the well-heeled town, all gastropubs, old-style hotels and fancy delis, and drove a further mile towards a well-known local swimming spot. With the help of my map, I deduced that Roger would have passed through here on his long swim out of town, when he had crawled and paddled through the shallows, exchanging happy nods with anglers and locals out walking their dogs.

The low sun, which had hung at the top of Tom's windscreen all the way from Hertfordshire, was enclosed by cloud within a minute of us getting out of the car. It made little difference to the temperature, but psychologically that lack of sunlight was a killer. I gathered my things and packed up, ready to tramp down a bridleway towards the banks of the Test. It had obviously been raining here solidly for days – the verge was sodden and huge muddy puddles blocked our path. The only way to negotiate them was to splash through and deal with the messy consequences later. A riverbank is not a place for vanity.

The wide path slipped straight into the fast-flowing river, a wooden bridge to its left leading pedestrians over to the other side. This stony little beach was as good a place as any to get in, so we began undressing quickly and struggling into our wetsuits. Each of us was out of practice in the precise art of putting on neoprene, and it took a good ten minutes before we were all sucked in and ready to go.

Joe and Tom stepped towards the water, kitted out in boots and gloves to stave off the cold. I, however, had made a horrid realisation. My neoprene shoes, which had seen me through so many dips over the past year, had gone missing. They were nowhere to be found in my bag and Tom had definitely emptied the boot of the car. Neither did I have gloves. As Roger says, the cold on your hands and your feet will drive you out of the water faster than anything else. I'd learnt this the hard way on the Windrush, and here I was again, ready for another soaking that would leave my feet feeling as if they'd been injected with local anaesthetic.

Joe and Tom headed off to explore. The water moved fast around their legs, the pair of them having to lean into the strong current as they made for the middle of the river. It was shallow, not even waist high, but good enough to class as a winter swim.

I decided that despite my lack of protection, I should join them. I took two steps in and leapt back out in agony, the cold screaming up my legs and into my lower back. There was simply no way I could get in and enjoy the water, so I sat myself on a convenient grassy mound and watched Joe and Tom splash around, finding places where the riverbed dropped, letting them slip under and swim hard against the unpredictable push of the Test. I'd have to practise the art of feeling the water without being in it that I had perfected up in Scotland.

I was happily watching when Tom waded back and handed me his gloves and boots, his dark beard glistening with river water. We swapped places and he took pictures while I set off on a mission. Joe had already tried and failed to swim all the way from one side to the other, finding himself run aground and washed away downstream, human flotsam unable to tame the river's power. Now I gave it a go. The noise and confusion of the white water by the wooden bridge was overwhelming, and as soon as I lifted my feet and tried to swim I was swept away. I clawed at the still visible chalky riverbed and managed to half swim, half crawl to just past midway before it became clear there was no way I could make it.

Standing up, I didn't feel disappointed; rather, delighted. Despite the fact it was deep midwinter, we'd managed to make it out of London and into a distant wild-swimming hole. A pair of golden retrievers were playing with Tom on the bank as I walked back over, struggling to stay upright where chalky mud gave way to slippery rocks. I watched as I sank backwards and found a slightly less turbulent stretch closer to the river's edge, where I could starfish and let the water lick the back of my head. Another river baptism.

Heading in to dry off, the two dogs gallivanted into the drink, unconcerned by the cold.

'A helpful dog laundry,' said their owner as they scurried back out, shook themselves off and bounded away towards the road.

After twenty minutes of struggling with wet neoprene and balancing precariously on old plastic bags so as not to cut our feet on the wet gravel of the towpath, we strode back to the Jag and dumped our things. In Stockbridge we ate cream teas, a summery treat to follow a summery activity, even if it was now starting to blow a gale and rain was falling on the town's main road.

Doing this now, in the depths of winter rather than holding out for good weather, fitted neatly with my new approach of following *Waterlog* in my own fashion, observing any changes while I was enjoying myself, not just rushing around and taking dips in order to box-tick my way around Roger's favourite swimming holes. I was doing it because it made me feel more alive, more human, with anything else coming second. OK, I hadn't gone for a mile-long splash out of town like Roger, the push of 'Mother Test' at my back. But the happy nods and grins we'd got from locals who'd walked past as we swam proved that getting into the river here was not something to be denied, rather another way to enjoy the water, even in the depths of January.

CHAPTER TWO

March

~~~~~

Highgate Men's Pond, London – Burnham
Overy Staithe, Norfolk – River Bure, Norfolk

As winter continued I went for a series of swims in the men's pond at Highgate. After the enjoyable soaking at Stockbridge, I wanted to get acclimatised for early spring swimming without having to resort to the wetsuit. I may have been after a more languid look at *Waterlog*'s rivers, lakes and lidos, but at the same time I was desperate to see as much as I could in the warmer months. My wrist and my mind were working well and I wanted to make up for lost time, to travel and learn more about what Roger had seen.

Highgate was the perfect place to relearn how to stay in cold water for long periods. It was close to home and near to one of my favourite places for an afternoon tea in London. With my new-found ability to recognise when I felt guilty and anxious about indulging in such activities despite having done all of my work, and allowing myself to go and enjoy them anyway, I took up this new approach with gusto.

On one of my lunchtime trips, one of the daily regulars told me that this was the coldest he'd known the water to be in his eight years of doing the whole winter season.

'It's been more consistent this year,' he said. 'I've experienced it colder but it's been sticking stubbornly around 3°C.'

I can confirm it was very cold, good enough only for the very shortest of swims along the jetty, but enough to get my blood pumping and my body set for the next few months of watery adventures.

I got to test my new-found hardiness in early March, when I returned to the north Norfolk coast. My day on the wide stretch of beach at Holkham with Tim a year before had stayed with me for a long time afterwards: the distant churn of the waves, the strong breeze and the skies that seemed as big as anything I'd seen anywhere else around the world.

I had also missed out a swim of Roger's on my last visit, off the beach further round the coast at Burnham Overy Staithe, and wanted to sink into the water and see whether it differed just a few kilometres away from Holkham.

Tim was with me again, as were Molly and her old friend Tom. We met as usual in Norwich, Molly driving the hour north to the village of Burnham, past its inland harbour and along a high wall which protected Overy Marsh. When Roger came here, boats chugged back and forth from the sea, 'boat people' sitting in dinghies eating sandwiches and enjoying the summer sun.

The tide was well on its way out as we walked the zigzag mile towards the dunes, and the muddy creeks were littered with debris. A recent storm surge had destroyed boardwalks all along the Norfolk coast, their remnants washed up here and there, standing in the mud like ancient shipwrecks. The body of a headless seal lay rotting on the grass, while crows squawked overhead, the broken bodies of sea birds everywhere we looked. The macabre atmosphere was broken only by lapwings pee-witting overhead.

As at Holkham, emerging through the rolling dunes at the edge of Burnham Overy Staithe was a wondrous experience. The twenty-foot schlep up the loose sandy dune was rewarded with the most spectacular view of the harbour entrance as it met the North Sea. Great big inviting pools dotted the beach.

Despite my exertions in Highgate, I had brought my wetsuit along as backup. It was still March, after all, and not nearly warm enough for anything approaching a serious swim without neoprene. I mentioned this to Molly, who as ever took up her hectoring about the evils of wetsuits. None of my companions would be getting togged up, so why should I? Tim joined in the tirade while Tom stood back. I let myself be peer-pressured into going in bareback, despite the first snivels of a cold leaving my nose twitching. I knew it was stupid, but the chance to get that sweet hit of adrenalin was too good to miss out on.

My only concession to the cold, other than my thin summer shorts, was my new pair of swimming shoes. These gave me a modicum of protection as I strode into the shallows, keeping my feet warm while the others screamed blue murder. It was a windy day as always on this long sweep of coastline, but the waves were unusually subdued compared to twelve months before. They didn't burst against my chest and send shivers up my spine. And unlike other North Sea swims, I could see the seabed, the little sand valleys staying firm under the attention of the water.

Slipping under, I panted like the dogs I'd met on the Test and swam out further and further, going for a few minutes longer than I'd been managing at Highgate in recent weeks. There was no chance to wallow here as Roger had done, and the outgoing tide prevented us from swimming into the brackish waters of the harbour. Instead we raced back out and rubbed the wet sand from our legs, pulling on layers as the sun began to slide from view. My arms were bright red and my ears burned up as the blood rushed back towards my extremities. I could feel my chest heave and my nose fill with snot. I'd hastened the cold I knew had been brewing, but the high was so acute that it didn't matter.

The long walk back warmed us up, the late winter sun offering some extra heat too. Back over the marsh, we stopped to watch lapwings and little egrets feasting on invertebrate treats in the mud revealed by the outgoing tide. A short-eared owl took off and caused all other birdlife close by to scatter. It glided away inland and we tracked its flight path, catching a glimpse of a marsh harrier riding high on the thermals above.

*   *   *

By now I was reviving the trip's momentum and started laying more concrete plans. Each week on my calendar had a swim pencilled in, although I made sure to tell Keeley that I wasn't being too inflexible about it and wasn't going to beat myself up if things slipped or I had to change the timetable. As more cells on my spreadsheet turned green, I began to see it as a fun part of the trip rather than a way of turning it into a joyless task. Looking at the list of swims left, I began to wonder what each of them had in store. What would the weather be like? How would I get into the water? How cold would it be? What would have changed in the intervening twenty years since *Waterlog*? I began snapping up OS maps and carefully starring spots on each of them where I thought Roger might have swum.

After our swim at Burnham I'd developed a chesty cough and cold which took the best part of two weeks to shake. The weather was still doing a passable impression of winter, so I didn't worry about not getting back out there and instead dosed myself up on honey and lemon, scouring maps in my dressing gown, sleeping and making sure to say yes to any work that came my way in order to fund my *Waterlog* trips.

Ready to get back out on the road, I made a beeline for East Anglia. I was keen to try and get as many of the swims around Roger's home done in the spring before looking further afield as summer spread north across the country. I chose one that wouldn't require too long a drive for my regular chauffeurs.

Molly, Tim and I were in search of John's Water, an elusive mill pool a few miles west of Aylsham on the River Bure. Roger is deliberately vague about this swimming hole, in a bid to protect it from hordes of wild swimmers descending in summer, but with *Waterlog* in hand and a decent map I'd been able to track it down successfully. Roger came here in the October of his journey, and I was fully expecting the water to be every bit as icy as he had found it. It was a grey day and the temperature was on the low side for this time of year, so I had packed my wetsuit. Roger eschewed his neoprene outfit on his visit, and while I knew Tim and Molly would disapprove, I was keen to have a longer swim and do some exploring downstream, not to mention stay healthy after being laid up thanks to my willingness to go in without protection back in Burnham.

I was chuffed to find the pool exactly where I thought it would be, matching precisely Roger's description. We pulled up alongside an open-sided cart shed mentioned in the book and hopped out to get changed. A mill race rushed out from under old farm buildings, the road kinking south and away behind high hedgerows. I fancied that little had changed here in a hundred years, let alone the twenty since Roger's visit.

The shed, the perfect place to get togged up for a swim, was covered in graffiti, its floor dotted with crushed cans and cigarette packets, the marks of the kids who clearly came here to drink, smoke and, perhaps, swim. But being rural Norfolk rather than urban south London, the phrases were a touch more prosaic. Tim was breathless with laughter when he saw the biggest tag, engraved in huge capital letters.

'JOSH PARSLEY IS THIN.'

We trawled the walls for more gems. 'I pissed here' had an innocent charm to it. The mean streets of Camberwell felt a very long way away. While Tim and Molly read a few more, putting off the inevitable, I went and got suited up in a dry corner of the shed and allowed myself a moment in the Bure alone. I dropped in twenty metres or so downstream from the mill race, the water whipped white and speeding beneath the old farm before eddying into a deep, inviting pool. I swam towards it and saw the gravelly beach from where Roger would have strode in.

I remembered his words about swimming into the turbulent water here, so I did so at speed, well out of my depth, allowing the water to turn me around and fire me off downstream. I was in my own natural water flume, free and far more enjoyable than the hellish rides found at tacky theme parks. The wetsuit and my blue silicone cap cut out the cold and I kept swimming back for more, speeding away into the shallows before wading back towards the deeper water and doing it all over again.

On my fourth or fifth time round I saw Molly edging towards the water down the gravel beach. Molly's hardiness had impressed me every time we'd swum together in the past year, and her entrance here was no exception. As soon as the water touched her toes she took big strides, going deeper every time before launching forward fast and refusing to scream. Despite being inoculated from the cold by thick rubber, I knew how freezing it was, my hands red raw without the protection of gloves.

Tim, naturally, went for the more extreme option. Cursing as he walked in, he reached thigh depth before beginning a count to three. On two, he tombstoned face forward, surfacing and shouting.

'It hurts. It hurts.'

These aren't exactly the words you want to hear on an isolated river on a cold day, but Tim was fine. It was the shock of the water that had caused him to shout, rather than any hideous injury. I let the pair of them get on with their own swims, explaining my flume ride before shooting off once more and going for a wander.

The Bure was very shallow just beyond the cart shed, no more than knee deep. Water crowfoot swayed around me, with tresses of watercress everywhere I trod, much as Roger had found when he came here. I was pleased that this spot seemingly remained unknown and hidden, too far from Aylsham to walk for a casual swim. Only the graffiti attested to anyone being here recently, and compared to other rural swimming places there wasn't too much litter, in the water at least. That added to the Pre-Raphaelite vibe as I walked further and further along the centre of the river, away from Tim and Molly's hundred-mile-an-hour chatter, both of them clearly enjoying strong endorphin highs. The wetsuit wouldn't afford me one of those, but at least it let me lose myself deeply in my surroundings without feeling the nip of the cold around my ankles and across my chest.

I walked back the same way I came and enjoyed a couple of last rounds on the flume before climbing out and divesting myself of my second skin. I got dressed and sat in the shadow of the cart shed eating leftover quiche and drinking tea from a flask. Happily, this is a place that Roger would definitely have recognised down to the last detail, although perhaps not the reminder about Josh Parsley's waistline.

CHAPTER THREE

April

~~~

Highgate Men's Pond, London – Hathersage,
Derbyshire – Well Creek, Middle Level
Drain and the Great Ouse, Norfolk

Back in London I continued to use the men's pond as my alternative to Roger's moat, readying myself for May and the opening of the mixed pond on the other side of the Heath. Spring was well and truly underway, the light pushing hard against the curtains on murky mornings, and I wanted to swim every day that I could. Trips to the pond were becoming a ritual, with each part of the routine refined day by day. I would arrive around 9.30, walking up from the train station in Kentish Town, changing quickly in the enclosed metal shed which acted as a pleasant sun trap, making getting out of clothes less tortuous than on exposed Norfolk beaches and riverbanks.

Despite the warmer weather, coconut matting was still down on the jetty, meaning the walk from clothes to water was a little less painful on the feet. The ropes however, had been pushed back out, swimmers now able to stroke further from the safety of the changing area thanks to the rising water temperature.

The water had reached double figures by early April, when I took my last swim there before getting back out on the road, and I was able to enjoy a comfortable ten minutes before the goosebumps on my chest told me it was time to get back to the warmth of my coat and the life-giving steam of a hot chocolate at the resolutely old-school café at the bottom of Parliament Hill.

I slapped wet footprints over the matting and across the concrete floor of the changing area, drying off with a starchy towel, feeling happily braced. Adding this swim to my routine was working wonders for my anxiety. It gave life an added clarity and seemed to create more purpose, a necessary break from the working day. This was what I had hoped swimming would give me when I set out to retrace Roger's journey. It didn't fix things in and of itself, but it gave me the warm feeling of contentment I needed to be able to face up to my worries, and to deal with them by talking and listening to others. I imagined this is what the moat afforded Roger – a space to both indulge a passion and work out the kinks of day-to-day life in the most private way possible, before facing them head on. I was using swimming as an adjunct to other techniques, from breathing exercises and running around my local park to yoga and meditation, to combat worry, rather than expecting to find all the answers in the water.

This approach had worked well on all of the swims I'd enjoyed since returning to the water, especially on the Bure and at Stockbridge. With this more rounded take on things in mind I took the train north to 'the Pool in the Peaks' in Hathersage on something of a whim, again choosing to push work around so I could squeeze in a swim. This was a perk of freelancing I had rarely used before, and I told myself that I had no one to answer to but myself. It felt liberating not to berate myself for choosing to do something fun and not see it as unproductive or a waste of time.

The heated outdoor pool in Hathersage opens all year round and I was particularly looking forward to seeing whether it remained a local institution, as Roger had found on his visits, not to mention taking a dip that didn't leave me shuddering with cold afterwards. My predecessor spoke of 'spectacular views of the Peaks on all sides', but it was a proper pea-souper when I arrived with my uncle Dave, who had driven down from his home near Huddersfield to join me, the only view that of the empty bandstand and the odd plastic picnic chair laden with towels and swimming gear.

The temperature had also dropped, meaning steam was rising as I paid the £6 entry fee, the smell of cooking bacon rising from the adjacent café and a handful of swimmers ploughing out lengths, even though it was a cold Tuesday morning.

Since Roger's swim here, the parish council, which runs the pool, has fixed up the changing rooms and ensured the bandstand conforms to the EU standards of which it had fallen foul back in the late nineties when Roger came. It holds regular night swims with live music to accompany those countless laps, plus charity events and garden parties over the summer. The heating is switched off over the winter, but swimmers still come for regular dips and to catch up with friends and neighbours.

I slid into the luxurious 28°C water at the deep end, eavesdropping on conversations about the school run, lunch meetings and weekend trips into the hills while I demisted my goggles. I swam off on the must-do forty lengths of a kilometre, finding a steady rhythm while a lifeguard used a mop to clean the sides of the pool. I caught a glimpse of Dave in the general swim area, nosing out a few lengths.

The same convivial atmosphere Roger had found here was alive and well, it appeared. I'd be lying, though, if I said I wasn't delighted when, one by one, my fellow swimmers – Dave included – vacated the water and left me on my own to enjoy the glassy surface, just as I had at Parliament Hill a year before.

After I'd reached my arbitrary swim target, I joined Dave for tea in the impressive grandstand which lines one side of the pool. A set of old church pews provided corrective seating, forcing visitors to sit upright and pay attention. At one end there was a banana box stuffed full of books for sale for £1, the proceeds going to the upkeep of the pool and its grounds. I passed over the dog-eared copy of cricket commentator Brian Johnston's autobiography and instead stuck a quid in the collection box without taking a tome.

It's essential that lidos like this stay central to their communities. In London, lidos have enjoyed a recent boom, with the reopening of Charlton and the ever popular London Fields joining well-known spots at Brockwell, Parliament Hill and Tooting Bec.

Every summer, queues snake around the block to get into these establishments, a sign that the 'healthier, happier, more sensual days' Roger hoped for when he found lidos left to rot in the late nineties are most definitely here. Ambitious projects such as the new outdoor, all-natural pool in King's Cross and plans for a bath on the Thames at Bankside show that swimming is once again becoming an essential part of our daily well-being, not just physically, but mentally and emotionally too. It makes us feel both fitter and calmer.

But it isn't just in the capital. Hathersage is going strong and new funding has been found for the stunning art deco Saltdean Lido in Brighton. Cheltenham's beautiful lido is also basking in huge popularity. It's not just the exercise. It's the sense of community, where everyone is stripped down and doing the same thing, coming together to talk, relax and enjoy the weather, remembering that life is at its best when it's spent idling and taking time to enjoy bright and beautiful surroundings. This was a lesson it had taken me a long time to learn, but I realised that it was such places, these communal baths and pools, that really made me feel at peace when I swam. The idea that other people enjoyed the same thing as me felt magical, as if we were all in on a badly kept secret. Even on a cold day in Hathersage, it was impossible to escape the feeling that the swimming revolution Roger had dreamt of when writing *Waterlog* was finally happening across the UK.

Rather than staying up north, where winter still seemed to be clinging on, its icy prints all over the puddles of towpaths and the shallows of lakes, I swung back south to meet Tim for an altogether different trip than my one to Hathersage. Back in Norfolk, spring weather and high skies made for a less claustrophobic atmosphere than the claggy hills Dave and I had driven over after our swim at the pool in the Peaks. It was good to see proper daylight and to be heading for some cold, open water. Best of all, I was once again sharing it with someone close. It wasn't lost on me that all of the swims I'd done in recent months, even the journeys when I was unable to get in and indulge, had been enjoyed in good company. That sense of collective joy was addictive, and something I didn't want to lose as the journey's momentum continued to grow. The fact that Dave, Tim, Molly and everyone else I had swum with were willing to come with me at short notice was very special. It was a strong antidote to the loneliness I had often felt when working at home, alone.

There wasn't a cloud in the sky when Tim and I met in Downham Market and drove towards Well Creek and the village of Outwell. Roger swam here after bathing in the Little Ouse at Santon Downham and the whispering Wissey near Ickburgh, before heading north towards Hathersage and onwards for his date with Jura and the Gulf of Corryvreckan. Not for the first time, I had that feeling of doing this trip arse about face, having done, or at least attempted, all of those dips in the past few months. The main thing was I didn't care.

We pulled up by a pretty church in the centre of the village, trees in full blossom in the neatly kept graveyard, and set out on foot along the narrow road towards our two intended swimming spots. As I'd found on my trip to the Lark, the Fens can be overwhelming, a vast space in which anything is possible and you are just a speck in an empty landscape. The map in my hand was streaked with straight blue lines, criss-crossing each other and promising boundless swims as long as our bodies and minds craved them.

I kept such bucolic notions to myself, because in reality I knew that we were really heading for a wide drainage channel and a shallow canal where the two bodies of water crossed at an aqueduct. Tim seemed buoyed by the good weather and the thought of a chilly swim and I didn't have the heart to tell him that this wouldn't quite be the same as the day he'd flung himself into the Wissey from a rope swing.

I was surprised he hadn't realised. I had floated a trip to Well Creek the previous summer to both him and Molly, and even sent them a picture of the aqueduct, promising it would be a unique and different take on all the sea and river swims we'd been enjoying. Molly's reply said it all.

'I'm not swimming in a canal, mate. It looks shit.'

With that, I'd shelved my plans for Well Creek. But with Molly unavailable, I'd coaxed Tim into thinking this would be an idyllic break from the book he was in the midst of editing. To be fair, the walk from Outwell down to the aqueduct was beautiful, barges moored at intervals and mallards snooping under the water for an easy meal. The day was still and fresh.

Arriving at the aqueduct, we were greeted by tall fences coated in anti-climbing paint and designed to prevent swimmers from slinging themselves into the depths of Middle Level Drain, which ran at a stately pace beneath it. 'No swimming' signs dotted the banks, alongside dark warnings of £5,000 fines for anyone who trespassed on the sluice gates between aqueduct and drain.

Well Creek itself looked in a sorry state. Its banks had burst during the recent storm surge which had also battered the coast at Burnham, and the water was a filthy light-brown colour. The only people who could see us were the drivers of HGVs which thundered along the adjacent road, but Tim and I both baulked at the idea of paddling along its narrow course. Roger had made it sound like the perfect swimming hole, when in fact it was anything but.

Instead, we crossed the creek at a nearby bridge and dropped down to Middle Level Drain to at least attempt one of Roger's two swims here. On his visit Roger had encountered a group of teenagers 'clocking up hundreds of pounds of Environment Agency fines' by jumping from the sluice gates, but our only company was a sole mute swan about 200 metres downstream.

We had picked a spot east of the aqueduct, where Roger had swum west. Despite having to negotiate a steep bed of stinging nettles and standing on a retaining wall littered with old fag packets and crushed cider cans, I was able to concur with my predecessor when he said this 'was the most beautiful drain I had ever seen'. Early season oilseed rape swayed on the far bank, and the now high sun lent everything a distinctly midsummer air.

I didn't allow myself to be fooled by this intimation of heat and yanked on my wetsuit before slipping in from the wall and heading east, looking far off down the straight channel towards where it met the Great Ouse south of King's Lynn. It was like nowhere I had swum before, the arrow-like channel so different from the swooping meanders of the little rivers into which I'd thrown myself over the past two years. I felt suddenly tiny and alone, that familiar Fenland feeling returning, although this time it made me feel more alive and less inconsequential than it had done back on the Lark. Loneliness didn't cross my mind. There was just me, an endless blue sky and the quiet hiss of the farm fields as the breeze ruffled through them.

And, of course, Tim.

'Er, mate, what's it like in there?'

I turned back and gave him a quick report. Cold, deep, beautiful.

With that, Tim, in his maroon swimming shorts and nothing else, sat himself down on the wall and flopped in, immersing himself as he went. I felt bad watching him gee himself while I'd donned my neoprene. I had promised him an Arcadian wild-swimming adventure, but this was definitely not what he had had in mind.

He swam across to me with his usual ebullience, hollering for all the Fens to hear as we trundled back and forth across the drain, a surprisingly strong current, not visible from the road, pulling at my arms and legs. I hopped out and Tim followed, a cool gust of wind reminding me that he would be feeling the cold far more than I was. I passed him a towel and he rubbed himself down furiously, doing the strange, monosyllabic chuckle he always does when he's having a good time. Hearing it made me realise I didn't need to feel bad about bringing him here.

My wetsuit now a sopping mess around my ankles, I was more than up for decamping to Downham Market, finding a café and reading the paper. But Tim knew there was another *Waterlog* swim just a five-minute drive away and was not letting me off that easily.

I found that, unlike Roger, my urgency to return to the water after one swim was never great, but in Tim I had the ultimate companion for egging me on further into the journey. Tim's peer-pressure antics always meant having one extra drink or another pull on a joint when we were students, often with me being the guy having a nap in the corner while the house party kicked on into the small hours. Now his urging was a lot kinder and led to a lot more fun. Plus it wasn't as if these flat stretches of Norfolk farmland were within spitting distance of my Camberwell flat. There were still dozens of Roger's swims left to do, and getting here took time. Tim's gentle coaxing was the necessary shove I needed to keep going. It was another reason why sharing this trip was becoming so vital.

Dried off and packed up, we drove to nearby Salter's Lode, parking up and setting out towards Denver Sluice, the towering gates of which hold back the Ouse and the various relief channels that mark this watery, reclaimed place. We walked a few minutes along the high levee of the Old Bedford River, getting ever closer to the sluice, where brown, gloopy water roiled white and poured forth towards the Great Ouse. Swimming here would not only be a logistical nightmare, it would also be dangerous. Thankfully, Roger's chosen spot was a little further downstream from the gates, so we turned and headed there, glancing down the fifty-foot banks towards the fast-moving water with excitement. My urge for a dip had risen again.

We passed over a series of lock gates and crossed Well Creek where it flowed into the Great Ouse, far less grimy than it seemed a few miles upstream. The river here was tidal and the water was oozing out towards the Wash, leaving the thick brown muddy riverbed exposed to the spring sunshine. We alighted on a spot opposite a convenient beach and inched down towards the water's edge, my hands scratched by errant thistles as I went.

I decided not to dally and pulled out the wetsuit, dolling myself up in record time, surprised that the damp neoprene didn't make me feel queasy. While Tim dug around in his bag looking for his shorts, I made for the Ouse, attempting to edge in gently but slipping on my backside on the wet, slick mud and entering the murky water feet first.

It felt so different from the drain of an hour before, less industrial despite being the colour of over-stewed tea. The water was thick and silty in my hands and pushed me downstream at Phelps-like pace. I tried to swim across to the beach, which was bathed in afternoon sun and looked like the perfect place to flop out after a hard swim, but the sheer pace of the Ouse pushed me on further and further. I let it take me, whirling my arms in long, joyous strokes as I looked up at the high green banks. Although the road ran parallel to the Ouse, the dyke was so high that any car noise was muffled and impossible to hear above the rush of the river.

I spun myself around and tried to swim against the heavy push of this great river, but made next to no progress. I was stuck stock still in this fashion when I saw Tim inadvertently slip as if on a park slide and crash into the water. For once, he didn't shout, the silt keeping the Ouse warm and Tim quiet.

Getting out proved to be far harder than getting in, the slippery banks offering no purchase to the wild swimmer clad in a wetsuit and neoprene socks. With great difficulty I pulled at young reeds and cut my hands on more thistles, finally making it back to my bags more exhausted by the exit than the swim itself. Tim swam on, lost in a dream.

Back at our bags on the high bank, we took our time getting dressed. I unzipped the chest pocket of my coat and went to put on my wedding ring, which I had taken to pulling off when I went for a dip, just in case it slipped off while swimming. It wasn't there. My face flushed with panic and I began emptying pockets and tearing through my rucksack, flinging wet towels and muddy boots every which way.

'It's gone. Fuck, it's gone.'

Tim looked at me, his face a picture of calm.

'What's gone?'

'My wedding ring. Oh Christ, what the fuck am I going to do? It's gone. I knew I should have kept it on, it never slips off. Never.'

My anxiety wouldn't subside. I was reaching the outer edges of a panic attack. Any breathing techniques were useless to me. My frantic search went on. I delved into each pocket of my bag and scrabbled around on the rough grass, cutting my already bloody hands on more thistles, hoping to see a glint of platinum. I plunged my hand one final time into the jacket pocket I was sure I had left it in and felt metal. I pulled the ring out, pushed it onto my finger and took deep, heaving breaths. It had been in there all along.

Tim looked on as I packed up, mortified. Like Molly, Tim knew I had sought help for my anxiety. Tim also suffers, which meant he was adept at keeping me calm as I stuffed everything away again and we began walking back towards the car.

I apologised. And then apologised again.

'Mate, you don't have to say sorry. I guess the only thing is, you have to try and think what the worst thing is that could have happened. The jeweller you got it from would have had your size, you'd have had to spend some money to replace it, and that's that.'

It was exactly the kind of situation I had spoken with Mark about. Rising panic never fixed anything, but in the moment, it felt like the only thing that could make things better. I had forgotten to say 'fuck it', to recognise the situation as a fleeting moment that would pass. It was an important lesson.

I tried to recapture the high I had felt in the immediate aftermath of the swim, but instead felt embarrassed. It was instructive to know that these things could still happen and that I was still learning how to deal with them.

I managed to calm myself properly as we loaded up the car, silently reciting Mark's essential mantra as we drove over the Great Ouse and around to the gates of Denver Sluice. We walked back and forth across them, the water appearing calm on the surface, but full of violent potential as it rushed through the gates and down into the Ouse.

Like Roger, I found it hard to comprehend the idea of hidden little rivers like the Wissey, Lark and Little Ouse all winding up here in this great watery Fenland holding pen, ready to be unleashed for a turbulent trip into the North Sea. I loved the thought that the crystal-clear Wissey, just a few miles east, and into which I had waded a few months before with a broken wrist, could become something so much more powerful when it teamed up with other, similarly unthreatening, waterways. Watching the water behind Denver Sluice and looking east across the Fens, I slowed my breathing and fingered my wedding ring, anxieties allayed for now, the water soothing me. This was still a journey I was travelling on and one which was unlikely to ever end.

CHAPTER FOUR

May

~

River Wensum, Norfolk

The tea-coloured Great Ouse had been something wholly new for me, a challenge and a variation on my previous *Waterlog* swims. It had taught me I could tackle some of Roger's more extreme adventures. It had also served as a timely reminder that my anxiety wasn't disappearing any time soon. That needed work as much as Roger's trail needed following. But as the days began to lengthen and warm, nerves and worries about long trips and days away from the daily grind slipped away.

I felt an overwhelming sense of excitement about what was to come as summer finally slipped out from behind the clouds. My brief panic had subsided.

I began planning a long trawl through Devon to Dartmoor, and its deep, hidden salmon streams, a three-day adventure on which I'd be joined by Keeley, Tom and Joe. But before heading south I made my last East Anglian trip for some time.

I had wanted to swim in the Wensum ever since I started laying plans for my reappraisal of Roger's journey, even though he himself hadn't swum there. His descriptions of the daredevil Sonny Goodson jumping from the 69-foot parapet of Norwich Art School into just 12 feet of water in the Wensum below got me thinking about a long, soothing dip in this river which winds its way through the city I once called home. I had no desire to hurtle off a building I used to pass almost daily as a student, nor to swim in what had become a rather industrial, dirty stretch of water.

Thankfully, Molly had found an ideal spot a few miles upstream where we could enjoy a dip away from prying eyes in much cleaner water. We met at her flat in town, which overlooked the river and where she had seen otters playing in the shallows just the week before. I was jealous of her proximity to such a pretty stretch of water. Tim joined us, checking to see how I was after my recent panic on the Ouse, and we set out at a brisk pace along the Marriott Way, skirting past a used car garage and an industrial estate before hitting a wide path which allowed us to walk easily three abreast. It was mild, and we all knew that if we could work up a proper sweat the cold of the water would be much easier to bear.

Molly walked us to an opening in the trees and parted them to reveal a steep, grassy bank which led down to the Wensum below. It looked still and deep from high up, but as we moved down I could see it slowly trundling towards Norwich. I imagined it becoming brown and turbid as it mingled with the Yare downstream, passed through the Broads and headed out into the North Sea near Great Yarmouth. The Ouse had left an indelible mark on me, letting me see rivers in their future state as I gazed at them in the moment.

The early summer sun's rays barely reached this shady spot, and so we nattered for a few minutes before Tim began pulling off his T-shirt. I did the same and was soon following him into the water, grateful for my neoprene shoes, the riverbed rocky and painful beneath my feet. It was, unsurprisingly, freezing. Coming after a series of wetsuit dips in the Ouse and Middle Level Drain it felt like my first ever wild swim, the water pushing air from my lungs before I finally got a grip and managed to find a steady rhythm, suspended in the current. A perch rose and flopped out of the water before sinking back down to the deep.

Looking upstream, I could see the tempting blue flash of a rope swinging from a low-hanging willow branch. But the current was too intense and my arms too cold for me to get to it, let alone attempt to climb out along the worn bough before throwing myself into the unknown. Roger probably would have, but seeing as even Tim said he didn't fancy it, I didn't worry too much about my unwillingness to try.

Molly joined us and we each swam our own short course lengths, ploughing up and down imaginary lanes. Everything was tinged with spring. The fresh water, the late blossom, the young leaves pushing for the light above the canopy. Possibility was everywhere I looked.

CHAPTER FIVE

June

~

Lyme Regis, Dorset – West Dart, Devon – River Swincombe, Devon – Chagford Pool, Devon – River Erme, Devon – Mothecombe Beach, Devon – Cirencester Open Air Pool, Gloucestershire – Sandford Parks Lido, Gloucestershire – Hampstead Mixed Pond, London – Henleaze Swimming Club, Bristol – River Frome, Somerset

The leaves were a darker, deeper shade of green a few weeks later when I decamped to Dorset to get acclimatised for my Dartmoor trip. Summer was on an intermittent hiatus when I arrived in Lyme Regis for a family holiday, but my first task was to drop my luggage at our rented cottage, put on my swimming shorts and talk my dad into taking a dip in the pools which dot the beach from Lyme Regis to Charmouth.

The water here is always calm when I visit and the saltiness of the English Channel on my lips gave me a taste that I became greedy for. Over the next three days I swam twice daily off the town beach, breaststroking out to the furthest buoy before a rope prevented me from entering the channel where fishing boats and yachts putter in and out of the Cobb harbour. My body stopped fighting against the cold press of the waves and soon came to embrace my getting in and out as I pleased. After a winter of wetsuit dips I was finally ready to ditch the neoprene for good, at least until the first frosts of autumn.

It was raining. Big heavy drops hit the windscreen of Tom's Jag and streams formed down the middle of Dartmoor's steep, narrow lanes. June had arrived but we had been pitched back into April, fast-moving clouds tracking across the sky when it appeared through a break in the trees.

Our mood was lifted by the sight of runners, scores of them, struggling along outside, marshals in high-vis waving us down single-track lanes whenever there was a big enough gap between athletes. A roadside sign welcomed them all to the Dartmoor Ultra Marathon, a punishing 32-mile run through one of southern England's hilliest places. Suddenly, getting into a series of upland streams and rivers didn't seem so hardy after all. Everyone looked knackered as we drove past, but we were just getting started.

We pulled off the running route and came to Hexworthy Bridge, where the West Dart flowed underneath at a nippy pace. The rain had let up, so Keeley, who'd had to miss our family trip because of work, walked with me to the top of the bridge and looked back down into the drink. We held hands and kissed as the rain started up again.

Giant slabs of rock slid from the banks all the way down to the riverbed, which was clearly visible even from such a great height. The water was a golden orange colour and put me in mind of the Jura burn I had dipped my hand into all those months before.

Tom and Joe struggled gamely into their wetsuits while I used a towel to shield Dartmoor from the brilliant white of my backside and got into my shorts. I took a quick jog over to the Dart, following a shingly beach out into the water, which shelved quickly away into blackness. The cold didn't trouble me unduly and I swam off downstream, the odd bubble rising to indicate one of the native trout had swum off owing to my impertinent intrusion.

Roger spoke of the sweet relief of the Dart when he came to Hexworthy Bridge, diving in after a long car journey from Suffolk.

I felt his joy, albeit on a slightly smaller scale, after our hour-long drive from Exeter. The cold water eased out the cramps in my legs, and I could feel the knots in my back loosening up under the weight of the speedy stream.

I joined Tom and Joe exploring further upstream, a dipper tracking our progress and swooping ever onwards, rising quickly from the rocks as soon as we caught sight of him taking a rest. His tail splashed in the white water before heading off for more adventures away from our prying eyes.

Rubbered up, the guys were in a much better state for wading and nosing around, and so I left them to it and dropped back into the river, letting the Dart carry me at a fair lick through a deep eddy and away under the bridge. It felt like my River Bure flume all over again, although this time with the added bliss of the water scouring my skin without the protection of neoprene. I swam hard against the current and back to the beach, where Keeley stood hunkered beneath an umbrella, a towel tucked under one arm and a flask of tea at her feet. I had hardly noticed that it was teeming, rain streaking down the windscreen of Tom's parked car. Keeley poured me a cup and help towel me down, fussing around me happily as I began to shiver.

Buzzing after breaking our Dartmoor duck and relaxing on the vast leather seats of the Jag, I pulled out the map and declared that we were now going in search of Roger's Sherberton stream. I had a place marked that I thought could be my predecessor's secret spot, whose location he'd refused to divulge. Roger said it was 'a place where the Dart is joined by an unusually cold moorland current'.

The Jag, more suited to city streets, struggled up the stiff gradients of the national park's knackered roads and we clattered over a cattle grid towards the hamlet of Sherberton itself. A promising stream ran parallel to the small, untended road and we ignored various 'No Parking' signs, stopping to have a closer look.

A set of submerged stepping stones crossed this little waterway, but it was no more than knee deep. Roger spoke of his place having a ten-foot deep pool where he had spied salmon swimming against the current by the dozen. My map-reading clearly needed some work.

We drove back through Hexworthy Bridge and out onto open moorland. That same little stream we had checked out in Sherberton appeared to meet the Dart further north, although getting to this spot where the river widened was going to require a lengthy tramp from the road. Ditching the car, we stuffed our wet swimming things into bags and headed down a steep, boggy track, the rain making the path almost impassable. Nestled into my waterproof, I thought of those runners, splashing out mile after mile with no respite in sight.

Soon the Dart was upon us, moving fast towards where we had swum an hour previously and offering up wild-swimming spots at what seemed like five-metre intervals. There was still a mile to walk, and Keeley had to gently remind me that if I got into the water here I probably wouldn't get to sink my shoulders in Roger's chosen place. I grudgingly agreed, knowing she was right.

By now the weather was finally on the turn and we found the confluence of the Dart and the pretty River Swincombe, the little stream we'd explored earlier, to be the most perfect swimming spot imaginable.

A long set of stepping stones stood proud in the shallows, the sweeping beach marked here and there with crusty cow shit. The Swincombe didn't rush into the Dart in a torrent, like Roger said, but just upstream I could see the water deepened into pools which looked dark and mysterious, the perfect place for spawning salmon. I was sweaty and tired of trying to recreate things perfectly, and so got changed and splashed in. There may not have been a torrent, but it was certainly 'unusually cold' in this place, far more so than down at Hexworthy. Even after a week of countless cold water swims, the breath was knocked out of me as I dived to the bottom and resurfaced gasping hard and fast. It felt fantastic.

Keeley, Tom and Joe had watched sceptically as I waded in, reluctantly agreeing to my hectoring about wetsuits and summer weather. Each of them stripped down to their swimming gear and looked on as I called them in, promising it would be warm once they took the plunge.

They tiptoed across the sharp stones of the beach and shared looks of bewilderment as one by one they entered the fast-flowing stream. I swam on my back, watching as they finally dunked themselves and rose spluttering, laughing obscenities at me about the cold. It may have been my fault for starting this adventure, but it wasn't as if I had a say over the temperature.

I had left the snorkel I'd bought in Lyme Regis in the car, so had to make do with taking deep breaths and peering down into the deep pools with the standard-issue swimming goggles I had remembered to stick in my rucksack. There were no salmon I could see, perhaps because of four interlopers creating such an almighty racket about thirty yards downstream.

I left the others to acclimatise and went off towards where the Swincombe began to mingle with the Dart. It was shallow, the riverbed shelving from the confluence into the deep pool I had just been exploring, a pair of weeping willows draping their spindly fingers across the Swincombe. I eased the tresses to one side to find a stream no more than a foot deep, the willows' roots swaying gently in the current. I couldn't think of a better place for a resting salmon to hole up, but alas I wasn't in luck. It all brought to mind the long tresses of Pre-Raphaelite water crowfoot in the River Bure back in February, except today I wasn't in a wetsuit and the now searing summer heat meant I wasn't in need of a flask of tea and the immediate attentions of a car radiator to warm me up.

As in the Fens, I felt like a tiny speck on the landscape, far away from everyday reality. Nestled deep in this Dartmoor valley, unreachable via my smartphone, I remembered that true escape was the essence of wild swimming: escape from needless worries and anxieties, from fear, from being hassled. But I was also reminded that as much as being in the water is about escape, it is also about joy. Sharing swims like this made me happy, especially seeing people who would previously have never done something like this taking time to swim back and forth, totter over stepping stones and jump into the deep. Coming to these places made me realise that this was what made my life worth living.

Looking at Joe, Tom and Keeley getting out and chatting, I saw that wild swimming was something that anyone could do and love. Sure, they were cold, but they looked more than content, joking and towelling off damp hair, ready to go where Roger pointed. Four years ago I couldn't have imagined myself ever being in a situation like this, and now it was all I ever wanted to do, a way of keeping demons at bay, of spending time with people I cared about. I had Keeley to thank for taking me to Hampstead mixed pond in the first place. She waved from the bank as she waded out and gave me a thumbs up, her hair tied up high to stop it from getting wet. I fancied I could see her blue eyes brighten in the sunlight. It was wonderful to be sharing a swim with the person I loved most.

The Dart had fast become my favourite river, a place I knew I would rave about to anyone who cared to listen when I told them about my latest swimming escapades. But there were more places to see and time was limited. My planning had been meticulous for this trip, despite the jolly, laid back nature of it, and after eating a pub lunch and guzzling bitter shandies, we drove north across Dartmoor for an end-of-day swim in the pool at Chagford. This little lido sits flush against the banks of the Teign, high reeds visible above the fence which marks out the far side of the 25-metre pool. Its big draw is the fact that the water comes from the river via a mill leat and, although chlorinated, it tastes suitably fresh when you accidentally take a gulp.

The swimming here was dreamy and fun, a little more ordered than the chaotic flow of the Sherberton stream but none the worse for it. A group of local kids in rubber rings played in the roped-off shallow end, while a bunch of teenage lads performed handstands and lifted each other out of the water, egging each other on to dive and cannonball into the deeper water at the far end. A brutal game of splash erupted, but the lifeguards looked on, impassive.

Joe and I, both fans of ploughing out lengths during the week back in London, settled into a steady rhythm of front crawl and breaststroke to warm up, while Tom and Keeley pottered along at their own pace.

Afterwards, drying off in the sun and drinking tea from an official Chagford Pool mug (50p hire charge), I fell into conversation with Sue, one of the relaxed lifeguards. She explained that she had moved to Chagford in 1985 and started working at the pool around the same time. She had fallen in love with the place and never left. I told her about my *Waterlog* mission.

'You'd be surprised by the number of people who do what you do,' she said.

For a moment, I had a sudden panic. Was there a rival Roger acolyte going around the country, swimming in every spot and obsessively logging their experiences?

She said that it was more that people came to the pool because of its mention in *Waterlog* and various wild-swimming guides. A pathetic sense of relief surged over me. She said a growing interest in outdoor swimming, plus the fact that the nearest indoor pool was an hour away in Exeter, had saved this wonderful place from going out of business.

Like Hathersage, I loved the self sufficiency and community atmosphere at Chagford. It was resolutely old school. The changing rooms had been done up in 2000 and a new tank fitted earlier in 2014 to stop leakages, but it felt timeless. When I told Sue how good it was that the eaves of the recently renovated changing rooms played home to nesting swallows, she agreed.

'It's great that they're here. The only problem is having to clean the shit from the changing room floors.'

The following morning we left the moors behind, Tom carefully steering the Jag down single-track lanes towards Mothecombe and the Erme estuary. After being cooled by the Dart and exercised in Chagford, stopping at this outstanding stretch of coastline had felt like a logical next move for Roger, and I could see why. The surroundings were wholly different to those of Dartmoor, but the sense of isolation was just as vivid. The V-shaped Coastguards' beach which jutted out from the Erme looked astonishing from up on the clifftops.

Roger swam here on the rising tide, pushed inland and towards the narrow, verdant, vertiginous walls which the river had carved out after tumbling its way through Dartmoor. On his trip, surfers sat waiting to ride in on the huge rollers which battered the sand bar that divided sea from estuary, but those with boards were only just making their way onto Coastguards' beach when we emerged onto the sand, the tide just about slack. We walked hurriedly across to where the stream-like Erme stood limpid and slow flowing, reduced to a shallow trickle.

Tracing it inland, I couldn't help but find the Erme less than tempting. The beach itself was beautiful, but the river was an off-green colour and chock full of weeds, just as Roger had described. But with the weather so good and no chance of coming back any time soon, we were left with no choice but to swim.

After changing behind some convenient dunes next to Boult Hill Plantation, we made our way into the still, shallow water. Roger had talked of hurtling with the current and being washed up by the old lime kilns which we could see in the distance, but our experience was set to be a wholly different one. I waded in and grimaced, the cold numbing my feet. I heard Joe, Tom and Keeley muffled growls and splash on behind me. By now we were deep into the estuary mouth, with boats moored ad hoc along the course of the river.

The riverbed suddenly bottomed out and I was able to swim against the easy current, turning to look out along the green tunnel towards the whip and thrash of the English Channel. The surfers were now taking up their places in the distant waves, a sure sign that soon this whole stretch would be flooded.

By now we were all warming to the task. The morning sun had breached the tree tops and was heating the water nicely. Having swum so much in recent days, it felt like this was my natural element, as if I belonged more in the water than on dry land. I imagined this was how Roger felt come the end of his journey: that walking on sand, rock and stone was a poor substitute for getting into the water and being part of the scene. I tried to remember how I had learnt to have a feel for the water without getting in, but at that moment, only being under the surface was going to do it for me.

As at Sherberton, I felt so very far away from anything. The idea of getting into Tom's car and driving back to a city of millions of people seemed faintly ridiculous, as if this place and my home weren't in the same country but on different planets. The only other people close by were those I was with, at least that I could see. The boats seemed empty and the surfers were pinpricks against the horizon.

I swam onto the little beach next to our swimming spot and allowed the sun to dry me off. I contemplated the water: the same stuff I had dismissed as off-green was now a sparkling azure, clear where the guys still swam and chatted. It made this place all the more tropical and added to the sense of 'dream swimming' which Roger spoke about.

My contemplative mood was quickly shattered as we began our walk back towards the causeway which led up and away from the beach. The tide was rolling in rapidly, surfers zooming into view and fast-moving water pushing us closer and closer to the rocks and higher ground. Suddenly, people emerged from every corner of the estuary. Dog walkers, kite flyers, swimmers – all of whom had somehow been hidden from view – were making their way to the same place we were. Perhaps this wasn't the isolated place I thought it was.

Did it matter? I had felt that sense of isolation so strongly that it was impossible to deny it. I pondered this as we formed a queue to reach the path that led up to the cliffs and the access point for Mothecombe beach. The water was now licking the edges of the estuary, but everyone around me seemed so delighted. They had made it here early enough to frolic on the sand or in the water and didn't seem disappointed by the fact that nature had curtailed their fun. Quite the opposite. There was the same sense of shared experience I had found in lidos around the country. We made it here separately and now we were all leaving together, most of us heading to share more time on nearby Mothecombe beach.

It was a public day on this private beach, the landowners allowing all and sundry to walk down the sunken path which cut down from the Erme estuary and out over the dunes onto the most magical of sandy bays.

England was at play here, despite a high sheet of grey cloud sliding landwards. Windbreaks formed makeshift camps for extended families, dads built elaborate sandcastles, grandparents slept in the artificial shade and kids ran into the foamy shallows.

The waves were pounding the beach, throwing up spume and making the water look unswimmable. A pair of surfers could be spotted at intervals as the crests of waves subsided, sitting far away and waiting for the perfect roller to bring them back to shore. I clambered back into my clammy shorts, already caked in sand from my excursion in the Erme, and legged it with the others straight into the sea.

Thigh deep, I took a quick dive under and got wiped out by a thunderous white wave hurtling into land. I got up, waded back out, and did the whole thing again. Keeley laughed as I repeated this cycle, before we finally managed a few strokes to meet Joe and Tom, who had settled into a game of wave-jumping. It was an impossible task. Just when you thought you'd escaped one monster, another, larger one appeared as a harsh reminder that the sea is the boss.

Delirium soon began to settle in and we fell into hysterics as, one after another, we got an absolute battering. People would surely pay good money for this kind of pounding at a fancy Turkish bath. I looked around and realised there were dozens of people enjoying the same game. Just a few feet away a hulking giant of a man, his bald head reddening in the June sun, disappeared beneath the drink with a deadly serious look slapped across his face and emerged grinning like a buffoon.

Even as grey clouds slanted across the sun and rain began to fall, the beach didn't empty and the water remained a human soup. A group of kids, no more than ten years old, were jumping waves too, albeit in slightly shallower water. I felt I had happily regressed to their age, my only concern being dodging the next breaker. There was nothing else.

After half an hour we emerged, skin puckered and red, facing up to the realisation that our Devon jaunt was over. Ahead of us was a long drive back to the Smoke, but our memories of these special swims wouldn't fade fast. For days, all I had been concerned with was water, the very nowness of it – perhaps this was the 'third thing' about it that Roger mentions at the start of *Waterlog*, the thing other than hydrogen and oxygen. So much swimming was having a huge affect on me, and in a positive way; I felt happier, less anxious and more content, as if the journey was finally showing me the way now I had stopped trying to ape Roger and do things at my own pace and in my own way. Swimming was most definitely helping, especially in such good company.

I took just enough time back in London to clean and dry my shorts and towel before getting back on a train and heading out west, this time to Cirencester and its open-air pool. I was going to meet Tom, my best friend with whom I'd swum in Burton Bradstock at the start of my *Waterlog* adventure.

Tom hadn't been on as many swims with me as either of us would have liked, and this was a chance to make up for lost time. He'd made a mix CD specially and slipped it on as we drove out of his home town of Oxford. Tom Petty blasted out of the little speakers in his Mini.

Tom and I had bonded over music while students. It was a shared language, something which we could always come back to. The first time I'd met Tom, the first thing he asked me was whether I wanted to hear a pirated copy of the new Radiohead album. He was going to play it on his university radio show and handed me a flyer, telling me what time he'd be broadcasting his ill-gotten copy of this most sought-after LP. It wasn't long before we had a show together, delighting and confounding the student body with second-rate Britpop selections, Jeff Buckley album tracks and the occasional soul classic.

As the trip had gone on, I'd unintentionally embarked on a parallel journey into the world of songs about swimming, sharing my discoveries with Tom, whose excitability was infectious. I listened to my playlist religiously whenever I took trains to meet Tim and Molly, and had done so today as I'd left London. I was obsessed with Kate and Anna McGarrigle's version of Loudon Wainwright's 'Swimming Song' and the lazy flow of Nick Drake's 'River Man'. The latter had a slow, gliding rhythm which for me always evoked my first river swim on the Granta. It coloured that day, and my earliest swims in Roger's in wake, in a sepia tint which grew with time.

At that moment I was particularly obsessed with a solo artist called Mutual Benefit, whose EP 'Love's Crushing Diamond' had just been released and featured songs focusing on swimmers, rivers and the search for tranquillity. I had listened to the twenty-minute suite on the way to see Tom that morning. I found that the words of the final track, 'Strong Swimmer', filled me with the essence of the water, the way it nuzzled and gilded every pore of my body. It was that same elusive touch when I was in or near the water. I listened to it before and after I went swimming, to prepare myself for the water and to amplify its beauty.

These lines in particular stood out:

> *I clear my mind of joy and sorrow*
> *river doesn't know tomorrow*
> *rolls along with such simplicity.*

I felt it summed up how I felt in these months after I had broken my wrist. Every time I thought of or was near water, my mind was at peace, the river or the sea or the lido buoying me up without judgement, making everything simple. Helping me see the world anew.

I wasn't afraid to tell Tom about how I felt about this. We'd been the closest of friends for almost fifteen years and I told him about the record, which of course he'd already heard, and how it made me feel. He knew too about the help I had been receiving from therapy. I told him how much I was loving spending time with old friends, how the journey was taking on a more profound and rounded meaning than

I could ever have hoped. I gave his leg a squeeze as we headed off down the A34. It was great to see him.

Summer was officially here and, as the miles passed, the excitement began to grow. It was a beautiful day and we were going to cool off in the most perfect place imaginable. I had done plenty of research about Cirencester's pool and was set for it to be every bit as splendid as Roger had found it almost twenty years ago. I wasn't disappointed.

We reached the pool via a narrow alleyway, crossing the bridge over a small stream and handing over £4.50 each to one of the attendants, who dropped the change into an old ice cream tub. There was no contactless payment option here. The 'old-fashioned charm' that Roger had enjoyed was very much in evidence: the blue-washed walls, the breeze-block changing rooms and the wire baskets for stashing your clothes were all still there. The only concession to modernity seemed to be a single electric shower, doubtless installed in case anyone wanted a quick warm-up after a dip on a day cooler than this.

The water was heated to 26°C and there was no segregation. Serious swimmers mingled with kids splashing in the shallow end, while locals trod water in the middle of the pool. Best of all, it was absolutely packed. It was a weekday lunchtime, but it felt as if half of Cirencester had sacked off work for the afternoon and decided to come down to have a swim and drink tea from the Tuck Shop, its serving hatch doors flung open to reveal an array of unhealthy treats for post-paddle enjoyment.

The water here was natural, like at Chagford. It came from a nearby spring and felt silky on my skin as I slowly worked my way through a series of lengths of breaststroke. My whole body cast a long shadow along the white-washed bottom, and occasionally I caught sight of Tom, wide eyed and goggle free, going about his own exertions.

The view was none too shabby either, the old Cecily Hill barracks looming on one side and making the whole place feel like a castle's private playground. I loved that a community-run pool such as this could still be popular, that Roger's call to arms and the work of other outdoor swimming campaigners had ensured that being outdoors like this on a summer's day wasn't a niche activity for English eccentrics, but one that anyone could do as long as they had a spare half hour. The people of Cirencester certainly seemed to think so.

I barraged Tom with this swimming manifesto as we left the pool and went to find somewhere for lunch. He listened to my ceaseless chatter about how this country seemed to be in the grip of an outdoor swimming renaissance.

Cirencester's water had quickly reawakened the joy I'd felt when I emerged onto Mothecombe beach. I'd become an evangelist, preaching to anyone who would listen about how and why swimming could make us all happier and healthier.

At this point I was desperate to find another swim. It was early afternoon, a Friday, and I couldn't think of a better time to carry on my mission. No work was going to get done today. Back in the car I mentioned to Tom that I needed to swim at the lido in Cheltenham, hoping he'd be keen to go, but not expecting him to push on further west and out of his way.

'Let's go now,' he said. 'Come on, when are you going to be down this way again?'

Tom was just one of a growing band of cohorts who were seemingly ready to drop everything to join me for a dip. Keeley, Tim, Joe, Tom and Molly didn't simply shrug when I told them of my plans – they actively embraced them. It made the mission fun. I was enjoying the company and the way swimming brought me closer to people I loved and taught me new things about them every time we headed for a river, lido, lake or beach: About their fearlessness in the water, their willingness to follow my dodgy map-reading, and their varying abilities behind the wheel (admittedly always better than mine).

By the time we reached Cheltenham it was 3 p.m. and the whole town seemed to have the same plan as us. The lido car park was full and a queue filed out from the turnstiles. We crawled along Georgian terraces, found a place to squeeze in Tom's Mini and walked the ten minutes back to the pool.

Cheltenham Lido is arguably the most beautiful example of an out-door pool in the UK. Its wedding-cake fountains were spraying forth as we entered, the huge pool opening out among beautifully manicured lawns, where all of Cheltenham seemed to be sunning itself. The lido was given a full makeover in 2006/7, having been saved for the town by a group of dedicated trustees, and it retains the charm which Roger found when he visited in the late 1990s. Its grand café, with its stunning portico, was rammed, and the lawns were barely visible beneath damp towels and sizzling skin. A short slide played host to a never-ending rotation of kids, screaming as they dropped into the drink.

The serious swimmers were roped off to one side, three lanes marked out for those who had come to go back and forth rather than loll and splash. A group of teenage boys, bodies perfectly sculpted and side partings razor sharp, wandered past, pretending not to stare at a group of girls who swung their feet in the deep end. Their studied indifference was a sight to behold.

I dropped into the medium lane and tried my best not to tap the feet of the woman swimming slowly in front. No joy. I switched to a speedier front crawl, overtook her and tumbled back at the end of the fifty metres, only to find myself being tapped by a more athletic swimmer behind me.

Regulating my speed in a busy lane was something I had yet to master, and I parked myself in the shallows waiting for a decent gap to emerge. I could only envy Roger, who'd come here early in the day and had the whole lido to himself. I could wait here until closing and that wouldn't happen. The working day was coming to a close and the temperature was showing no sign of dropping, more and more locals arriving to blitz away the stresses of the week with a soothing swim.

After a few haphazard laps, I lay down on my towel along a low wall and allowed myself to dry in the June sun. My chest heaved with the effort of my swims here and at Cirencester, both having been far closer to a workout than the swims in Devon a week before. But that was what I loved about this whole thing – the sheer difference of every dip. In the space of a week I had been cooled off in a raging Dartmoor river, swum in the azure waters of a faraway estuary, been battered by the surf of the Atlantic and swum in a series of beautiful outdoor pools. The spread of swimming options made me happy. There was of course a tinge of melancholy to all of this. Roger hadn't got to see these changes happen. He had died just as people were coming round to the idea of wild swimming not being a subversive activity. I knew that if he'd been sunbathing here with me, or more likely swimming a 'token mile' while I marvelled at his stamina, he would have been delighted with such progress.

By now there was no excuse for me not to swim every day. The days were long and bright and the sun was warm from 6 a.m. I had built trips to Highgate men's pond into my routine, but now it was open I started using the mixed pond as my moat instead, delighting in being there before anyone else on scorching hot days and being home and hosed by 10 a.m. The only thing that could have made the routine better would have been a house overlooking Hampstead Heath.

Every morning I'd take the long walk from Kentish Town up the hill and onto the Heath, past the tennis courts alive with Murray wannabes thwacking balls as if they were knocking up at Wimbledon, and on over Parliament Hill. The long view south across the city was always hazy, a nasty smog clinging to the Thames and obscuring the Sussex hills. Dog walkers and runners paraded up to the viewpoint while I took the briefest of glances at London before hurrying downhill to my date with the water.

Swimming at this popular place on a June morning, with only the local mallards and the lifeguards for company, was heaven. There was something marvellous about jumping in and swimming out to the far rope, knowing that within three or four hours the pond and its narrow bank would be teeming with people desperate to cool off and escape the mugginess of London in high summer.

Pushing my head into the deep green water and watching the air bubbles surface, I thought back to my trips here last summer, when Molly and I had queued to get into the water. Everything was so different earlier in the day. Not necessarily better, but certainly more peaceful and more conducive to deep, meditative contemplation. Each morning swim set me up for the day and got me dreaming of upcoming trips to Roger's chosen *Waterlog* waterholes.

On the days I couldn't make it all the way north to Hampstead, I'd struggle out of bed at 6 a.m. and cycle the five minutes from my home to Brockwell Lido for a few short laps. The vibe there was altogether more serious, twenty or so early risers quietly steaming back and forth and getting their exercise in before decamping to the office. But at either place I left with the sense of being restored to my senses, my wilder, anxious edges smoothed like a pebble on a riverbed. Coming home I felt relaxed, but energised.

Boarding the train alone at Paddington, I had worked myself up into a real state about the day's impending swim. I thought back to the dips I'd enjoyed with all my friends in recent months and felt sad about not having anyone else to share this trip with. It was the first one I'd done alone outside London since I'd broken my wrist. Without anyone else to talk to as the train clattered west and on towards Bristol Temple Meads, I allowed my mind to race away with itself. Why was I doing this anyway? Roger had done it and done it better, so why was I bothering? Who really cared about such a wasteful adventure? Shouldn't I be at home doing something more productive?

I brooded and stared out of the window at the grey June morning, well aware that I was being ridiculous and overly dramatic, but allowing myself to wallow in it anyway. These swims needed doing and I had to accept that people couldn't always spare time to come along with me.

It didn't help matters that this wasn't simply a trip to a river where I could jump in alone and munch on homemade sandwiches in sweet repose afterwards. I was on my way to the Henleaze Swimming Club, a private quarry pool where I was due to meet the club's staff and undergo a swimming test before the swim proper. The thought of having to meet and talk with strangers seemed like a hideous ordeal. It didn't matter that they were fellow swimmers. I was not in the mood to be social.

Roger wrote about a shining lake at Henleaze, with well-kept lawns and a 1920s ambience. But reading his passages about Henleaze I only found myself pining for swims gone by: the vim and vigour of the Dart, the churn of the North Sea at Walberswick or the simple pleasures of an early dip at Hampstead. As the London suburbs rolled past the window and the Thames came into view through Slough, I picked through *Waterlog* and found a line to suit my current mood.

'A solitary, fugitive affair', is what Roger called his journey as he drove the hundreds of miles from Suffolk to Devon for his Dartmoor dips. Like him at that point in his adventure, I was in so deep that I could no longer back out, but the end was nowhere in sight. My swimming to-do list seemed never-ending and appeared to grow longer every time I crossed another one off. It was as if Roger was setting me a challenge, showing me that this wasn't simply a vanity project, but a worthwhile slog that would come good in the end, despite revealing its difficulties to me almost as often as its joys. I needed to remember that I was meant to be having fun and indulging a hobby.

I tried to keep this thought in mind as I took a lumbering double-decker bus from Temple Meads station through Bristol city centre and out to Henleaze. I felt nervous alighting in this distant suburb alone and walking through the tall, cast-iron gates of the swimming club. I should have remembered Tim's wise words after I thought I had lost my wedding ring. 'What's the worst that can happen?'

Alison, the club's secretary, met me at the entrance to the little wooden clubhouse, where I signed my name in the visitors' book, an old ring binder stuffed with foolscap. She made me feel very welcome and introduced me to a whole crowd of locals, telling them about my mission to swim all of *Waterlog*. Nods of approval greeted this. I was among friends here, the shared experience of Britain's lidos and lakes very much in evidence. I hadn't needed to be anxious at all; my worries had merely been in my head, just as they always were. After I raved about the pool in Cirencester and the cooling waters of the West Dart to a few of the hardy swimmers in the clubhouse, Alison pointed me in the direction of the men's changing rooms and Joe, the lifeguard who'd be giving me the fifty-metre swim test I needed to pass in order to enjoy Henleaze to the full.

I'll admit that this was one of the things that had been preying on my mind ever since Alison and I had begun speaking over email about my visit. I had never earned so much as a ten-metre badge to stitch onto my speedos. I hadn't even been able to jump in at the deep end without making a scene. I was no champion swimmer. In fact, I felt like I was a fraud. Well, at least that was how I felt as I waved to Joe, a lithe young student who stood over six foot and clearly swam 1,000 metres before breakfast.

I put on my shorts in the open-air changing area, deciding it wasn't wise to have a go on the parallel bars, which had seemingly been placed there to help swimmers work up a sweat before trying out the lake's myriad diving boards. Joe stood waiting at the water's edge.

I asked him the temperature.

'Seventeen degrees Celsius. Now if you can swim to that yellow marker and back, that'd be grand.'

He pointed to an old police cone a little way along the bank. It didn't look more than ten metres distant, but I didn't complain.

I swam quickly and in my neatest breaststroke, putting my keenness to impress Joe down to my relatively new-found ability to get from A to B in the water without impersonating a Labrador. I doubled back and surfaced at the steps where I'd entered. Joe looked down and gave me the thumbs up.

'Well, you've passed with flying colours,' he said, deadpan, before outlining the rules of the lake. No swimming beyond the rope at the far end, no climbing the quarry walls on the far side.

'Feel free to use any of the diving boards,' Joe added as I set off.

The towering green platforms loomed over to my right, the highest ten-metre board removed because the lake wasn't deep enough to accommodate the most daring water nymphs. The middle platform, at seven metres, looked terrifying.

I aimed for the general direction of the old quarry wall, where two swimmers appeared to be sitting beneath the surface. The water was green and cleansing, and I could see my hands reach into the deep, the light refracting as they stretched to feel the essence of the lake in front of them.

At the wall I found a convenient place to perch, my shoulders just above the waterline. I pulled myself high and strained to get a better look at the club from this perfect angle. There was nothing exclusive about this members-only place, but restricting numbers clearly had its benefits. The lawns were closely cropped and the buildings around the lake's edge looked spic and span, clearly given a fresh lick of paint every twelve months. Entry points around the water were well tended, with reeds cut back and shallow steps to make it easy to get in and out for those members who didn't want to dive.

I pushed off and swam a dozen lengths of the lake, alternating between breaststroke and front crawl. When I swam the latter, my path was haphazard, the only clue to my whereabouts being the high wheel of my arms and the clear blue sky away from the trees on the banks. More than once I ended up beaching myself in the reeds, looking around to see if any regulars had spotted my mishap.

At the clubhouse end of the lake, breathless, I realised that I couldn't come to this wild-swimming institution and not try out one of the diving boards. There was no way I was taking the slow climb up to the high platform, but a number of springboards which sat closer to the water did look marginally more appealing.

I hauled myself out and edged along to the front of a beautiful old willow board. In previous weeks I had taken to practising my diving skills, finally learning how not to bellyflop. But in front of the serious swimmers who dotted the banks and powered out lightning-fast lengths of the lake, I chickened out. Instead, I opted to jump, hearing the thunk and boing of the board behind me before I crashed in ungainly fashion into the lake below. I swam across to where Joe had given me my test and clambered out for the last time.

After eating my sandwiches and reading the paper on the lawn, I fell into conversation with Roy, one of the lake's part-time staff. We chatted about Roger's visit here and how *Waterlog*, coupled with the recent boom in triathlons, had ensured the lake remained as popular as ever.

The waiting list was down from Roger's time, with just 250 people in the virtual queue. But Roy explained that this was because of week-day memberships being introduced, allowing older and self-employed swimmers to come during the week for a cut price. In total, 1,900 members used Henleaze. It seemed a very small number, especially when there could be that many people at Tooting Bec Lido on a hot summer afternoon.

Roy said he had joined Henleaze when he had been a competitive triathlete, looking for a place to train when he moved to Bristol. At the time it was the only place in the city that catered to such outdoor types. He had swum all over the UK: in the spring-fed pool at Cirencester ('How soft is the water?' he exclaimed) and regularly at Parliament Hill Lido as a youngster.

'I used to compete there in the sixties,' he said. 'It was always an early season meet, April, and always freezing. It was the longest length you ever swam, although the cold made sure it was the quickest too.'

I thought back to my own dip there, the previous May. It had been cold then and had taken me an age to warm up afterwards. Roy still looked as if he was a bit handy in the pool. I imagined him in a white-water blur, powering out a few dozen laps at dawn.

Roy led me back to the clubhouse, where he sold me a copy of the lake's history for £5. Inside was a series of stunning black and white photos from its heyday, with crowds thronging the banks on gala days. I imagined it wasn't much different on a sunny Saturday in 2014.

Alison enquired after my next stops on my *Waterlog* odyssey, and I filled her in on my plans for an imminent trip to nearby Farleigh Hungerford and the river-swimming club there. She gave a nod of approval when I mentioned this hallowed swimming institution. I found myself excited by the thought of going there alone.

I passed back through the imposing gates and onto the main road back to town. I stood tall and realised that all my niggling morning anxieties had been washed away in the quarry pool. There was a lesson here: to never doubt swimming's redemptive powers and to remember that worrying about imaginary concerns never fixes anything. Coming to Henleaze had been a timely reminder of what I had learnt with Mark. I was ready for more solo adventures now and knew that there was nothing for me to worry about.

Farleigh Hungerford was the place everyone with any wild-swimming knowledge always mentioned when I told them about my retracing of *Waterlog*.

'It's the last river-swimming club in England, you know,' was the usual refrain, followed by happy tales of swimmers clogging the field next to the campsite which now looks after the club, pushing off from the raging weir and crashing into the water from the old diving boards.

The club's secretary, Rob Fryer, had found a certain fame in recent years. He could often be seen on popular countryside magazine shows espousing the joys of river swimming. His *Wild Swimming Europe* guidebook had become something of a hallowed text for aficionados.

I was increasingly aware that the Farleigh and District Swimming Club was perhaps the epicentre of British wild swimming. And being a summer-only affair, I couldn't put off a visit much longer.

I hadn't done too much reading up on the club, or the water of the Frome which flowed through it, before I took the train west. A cursory look at the club's Facebook page would have stopped me in my tracks. Dated August 2013, it read:

On 3rd August when we tested the water, the result was bad. We posted warning notices.

We re-tested on 12th August and the result had improved to the top end of 'poor' and we will be testing again soon. In the meantime we have to advise members against swimming. If you do swim please take precautions not to swallow any water.

Water is now flowing over the weir again, and the river looks beautifully clear, compared to the murky soup it had turned into in the hot, dry weather. This should not be taken as an indication of water quality, of course. We are hoping the rain we're having will improve things.

Ten months on and thankfully none the wiser, I arrived on a stinking hot afternoon, having walked the three miles from Trowbridge train station. I'd had to yomp through tall grass along the busy A366, thanks to every public right of way being either overgrown or cordoned off with lightly buzzing electric fences. So much for public access to the countryside. Solo jaunts weren't just a struggle because of the lack of good company. They could be a chore because of my inability to drive. I'd been spoilt by my friends and family driving me around the country.

Save for a single car in the shade of an oak tree and a towel and a pair of swimming trunks slung over a metal field gate, there were no other signs of life as I walked onto the banks of the club's swimming hole.

Before changing I went to take a look at the water. Since Dartmoor I hadn't seen a drop of rain, and it showed in the still, murky Frome. The weir was bone dry, which if I'd seen that Facebook post would have told me that things weren't looking too good for a swim. A couple were swimming at leisurely pace upstream, gamely struggling against the current and chattering away, oblivious to my presence.

Roger had had the swimming club all to himself when he visited, the weir raging and the need for swimming trunks deemed unnecessary. Unwilling to upset my fellow swimmers by going *au naturel*, I went and donned my shorts in an old tin shed which doubled up as a male changing area, the flagstones cold on my feet. I dodged a pile of fox shit, bundled my clothes into my bag and made my way back down to the water.

The old triple-tiered diving boards which Roger described were no more. Only the sad, decrepit frame remained, its red paint peeling off and fluttering away into the field. Rust nibbled at its feet. As at Henleaze, modern health and safety had done for this go-to spot for more daring outdoor swimmers.

The ash springboard which Roger had sprung off naked into the Frome was still in evidence, though. Its coconut matting was warm underfoot, and remembering my entrance into the water in Bristol the previous week, I tiptoed out to the far edge to take a look down into the depths. The river looked brown and dirty, and I suddenly felt very alone, with no professional help close by if I did somehow come a cropper after jumping in head first. Chastened, I walked back onto the grass and round to the weir entrance.

I had the water to myself, the couple who'd swum earlier now dozing on the banks with a picnic spread out around them. It was cold, far more so than at Henleaze. Swimming against the current proved surprisingly difficult, the Frome full of an urgency which wasn't at all apparent when I had stood staring at it from the great height of the diving board.

I soon reached that wooden entry point and decided to turn and swim back to the weir. Nose just out of the water, the five-foot-high board looked impossibly distant, more like a ten-metre platform than a piddly springboard.

I swam a few lengths of this stretch of the Frome, sticking to club rules about not swimming downstream from the weir (despite its beauty and the preponderance of inviting pools) and further upstream than the long meander which led away to the nearby farm, before hopping out and drying in the sun. I ate cheese and chutney sandwiches and gulped cold water, unwilling to leave now that I had settled into the slow rhythm of the place. That and the fact that to get home I'd have to walk the long road back to Trowbridge. I could have done with Tim or Molly being there to give me a lift.

After a few more minutes' lolling, I convinced myself that I couldn't by all rights say I'd swum at this famous swimming hole without having at least jumped off Roger's ash springboard. I walked back out towards it and eyed it from the safety of the bank. I inched along it, toes tucked over the edge, readying myself to jump.

I had just turned back when a loud party of picnickers appeared behind me, choosing an area directly behind the board to lay their blankets and eat before taking a swim themselves. I felt ashamed of losing my gumption at the last minute and swore I caught the pitying eye of at least two older ladies in the group.

I spun on my heels and took two long strides before closing my eyes and jumping, wheeling my arms and legs in ungainly fashion. I crashed into the river hard, smashing my forearm flat on its surface. I came up gasping for air, my arm smarting and legs sore, and swam the last few metres back down to the weir. My ears were still roaring as I reached for my towel and rubbed myself dry. I changed in the open, stuffed away my wet things and passed back through the gate. No volunteers had been down to collect the £1 fee, levied thirty times a year until you become a fully fledged club member. I felt a little guilty for getting a freebie as I trudged back up the A366, off to meet my train in Trowbridge, the day's swim already being sweated out in the June heat.

CHAPTER SIX

July

~

RAC Clubhouse, London – River Lune,
Cumbria – Ingleton Pool, Yorkshire – River
Doe, Yorkshire – Cowside Beck, Yorkshire –
Leeds to Liverpool Canal, Yorkshire

I returned to London happy but in need of a swim in clearer, cleaner water. I had started plotting a route through the Yorkshire Dales just for this purpose, but before heading north I got on my bike and rode from Camberwell to the RAC Clubhouse on Pall Mall. Roger came here with a friend to enjoy the rarefied surroundings after dips at Tooting Bec Lido and Highgate men's pond. Getting to those popular places was easy for me, and I had already visited them many times on my recreation of his 'swimmer's journey through Britain'.

Despite not having a friend with RAC Clubhouse access, I was kindly allowed to swim in the private, members-only pool by the sports centre's manager. I enjoyed the fact that, like Roger, I arrived on a push bike, decked out in cycling gear and carrying a backpack which was sprayed with dirt thanks to my lack of a mudguard.

Like everywhere on Pall Mall, the RAC Clubhouse is a place of privilege, something which has always made me feel uncomfortable.

Whenever I'm in such places I feel like an interloper, just a stroke away from being asked my business and escorted towards the exit. But as I pushed through the revolving doors, my clammy palms leaving prints on the freshly polished brass handles, I was instantly made to feel welcome. A chirpy security guard pointed me down a sweeping spiral staircase, past classic photos of The Beatles which adorned the wood-panelled walls, and on towards the pool.

The whole sports centre was restored in 2003, retaining the same Grecian splendour which Roger enjoyed on his visit in the late 1990s. Everything was marble and polished to a slippery sheen. I took a seat on a balcony which overlooked the water and awaited my compulsory tour of the facilities, parked next to one regular buried deep in the *Daily Telegraph* and another taking a mid-morning doze in a wing-backed armchair.

After being shown the imposing entrance to the Turkish bath (a ladies-only day, sadly for me), I was ushered into the splendid changing rooms. They represented a significant change-up from the tin shed and fox poo affair down at Farleigh Hungerford. Wood-panelled walls gave way to immaculate benches, above which hung tailored suits and brash polo shirts. A row of sinks were overlooked by free-standing mirrors, each one with a pot of razors, shaving foam and moisturiser.

I showered and pushed through a heavy door. A single lane was tacked out to the side of the pool, where a lesson was taking place, with the rest of it given over to half a dozen swimmers quietly splashing back and forth. I made my way down the marble steps and into the water, which was heated to an unnecessary 28°C. It felt like a tepid bath after my exertions down at Farleigh and Henleaze. A fountain running the length of the shallow end sprayed colder water, and I luxuriated in its cooling embrace before setting off on the first of my planned forty lengths.

Despite feeling sweaty from the overheated water, I soon fell into that meditative state where the only thing on your mind is the line of black tiles beneath you. I thought about how everything here looked polished and new – even the bottom of the pool seemed to have been scrubbed to within in an inch of its life. The leaf mould at Tooting and the flotsam in Hampstead were the very opposite of the experience I was having here.

On every breath, I turned my head to look at the high pillars and wondered whether I had been transported to Ancient Greece. The heat and the surroundings definitely made it feel more like a bath, the convivial atmosphere reaffirmed after I crashed into a lady and we got chatting about the need for more lanes to help us regulate our speed. It may have been posh, but the RAC pool retained all the good grace of Roger's 'swimmers' universities' that I'd found alive and well on my journey across the UK. That feeling of sharing my swim and relaxing with like-minded people was here just as it was at Chagford, Cirencester and Henleaze.

After a first-rate swim I took a blisteringly hot shower and, skin puckered, decided to enjoy my first wet shave in two years, courtesy of the RAC. I emerged onto Pall Mall with chlorine in my nostrils and my cheeks exposed to the elements.

I left London the following week, stubble pricking my chin, and took the train north to Yorkshire. I was excited to be swimming in good company again and was off to meet my uncle Dave, who would be ferrying me about the Dales and beyond, along with his good friend Jim. I had a series of swims planned across the north and wanted to start out at the infamous Devil's Bridge, just outside Kirkby Lonsdale. Roger's visit here forms one of the most evocative parts of *Waterlog*, with bikers stripped to their waists and daredevils flinging themselves from the high parapet of the ancient stone bridge into the River Lune below, narrowly avoiding the hulking rocks as they flew.

Pulling up, we found the place more subdued than that. Admittedly it was a Tuesday morning, but the only bikers here confined themselves to the car park, scoffing bacon butties and slurping tea from a snack van which seemed to have a permanent mooring at the bridge's eastern end.

Walking over the bridge, I soon saw why. A bench with a small plaque stood at the entrance to a copse which followed the river's stony bank, on it a tribute to a 22-year-old swimmer who had been killed while attempting a dive at this notorious spot. On the bridge I stood and peered over the side, the low walls, the fast-moving water and sheer height giving me a swirl of vertigo. My diving skills were slim to non-existent, but even if they weren't I would not have tried jumping.

Wandering down to the bank, I noticed a 'No Bathing' sign on the far side, where the water narrowed and zipped beneath the bridge, looping away from the town and off towards the sea. But further downstream I came to a gravel island, from where the Lune shelved deeply into a wide, slow-moving pool. There wasn't a sign to forbid swimming here, so I clambered out of my jeans and into my swimming shorts and took a few short strides before falling forward and swimming in ever-decreasing circles, allowing the current to push me one way before turning against it and pushing back with all my might.

The water had a dark orange glow and was very deep, shelving within a metre of the bank, so much so that I couldn't touch the bottom with my feet. Between the depth and the slow pace I could see why diving would be so appealing, even if there was no chance this would have been regarded as deep enough by modern-day standards. There was a reason the high boards at Henleaze and Farleigh had been removed after all. I swam off downstream and eyed some far-off kayakers, but there was no one else taking a dip like me. I had the Lune all to myself.

A black-headed gull sunned itself on a distant rock and I continued to swim while Dave and Jim sunbathed on the little gravel beach. Both had retired in recent years and spent a lot of time travelling together. They didn't look alike. Dave was tall and thin. Jim was short and wiry. But each of them sported a weathered teak tan, giving them an air of well-earned relaxation after forty years of teaching. Neither of them was keen to take a dip, but it was great to have them with me, to share my joy at getting into the water with people I knew, who understood what it meant to me.

To me this was the most perfect wild-swimming spot, but the hint of tragedy was inescapable. Roger seemed to have found the crazed atmosphere here wonderful, if a touch frenetic. But I couldn't imagine anyone coming here and tombstoning now.

There was a melancholy atmosphere to the place even as a wren darted past me and away upstream while I dried off. It's easy to overlook the dangers of wild swimming. It can seem such a peaceful activity, but I thought about that unfortunate diver and whether I showed enough caution whenever I went out for a dip in a river, pond or lake. Was I becoming too cavalier? And was Roger the same when he revelled in such boyish *joie de vivre*? It was an issue that *Waterlog* didn't really tackle, but one I had come face to face with in Kirkby Lonsdale.

I pushed aside these concerns as best I could as we headed back into the Dales, to the village of Ingleton and its delightful little outdoor pool. Normally my trips to the Yorkshire Dales involved spending a happy day traipsing through sheep's mess, hood up and rain pelting my face, leaving Dave to read the map and point the way. But the day was now blisteringly hot, and the thought of another swim after my dip at Kirkby Lonsdale quickened my step as I walked past pretty cottages decked with hanging baskets and up the hill to the lido, which nestles high above the River Doe.

I arrived just in time, as the pool only opens between midday and 1 p.m., before coming to life later in the evening for locals returning from work. I handed over my £4 entry fee and marvelled at what a spic and span spot this was. Tiered seating dominated one side, the perfect place to watch the occasional gala. The neat changing area had a single electric shower and new benches for stashing clothes and valuables.

I slid into the deep end and swam quickly, trying to squeeze as many lengths in before time was called. The water was 26°C, far warmer than the River Lune and much more conducive to a long, muscle-aching swim. I was just clocking up my thirty-sixth lap when the friendly attendant appeared at the shallow end and called time as I was about to take a deep breath and set off on another twenty-metre length.

Afterwards, hair wet and mind quiet, I took a look at the plethora of flyers for lessons and events on the noticeboard outside. Ingleton pool clearly still played a key role in this community in the summer months, but it was another favourite swimming hole that I had set my sights on next, something a lot wilder that could indulge my need for something illicit, just as Fladbury and the Itchen had done.

Beezley Falls, upstream from the pool on the River Doe, was billed by Roger as a Mecca for local wild swimmers and, as at Kirkby Lonsdale, daredevils. He described visiting late at night – the 'worn precarious bough' high above the dark, roiling black pool 'like a gibbet', a frayed rope, the turbulence around the rocks – before camping and returning the following day to find the that 'swimmers thronged the banks, above the waterfall, in the pool, on every rock'. It sounded exactly like the kind of place I wanted to spend a long, lazy summer afternoon.

Except when I asked locals in the village about it, they shrugged and pointed me in the direction of the pool where I had just soothed my sweaty limbs. One lady said she remembered hearing something about it, but that people didn't swim in the River Doe any longer.

This tied in with what Dave and Jim had told me. When I explained to them my plans to swim at Beezley Falls, they both said that it was on the private Ingleton Falls path, which cost £6 to use. Roger makes no mention of this and I was damned if I was going to pay for the privilege of walking on a path in one of our most beautiful national parks, a place where anyone should be able to come, roam and enjoy the countryside for free.

The path had an entrance on the far side of the village, but Jim and I attempted to walk up the banks from the Ingleton pool instead, crashing through bracken and brambles and tripping over fallen logs trying to find way to the falls without paying. Low alders and high nettles blocked our path, and it soon became clear that this was no way to reach the 'sleek black water' of Beezley Falls.

We doubled back and spread the local OS map out over a picnic table and tried to work out an alternative route. There was a northern entrance to the Ingleton Falls path – I could reach the River Doe there and try and drop in unnoticed.

We drove up the hill and left the car by a quarry. Jim and I set off over a field of tall grass while Dave hung back to enjoy the summer weather. A mistle thrush perched on a telegraph pole piped out its song as we passed through a field gate and on towards the river. Stepping stones poked up from the shallow water, leading to a ticket office where a warden dressed in a branded baseball cap and matching khaki shorts and T-shirt was collecting fees from unsuspecting walkers. There wasn't a path on my side of the river, meaning there was no option for me but to cross and cough up the exorbitant fee. Jim baulked, but not before I'd asked to borrow a few pounds to pay the fare.

As Jim turned back I strode on, passing the ticket office and the gatekeeper, who was engrossed in demanding money from a pair of tourists who were struggling to understand why they were having to pay to walk in a national park. He looked up as if to speak. I offered a loud 'Good afternoon' and continued walking down towards the waterfall.

Before I could even see Beezley Falls I was met by a huge 'No Swimming' sign and walked on to find the falls themselves cordoned off by a wooden fence. Down below was a swimmer's idea of heaven. The deep black pool, the rocks for flopping out on, the waterfall for pummelling tense shoulders.

But things had changed. There was no rope, and the oak bough which Roger eulogised had been snapped close to the tree's trunk. No young boys were queuing to impress 'a gallery of admiring teenage girls'. Instead there were signs. Everywhere. Ones warning walkers not to swim, not to leave the path at any point, that stones can be slippery when wet, and to keep a close eye on young children.

I hate this mollycoddling approach to the countryside and know that Roger would have too. He speaks extensively in *Waterlog* about this very problem, right from the book's first pages: 'Most of us live in a world where more and more places and things are signposted, labelled, and officially "interpreted". There is something about all this that is turning the reality of things into virtual reality.'

I pulled out my copy and found these words, using them to spur me on and flick two fingers at the landowners and anyone who thinks the countryside cannot be appreciated on its own terms. Beezley was out of bounds, the fences making it hard to reach, so I kept walking downstream. The next falls were smaller, but looked thoroughly inviting. A concrete wall, just off the path, made the perfect changing spot and, with no one around, I yanked on my shorts and waded in. The surface was a little scummy, but a few strokes in I was out of my depth, my skin singing in the cool peaty water.

I swam big circles of the pool, stopping to take pictures and lie on my back, looking up at the high clouds through the deep green leaves of the oak trees which hung over the gorge. It wasn't quite Roger's adventurous Beezley swim, but I was imbued with his anti-authoritarian spirit as I swam on, gulping and spitting out the water as I went. I felt invincible, happily alone and away from the prying eyes of the warden. I took great joy in saying 'fuck it' and getting in regardless of the rules and regulations.

My furtive dip lasted no more than a few minutes, but my skin tingled as I made my way back up the path. A couple spotted me pulling back on my boots and enquired about the cold and the strength of the current. Neither of them seemed perturbed or put out by the fact that I had clearly flouted the owner's 'no swimming' rule. Someone swimming in the river seemed like the most natural thing in the world to them.

By now I was really puffed up, delighted that I'd stolen a swim here as I had done all those months ago in the Itchen near Winchester. Not only that, I had got away with it right under the nose of the warden.

I was thinking these sweet thoughts, swinging my arms with my head down as I made my way back up the path and past the little hut which marked the end of the paid walkway, when a large boot blocked my way.

'You can pay here.'

I looked up to find the warden staring at me with palm outstretched.

'Oh, OK, how much?' I asked, knowing full well I was about to be unburdened of the cash I'd by now set aside for a couple of pints back in the village.

I handed over my shrapnel and decided politeness rather than briskness was my best approach. After all, I wanted to find out if this had been a paid-for path when Roger had come here. If it had been it was quite an oversight on his part to omit such a detail.

'So, how long has this been a paid for-attraction, then?' I asked.

'Since 1885,' came the reply. I was handed a pamphlet with my printed receipt, 'No Swimming' clearly written on the back in bold type.

I was shocked. But what about Roger's swimming paradise, his illicit late-night dip and the crowds swelling the banks on a summer afternoon? I told my interlocutor about my predecessor's visit and the swimmers he'd found frolicking in Beezley Falls.

'When was this? In the nineties? No, we don't have that anymore,' he said. 'We got rid of the rope swing and there's a very clear sign saying it's prohibited. Some boys still come up and do it when I'm not here, but they run off as soon as I appear. We have the pool in the village for swimming.'

By now it was obvious that I'd been in myself and the warden was warming to his theme, his distaste for wild swimming evident in his growing agitation.

'We had a death at Kirkby Lonsdale. People shouldn't swim here. It's extremely cold and it could be dangerous.'

I was furious. Of course it could be dangerous. But so could swimming off a beach on the south coast or, for that matter, striking out for the deep end of a pool when you're unsure of your ability. I walked off, struggling to conceal my rage – at the fact that this path was against everything the Yorkshire Dales and national parks were meant to stand for, and at the warden for using a tragedy in Kirkby Lonsdale to paint a negative picture of wild swimming, when the incident had clearly been a terrible one-off.

But as my anger settled I felt confused. Roger had depicted this place as a swimming idyll, which it no longer was and may never have been. The sombre feeling at the Devil's Bridge earlier in the day was also a marked change from what Roger had experienced. But then the awful events that had happened there and the warden's portent about 'dangers' in the Doe were what happened when people made bad choices. Not all wild swimmers choose to jump twenty feet into a too-shallow pool, just as not all walkers choose to go wandering off steep paths without first checking the terrain. To conflate the issues was to trivialise them and reinforce the taboo which still existed around swimming in rivers.

I trod carefully over the stepping stones and realised I was reeling from conflicting emotions: a buzz from the swim; annoyance at Roger for not telling the truth about how this place wasn't a swimming free-for-all; and frustration that swimming in anything other than a chlorinated pool was seen as a pastime for kooks and crazies, to be discouraged at every turn.

This mood burned inside me as we drove across the Dales and out towards Malham. My run-in at Beezley had dampened my excitement for more wild swims, but the sun was still high and there was plenty of time to go in search of Roger's famous tufa limestone pool in Cowside Beck, buried deep beneath Yew Cogar Scar.

Dave had studied the maps and even tried to look for the pool himself the previous summer after we'd talked about it at length over the phone, bounding down from the Malham side of the beck only to find the little stream shallow and lacking anywhere remotely swimmable. Like him, I had only Roger's descriptions and an OS map to go on, and left him and Jim high on the road at the top of the valley. My legs buzzed from the scratch of thistles and teasels as I stepped carefully down the steep-sided hill, ankle-cracking lumps stymieing my progress.

I had a few visual aids from my predecessor's account to help me: a spinney of ash, gnarled trees growing perpendicular to the walls of the scar, wide holes in the otherwise narrow stream. The drop was so steep that I couldn't see the water until I was almost on it, its light burble hitting my ears first. It ran white over rocks, black where it deepened. There was no pool in sight.

I scaled a creaking old fence, there to keep the sheep in check rather than stop walkers enjoying the right to roam, and walked a few metres upstream, back towards Malham. But this way there seemed to be no gnarled trees, no ash, no wide holes. And so I turned 180° and set off on a long yomp in search of this elusive bathing spot, somewhere to forget my unease about the afternoon's events.

A pair of buzzards circled high above, their occasional caws making me nervous as clouds began to bubble up and the sun went in. I kept walking along the beck's narrow bank, a dipper following my every move, darting ahead and leading me to what I thought might be Roger's pool. After an hour's clumsy trekking the valley began to open out, the beck beginning to meander in wide sweeps. I started to think I saw rocky outcrops and overhanging trees where there were none, imagining mossy pools where in fact shallow water rushed over limestone. I had clearly taken a wrong turn when I had reached the water. And so, with the evening fast approaching and my legs tired from the trudge and the three swims of the day, I peeled off every item of clothing, waded into the shallow stream and lay down, stark naked. It was shockingly cold, but my first ever skinny dip was the ideal way to soak off the disappointment and annoyance of Beezley Falls.

I was treading my way back to dry land carefully when I heard a shout.

'Put some bloody clothes on.'

It was Jim. Unbeknownst to me, he'd followed me along Cowside and had also failed to see anything like a tufa pool. We left the water behind, shooting off up the steep hill back to the road. Unlike other places on this trip where I'd struggled to match Roger's experience, I resolved to return and find the hidden pool and swim in its swirling embrace. I had the idea it could just be the best swimming spot in *Waterlog*, a soothing place to make worries and annoyances about feisty wardens disappear for good.

We spent the night at the youth hostel in Malham. In the common room, with a smattering of walkers and other outdoor types, we watched a bore draw and penalty shoot-out between Argentina and Holland in the World Cup semi-finals.

I woke early, swimming on my mind. My next swim was one I had been dreading ever since I first decided on following Roger's journey: a soak in the Leeds to Liverpool Canal at Gargrave. The Middle Level Drain on the Fens had been fascinating, if a tad murky, and I had eschewed the grimy Well Creek canal which ran across it. But having come so far from home, there was no point in missing out this far northern outpost of the canal network. I remembered Tim's gentle chiding and used it to drive me on.

Roger spoke of 'having' to swim in a canal. How could he swim across Britain and not? But as we clicked through a metal gate on the towpath and walked east from the town lock, I really wished he hadn't bothered. It was another beautiful day, warming up after a morning mist, and I had my swimming shorts on underneath my jeans, ready to whip them off and get in at the first convenient spot. The heat was making me itch for a swim, but the rainbow glint of boat oil on the surface and the dirty brown murk of the water was an off-putting sight.

The setting, however, was beautiful. We passed under a stone bridge, where two pretty cottages backed onto the canal. Each had neatly manicured lawns and blooming gardens, one with an old racing bike spray-painted yellow nestled in a flowerbed to mark the recent passing of the Tour de France through the Dales. I paused to take pictures, but was only putting off the inevitable.

A few hundred metres downstream, where the fields opened out and the shade of the trees subsided, I found as good a spot as any – a small inlet dropping towards the dark drink. I lay down my damp towel and began to get undressed as Dave broke out his camera and began taking snaps.

'Are you birdwatching?'

A lady with an inquisitive border collie had appeared from nowhere, looking us over with a curious smile.

'Yes,' we chorused. I felt too embarrassed to tell her my real plans, despite standing barefoot, and left Jim and Dave to chat while the dog eyed me suspiciously. He was wise to my game and I knew it.

After a few minutes the lady set off towards Gargrave. As she turned the corner, I took my chance, slipping in feet first and wading out to the middle. It was no more than four feet deep, with a rough, squelchy bed.

I launched myself forward, spluttering, sending a duck and her young scattering from the reeds on the far bank in panic. I could hardly blame them. I imagine this was the first time anyone had been foolish enough to swim here since Roger had done so. There was no way I was going to manage the 'token mile' of my predecessor, so instead swam hundred-metre lengths, back and forth. I kept my mouth tightly closed and my head up, and when I took in the summer sky, the ducklings in the distance and the lush green of the surrounding hills, I realised I was very much enjoying myself. I thought of the other canals I knew: the Huddersfield Narrow Canal through Marsden in West Yorkshire, the Grand Union and Regent's Canals in London. I was glad to be swimming in this one, with these surroundings, rather than those sometimes grubby affairs.

I dried off happy. My gloom after Beezley and Kirkby Lonsdale, and the failure to find the tufa pool, had lifted, even if questions about wild swimming's status and Roger's account of his trip remained. I had semi-conquered Yorkshire's *Waterlog* swims and returned south for something a little less alluring and a lot more industrial.

CHAPTER SEVEN

August

~~~

River Medway, Kent – Dungeness and Camber
Sands, East Sussex – Bamburgh Beach,
Northumberland – River Severn, Gloucestershire

Swimming in the canal at Gargrave had helped me steel myself for what was coming next. As the final planning of my *Waterlog* journey began to take shape, a series of less than beguiling dips was looming, ones I had left off the long list I had stuck to my office wall in the hope I'd forget them, but which were revealed whenever I idly flicked through the book's pages for inspiration and further guidance. The long schlep across the industrial River Medway to Fort Hoo was perhaps the least appealing, but one I didn't want to leave until summer was on the wane.

Like Roger, the thought of swimming in this polluted, busy river made me extremely nervous. My predecessor had a local boatman to take him across to the old island fort, but my only accomplices were a brand-new OS map and a deep sense of foreboding.

I took the high-speed train to Gillingham in Kent, London sweltering in one of its brief annual heatwaves as we reached top speed, slipping across the marshes and away from the capital's hinterlands. I studied the map intently, looking for a convenient way to get down to the water and a place where I could at least attempt to make the crossing unnoticed by passing boat traffic and the watchful eye of the coast guard.

I walked through Gillingham's backstreets, crossed dual carriageways and passed through an industrial estate, reaching the Saxon Shore Way. The bucolic name didn't quite match the surroundings. The Yorkshire Dales felt a long way away.

Then, beyond a tired-looking funfair, there it was. The River Medway. It shimmered far off in the distance, the near shore a mess of mud and shallow creeks, the tide having receded to make any kind of entry impossible. My planning had become so much better in the past year, but this really was a foolish oversight on my part. Even if I'd wanted to take a long swim, I couldn't have anyway. I cursed my failure out loud, but deep down I knew that this was a good result, that I had dodged a swim which by Roger's estimation wasn't actually that much fun. I decided to keep walking anyway, away from the town and towards the RSPB's Nor Marsh reserve further downstream. It was a hot day and I wanted to make sure I enjoyed the weather while it lasted.

As ever when a swim was denied to me, I felt a pang of longing for the cold embrace of the river, but had to remember to tune myself into the water and how it felt without getting in. After a while, I sat on the wall built to hold back the tide and watched the river come to life. The occasional sail boat slid away out to the North Sea, while black-headed gulls skittered over the mud, leaving tiny prints in their wake.

'Enjoy the view, mate, it won't be there for much longer,' said a cyclist as he rode past behind me, his tyres crunching over the gravel path. He meant Kingsnorth Power Station, which stood idle on the Isle of Grain on the north side of the river. But he could just as easily have meant the whole view.

The Isle of Grain was where London's former mayor Boris Johnson had once wanted to build a huge new airport, despite the protestations of environmental campaigners that it would destroy migration routes for the millions of birds who used the Medway as a staging post. Although this was once a heavily industrial place, there was a real beauty about the path which hugged the banks of the river. I couldn't understand why such vandalism seemed necessary. This stretch of river and its scattering of nature reserves brought happiness and relaxation to the hundreds of thousands of people who lived in this busy part of England. But what price happiness when a new airport can help the UK compete in the never-ending global race?

I thought about this as I walked on to Sharp's Head Bay and Horrid Hill, a short peninsula where children on school holidays were searching for insects and serious birdwatchers stood, binoculars clamped to their faces, watching far out across the river. Nor Marsh's abundance of birdlife would doubtless be ruined by the creation of an airport here. Our islands are so small and precious, and ruining what few wild places we have left seemed to me shocking as I watched people arrive to enjoy the wildlife or simply relax in the lunchtime sun. The scream of jet engines was the last thing I wanted to hear.

Despite my missed swim, I felt blessed to have come to this corner of Kent on such a glorious day and to have had a relaxing, joyous experience on the banks of the Medway. But my cravings resurfaced as I walked on and a series of potential swimming places was revealed to me. Horrid Hill offered its own delights, places where, if I'd had the foresight to check the tide times, I could have dropped straight down into ten feet of estuary water. But a few hundred metres on, an even more perfect spot homed into view.

It was a short slipway, at the bottom of which a small flotilla of dinghies stood tilted on the silt, waiting for the water to return them to their natural, buoyant state. Along its side was a small wood, where I could easily have changed into my shorts and struck out for a long, circular swim, around Horrid Hill and back into Sharp's Head Bay. But as I checked the tide times pegged to a nearby noticeboard, I knew such a trip was a fantasy. The long tidal range meant that it would be dark by the time the river lapped again in this sheltered place.

It would have been easy for me to see this trip as a failure to follow in Roger's footsteps. A year previously I most certainly would have berated myself for not doing things 'properly'. But, as on Jura, I didn't feel any guilt. Rather I was happy that I had come and seen the place as it was now and imagined how Roger would have felt here. Elation at the birdlife and local enjoyment of this rewilded reserve. Distaste at the absurd plans to turn what was now a popular natural environment into an international hub airport for no reason other than greed. I told myself this journey was in the spirit of my recreation of *Waterlog* – part homage, part personal mission to find my own place in Roger's tale. Feeling the water when I couldn't get into it, allowing the swims to come to me however they wanted to. On the Medway I found the calm I'd enjoyed in much less industrial, far more idyllic surroundings.

I decided to stay focused on Kent for my next of Roger's swims, and got together a gang of friends to join me for a bike ride and a series of summer dips on the other side of the county. Dungeness and Camber had always seemed so close to London, but I didn't want to tackle them alone, so I had let them slip down the list in favour of challenges on Dartmoor and across the north of England.

A week after visiting the Medway I once again boarded the high-speed train from St Pancras. I was joined by Joe and Tom, who had gamely swum in the Test back in January, along with James, another old work colleague and good friend. We zipped out of town and changed at Ashford, where we took the stopping service across into Sussex at Rye.

Doing the trip on foot would take more than a day, so I had arranged bike hire, but our steeds, rented from a garage in the centre of town, were in less than perfect condition. A loose pedal here, a clunky chain there. But despite that, and being blasted by a downpour as we biked through the ancient town and out towards the Camber road, it felt good to be cycling to a swim again. This was the first time I had done so outside London since my dip in the Lark near Ely a year earlier, and I had forgotten how sweetly biking and swimming dovetailed. I hadn't really enjoyed cycling since breaking my wrist and didn't go out on two wheels nearly as often as I had prior to the incident. The joint ached if I rode for too long, and every time I saddled up in London I had visions of my attacker looming over me as I tried to edge my bike past him. Riding outside the city, on quiet roads and dedicated tracks, was much more appealing. Within minutes I had worked up a sweat and was dreaming of sinking into those high waves at the bottom of the steep, shingly beach on Dungeness.

The ride was long, filthy and lots of fun, the gravel cycle path covered with deep puddles and my hired bike lacking anything as sophisticated as a mud guard. I could feel my backside becoming wet in the saddle as my white T-shirt became dotted with dirt. It felt glorious to be out, the wide-open skies of this strange corner of England leading us on towards the only place on these islands classified as a desert. The sun had cut through the early cloud, and the last of the showers had been blown out as we followed the road on a hard left-hand turn towards the church tower at Lydd, the crack of rifle fire from the MOD's coastal firing range sporadically sounding over the incessant, hefty wind.

Cycling was becoming tough in the harsh sea wind, but we pushed on, rabbits darting out from bushes to run alongside us. At one point a stoat skittered down the path beside Joe. I shouted in joy and almost got wiped out by a bramble hanging across the path. This was just what I wanted from a day out swimming. A challenge, good company and the promise of cold water.

Still, I had underestimated just how tough this trip would be, especially on those whose legs weren't used to lengthy stretches in the saddle. James and Tom brought up the rear, and we slowed to their pace before kicking on, a last few miles down the road towards Dungeness and a date with the English Channel.

The last stretch was brutal, a slog against a howling gale which blew over the flat sandy gravel and hit us square on. Roger arrived at Dungeness in his car and took time to enjoy the borderless garden at Derek Jarman's house, a gorgeous, off-kilter place to relax before a cooling dip in the ocean. But by the time we reached the Pilot pub, cycling past the nuclear power station and its tall warning signs about unauthorised personnel, we were shattered, and any plans I had considered to visit Jarman's old fishing cottage were forgotten. I bolted my bike to a road sign and managed something akin to a royal wave as the narrow-gauge Romney, Hythe and Dymchurch train clattered past, parents grinning as kids screamed with delight, most likely at the sight of four grown men trying to catch their breath after a brutal bike ride. All was well at the English seaside.

I looked around and found myself in a happy 1980s time warp. Everything around me reminded me of my childhood: pubs that hadn't been done up for thirty years, a Happy Shopper, friendly older people who looked like my grandparents eating sandwiches in their cars. It seemed that the hard road here had actually been a form of time travel, bringing me back to simpler times.

Glad to be off our bikes, we half walked, half waddled down towards the water, dropping level after level before reaching the clattering waves. A large family stood peering out to sea, but no one swam and, as I began to pull on my trunks, a voice piped up telling a child about the dangers of getting in the water here. Of strong undercurrents and the inevitability of death.

It sounded to me like a risk worth taking and so I moved faster, running into the sea while being watched like a zoo animal by the group back on the beach. I resurfaced after diving under to see them hurrying back to the car, averting their children's gazes in case I'd given them any ideas. Perhaps the spectre of Dungeness B's nuclear reactors away down the coast had given them further pause for thought. I didn't consider it as I took an accidental mouthful and swam out over the powerful rollers.

Roger called swimming at Dungeness 'some of the purest bathing on the south coast' and I was inclined to agree. It felt deep and heavenly and I revelled in the fact that I had given my body up to the higher power of the English Channel. This sea had done me good over the past year, and it was great to be back in its chilly reaches once more. I swam in wide circles, conscious that to go too far would doubtless see me swept out and into more turbulent waters.

Tom and Joe soon joined me, Joe practising his butterfly stroke while Tom and I splashed each other and took pictures with my waterproof camera. James, not overly keen on swimming, stood watching from the shore, stripped down to a pair of black shorts. His stocky frame appeared to wince as he edged himself in, but he refused to cry out against the cold as I stumbled out and lay down to dry off in the late summer sun. It was great to be in the water with these guys again, their willingness and happy abandon meaning my mood always soared when I was around them.

We parked ourselves in a row on starched towels and ate the treats we'd picked up in Rye: pork pies, cheese, fruit tarts. James, undoubtedly the most bibulous man I know, produced a bottle of wine, chilled by the windy ride, and we sipped from plastic cups and toasted our successful trip. We had managed to forget that we needed to turn the bikes back round and go for another dip before heading back to London.

The return leg was interminable, buffeting winds smashing into us head first and making our progress no faster than walking pace. As we struggled on, swearing into the elements, I could have sworn I saw Roger driving past in his knackered old Audi, following the same route he had all those years ago, back towards Camber. He'd have been quite cocooned from the gales hammering into the south coast. I cursed the fact that we hadn't come down in the Jag, my joy at cycling now well and truly eroded. The pedals were harder to turn with every rotation. The buzz of the adrenalin from the ocean had worn away to nothing and I grew weary with every mile we rode.

It was gone 5 p.m. when we slowed and stopped opposite the Pontins holiday camp in Camber, darting into the corner shop to buy bottles of water and waiting an age to pay while holidaying families stocked up on industrial quantities of ice cream. We locked the bikes up to a low wooden fence, scaled the high dunes and ran out onto the sands.

Kitesurfers flashed across the far-off surf, the tide a distant white line. I was put in mind of Holkham and its roiling waves, the simple pleasure of splashing through shallow pools and out into more challenging waters. I half ran, half fell over the soft sand, desperate once again to get wet.

Other than those intrepid adrenalin junkies, the beach was virtually empty. A few stragglers milled about around the café, where Union Jacks crackled high in the stiff breeze, and although it was late, there was still plenty of light left in the day for them to enjoy. It seemed as if this whole beach was being wasted, that those on holiday here had somehow missed a trick, opting to stay by the holiday camp pool when they could have been having fun out here.

When he visited, Roger found the same. 'As if unsure of the immense freedom before them, most people seemed to stay within range of the café, and I had gone only a few hundred yards when I found myself entirely alone,' he wrote.

We, ditched our bags in the middle of the vast beach and changing into wet swimming shorts. James volunteered to stay put and keep an eye on the bags as Joe, Tom and I set off in a race across the hard, ridged sand.

I ran through a large pool, hoping for a pre-sea soaking, and lost a leg in deep, tar-like mud, pulling it free and turning back to see I had turned the clear pool a dark, cloudy black. Joe and Tom were long gone, away to the tide line, while I stared and weighed up the terrifying prospect of Camber Sands gobbling me up unnoticed. I cleaned off the last vestiges of gloop from my toes and jogged on, more cautious now about my route to the water.

The waves were relentless and foamy, the water far shallower than the two-strides-and-it's-deep stuff round the corner at Dungeness. Whereas the channel there had buoyed us, here it beat us up. It felt like Mothecombe beach in Devon all over again, a chance to jump waves and perform tricks. Joe practised handstands as I grazed my knees trying to ride breakers back to shore and Tom waded out further, careful to avoid the kitesurfers who flew past at close quarters.

The sun was beginning to slip behind high cloud, cooling the sea and sending shivers up my arms. I jogged back, cracking over shells and disturbing plovers snacking on treats in the wet sand. Any disappointment about the holidaying masses not sharing this space was tempered by the fact that I'd been able to enjoy it in the company of good friends and good friends only. Sometimes swimming's private joys outweigh the happiness of being among a large group of like-minded strangers. My mood changed like the weather, it seemed.

Back on the puddle-strewn path to Rye, the sun slid down to the horizon as the turbines of Romney Marsh's onshore wind farm spun silently in the distance. Roger's Audi or Tom's Jag would have come in handy, but as we arrived back in Rye, I wouldn't have traded the sweet ache of tired limbs and my mud-splattered clothes for anything.

A while later I found a copy of *Derek Jarman's Garden* on the bookshelf of a restaurant. Jarman's stories and poems, accompanied by Howard Sooley's images, put me in mind of our swim that day, despite our not having gone to his garden. I remembered Dungeness's limitless, borderless possibility as it dropped down into the sea from the shingle beach. Jarman's open approach to his garden put me in mind of Roger's journey and reconfirmed my belief that there could be no rules about this trip. It was a way of seeing the world anew, without boundaries. To me, Jarman's garden was like Roger's watery pilgrimage. Boundless, without rules, something that could be aspired to but never perfectly copied. Idiosyncratic in the best possible way. Jarman's book made me excited all over again, ready to attempt the last swathe of swims Roger had in store for me.

In keeping with my haphazard take on Roger's own zigzagging mission across the UK, I next took to the water far up north, in the shadow of Bamburgh Castle in Northumberland. Kent had been a summery treat, but this far up the North Sea coast I could feel autumn's hand touching my shoulders. It was cold in the shade, and the protection of a thick jumper and a raincoat did little to warm me as I eyed the beach and the high waves smashing into the coast, the Farne Islands occasionally peeping up behind the tilting horizon.

Like Roger, I had come here from Scotland, although my reasons for being north of the border were not swimming related. I had talked Keeley into coming south for a day from Edinburgh, where we had been seeing friends performing at the Fringe. Train delays and expensive taxis meant we arrived in Bamburgh in less than ideal condition: tired, hungover and significantly out of pocket. Despite the joy I had felt down in Kent, I could sense that my single-minded determination to cross off all of Roger's swims was once again beginning to tip over into obsession, as it had done in the weeks and months before my wrist break. It was starting to feel like a necessity again, rather than being fun. My obstinacy and desperation to get as many swims done before summer ended was infuriating me, so I can only imagine how Keeley felt.

We walked down to the castle, around what must surely rank as one of the most picturesque cricket pitches in England and out onto the sandy path which led to the water. The thrashing of the ocean resounded in my ears, and I thought about the pathetic pair of swimming shorts stuffed in my rucksack. For the first time since March, I wanted the tight, warming cover of my wetsuit.

At least it was sunny. When Roger swam in the sea here it was a wet, late August afternoon, the power of the Gulf of Corryvreckan still fresh in his mind. The beach had been empty too, but as we brushed through the marram grass and onto the wide sands we were greeted by dozens of hardy beachgoers, each one wrapped up against the elements and determined to enjoy the brightness despite the breeze.

A few had strayed into the water. A group of surfers practised standing on the low waves of the near shore, while a lad no older than ten waded knee-deep in the breakers, his parents watching with a mix of anxiety and awe. A group of dogs splashed and barked while their owners walked on, trying to avoid the inevitable furry shakedown.

Having seen the roaring mass of uneven waves, Keeley wisely opted for towel-holding duties while I undressed in the shelter of a low dune. I had done enough of these kinds of sea swims around the Suffolk and Norfolk coast over the past two years to know that approaching the North Sea with trepidation was pointless. I dropped my head and bounded towards the water, my chest pricked with goosebumps, my pace slowed to a kind of lunar jumping as the cold water enveloped my feet, my ankles, my knees. As soon as the spume touched my thighs I threw myself under and swam as hard as I could against the rise and fall of the ocean. The whole scene felt wild and unpredictable, waves smashing into me from all directions and making anything like a proper stroke impossible.

Roger had managed a 'long cold-water swim' in a 'flat, calm sea' here, but I was the only person in the water without a wetsuit, and even if I had wanted to make a beeline for the Farne Islands, just clearing the white water would have been a challenge in itself. Instead I contented myself with swimming in and out of the shallows, watching the flash of windsurfers' sails cut across the horizon. Occasionally the white lips of breaking waves would subside and I would catch a glimpse of the lighthouse on the Farne Islands. I thought of the puffins there, heading out to fish in the same water in which I swam. Were there seals close by? And could they sense me as I swam and waded out further? These happy questions rose in my mind as the cold dissipated and I let myself be massaged by the water.

After fifteen minutes my internal swim clock told me it was time to get back to dry land and the warmth of a bowl of soup and a mug of coffee in the tea shop. Roger would probably have been beaching himself on the Farne Islands by now, communing with nature and generally being a tougher, more water-hardened swimmer than me. But it didn't matter. I had been here and seen the water in a way he hadn't, gleaming in broken sunshine, the beach busy and the waves altogether more powerful.

As I walked back towards Keeley, my towel a bright blue flag snapping in the wind as she held it high, a walker approached me, thumbs aloft, Macca-style.

'Well done, you brave man.'

Incapable of speech, I was only able to offer a laugh in return, smiling as I got to the back of the beach and began drying off.

All this time I had been watched over by Bamburgh Castle, its high walls and long parapets inescapable while in the water or on the sand. I couldn't recall having taken a swim in such majestic, medieval surroundings before. The pool in Cirencester, with the old barracks as its backdrop, was the only thing that had come close on the journey so far.

Roger called this place 'magnificent and sad'. And yes, there was an element of melancholy in Bamburgh, especially back in the village, where an effigy of Grace Darling lay in the churchyard of St Aidan's, a tribute to her bravery in rescuing stricken seamen. But at the same time it all felt very unreal and beautiful to me. The sand eddying over the beach with the wind, the high waves, the cut grass of the graveyard picked over by hungry pied wagtails. And that huge view of the castle and beyond, out over the unknown deep of the North Sea. No, I didn't feel sad here. I felt blessed to have found it at all, a blissful change from my previous jaunts, a place that appeared to make all its visitors happy.

By now I was growing acutely aware of summer fading. August was almost at an end, and my long list of Roger's swims seemed never-ending. *Waterlog* was still revealing its secrets to me after countless rereadings, pages of my tattered copy beginning to fall out after being packed and repacked ceaselessly over the previous two years.

One particular set of swims sat at the forefront of my mind. I had been planning a long trip down to Cornwall and the Scilly Isles all summer with Molly, but work plans had meant we'd already postponed the long drive twice. We pencilled it in a third time for the start of September, in the hope of an Indian summer and a chance to enjoy the county's best beaches and pools without having to battle with the school holiday crowds. I was excited, as this was to be my first ever trip to Cornwall, my ideas of it informed almost exclusively by Roger's writing. I kept thinking of his long, illicit swim across Fowey Harbour, of deep distant dips at Porthcurno and the Neverland of Bryher on the Isles of Scilly. I was so desperate to get down there and see it all for myself.

But first there were other swims to attend to closer to home, reworkings of Roger's adventures in places where changes had rendered re-creation impossible.

I'd returned from Northumberland with a gnawing sense of not having done enough swims his year, admiration mixed with annoyance that Roger had managed all of this in less than a year. So, bags packed and work quickly dispensed with, once again I took the train from Paddington and met Tom in Oxford. We drove west through Cheltenham, ignoring the temptations of the town's lido and heading to the Malverns instead. Roger's swing through these hills focused on the mysterious joys of hydrotherapy at Droitwich Brine Baths, having failed to find any 'lost pools' around Great Malvern itself, its famous springs refusing to give up anything like a convenient outdoor bathing spot to my predecessor.

But the brine baths were long gone, shut in 2009 due to corroded pipes, the upkeep of the spa deemed too expensive by the private healthcare company which owned it. A campaign group, Save Our Brine Baths, had hoped to raise £1 million and reopen the baths at its original site, but was forced in 2013 to accept that the building was in such disrepair that new premises were required.

A number of the people behind the brine baths campaign had managed to push successfully for the reopening of Droitwich Spa's salt-water lido in 2007. The lido had been left to rot after closing in the late 1990s, but was now regularly voted one of the country's best, at the vanguard of this happy renaissance. A new brine baths didn't seem far-fetched in light of this development. But with warm days about to be in short supply, I decided against a heated lido swim and instead directed Tom to a place where we could bathe in cold water in a less straitened atmosphere.

Roger complained of feeling 'high and dry' up on the Malverns, so I was feeling particularly pleased with myself for having turned to a wild-swimming guidebook and found what appeared to be the ideal outdoor swim: a cooling adventure in the disused Gullet Quarry.

We left the car on a gravel track, turning our backs on the huge views of the Midlands stretching east, and followed a muddy path up towards the water. Immediately it was clear that something was wrong.

Fresh fence posts and barbed wire were laid out at the top of the pool's perimeter, signs warning that it was an offence to swim here under a local bye-law. The old path down to the water's edge had been cordoned off, although a small group picnicked there, their black Labradors paddling out to retrieve sticks thrown into the depths.

A small remembrance plaque next to one of the stark signs spelt out the basics and a cursory web search on my smartphone did the rest. In the space of one week in July 2012, two young men had drowned here, attempting to swim across the wide lake and not making it back. Quarry and gravel pools are notorious for such tragedies, shelving quickly to cause a sharp drop in temperature that even the strongest swimmers struggle to cope with.

From reading old news stories it was clear that this twin disaster had caused quite a stir among the local community. They wanted swimming in the pool banned by law, and got their way. Some had even asked for the lake to be drained.

I thought back to the only quarry pool I had swum in on my journey, at the well-tended Henleaze Swimming Club. There, swimmers weren't allowed into the deeper water at the lake's far end and lifeguards kept a watchful eye at all times, stopping anyone going into that roped-off area. No such precautions existed at Gullet Quarry. Henleaze was a swimming club after all, this just a deep, isolated lake.

My mind also turned to the death at Kirkby Lonsdale and the stringent warnings of the warden at Beezley Falls. Perhaps I had been blithe in my assessment. Obviously I knew to use caution when wild swimming, but tragedies can happen to anyone at any time. Maybe jumping from high branches or swimming in cold water without the protection of a wetsuit or a lifeguard wasn't worth the risk after all.

I once again noticed that same melancholy atmosphere I had felt on the Lune in Kirkby. Making snap judgements about outdoor swimming based on one or two cases was never wise, as with all things in life, but did I show enough respect and take sufficient care when I went out on my own? And what would the families of those young men make of me undertaking such a trip? Would they think me foolish? Should swimmers avoid quarry pools altogether? I was beginning to think so.

Tom and I left and decided to find somewhere wholly different. Of course, as Roger had found, hidden swimming spots are none too easy to come by in this country of springs and salt water, and so we made for the most obvious place on the map: the River Severn.

Just outside Tewkesbury, we parked up at the Lower Lode Inn and walked upstream, past creaking camper vans and through a campsite where students and hippies were sprawled out enjoying the dying embers of summer.

Down a steep path towards the river bank, we found a handy anglers' staging post, wide enough for both of us to get changed. There was nothing as luxurious as shallows for wading in, instead a submerged post onto which I was able to lean my weight before sliding into the pacy water. It was freezing, the coldest I'd experienced all summer, so I swam hard and fast in a vain attempt to warm up. I made sure to stay close to the side of the river, the current of the central channel moving at a rapid rate and large boats looming in both directions. Tom followed, offering up a brief 'Oh my God' before swimming in the opposite direction.

After a few minutes' nattering about swims and winter plans, we pulled out of the dreary Severn and dried off fast, drinking tea between putting on jumpers, jeans and T-shirts. I realised now why Roger hadn't swum here. It wasn't what I would call pleasant, and could have been dangerous. My appetite for swimming had been dulled by the day's events and I settled into the passenger seat feeling conflicted, the cold of the Severn still pressing on my chest. Swimming had become a huge part of my life, but I could see why so many would see my approach to it as asking for trouble. I hoped that Cornwall might iron out these kinks and get my mind back to why I loved it so much in the first place.

CHAPTER EIGHT

September

~~~

River Fowey, Cornwall – Helford Passage,
Cornwall – Treyarnon, Cornwall – Godrevy and
the Red River, Cornwall – Porthcurno, Cornwall –
Marazion and St Michael's Mount, Cornwall –
Bryher, Isles of Scilly – River Wharfe, Yorkshire –
Hell Gill, Yorkshire/Cumbria – Cowside Beck,
Yorkshire – Hampstead Mixed Pond, London –
Bryanston, Dorset – Highpoint, Highgate – Burwell
Lode and Wicken Lode, Cambridgeshire

Summer had returned for a valedictory lap as we crossed the Tamar. I was about to spend the next five days swimming my way around Roger's Cornwall, before taking the boat west to Bryher and a long-awaited date with the Scilly Isles.

Molly had been behind the wheel for six hours and delirium was beginning to set in. Her little red car was a messy scene of discarded coffee cups, poorly packed camping equipment and sweet wrappers. Both of us were borderline manic as we drove westward towards Fowey, the car stereo cranked up, blasting out The Smiths, music completely at odds with the hot and hopeful weather. Between tracks we talked about the swims I had planned for us over the weekend, how the journey was coming to an end. My spreadsheet was quickly turning green and there were around a dozen or so dips left.

Fowey seemed like the logical first stop on our journey. It was the first of Roger's dips we would hit on our drive down from London and was also the one that everyone I had spoken to about coming here told me I needed to do.

Molly jerked the handbrake on and we spilled out of the car park set high on the hills above the town, stuffing our bags with towels and swimming kit as we bounded down the town's narrow lanes, the deep green glint of the harbour visible at every turn. Yachts, dinghies and ferries filled every available space. It was only now that I was here that I began to appreciate the sheer magnitude of Roger's achievement of swimming across this wide, boat-jammed stretch.

He'd tried it twice. The first time, the coastguard had stopped him mid-swim, ordering him back to dry land on what was initially meant to be a 'dry run' from Polruan on one side to Readymoney Cove on the other. The second time, he swam in the lee of an escort boat for protection, going one way and then the other before being collared by the authorities just as he was about to emerge victorious, receiving a telling-off that was 'the nautical equivalent of letting you off with a caution'.

My stamina and fitness had certainly improved over two years of tailing Roger. I was able to swim further, had more energy and had a far better sense of physical well-being than when I had first set out. But my willingness to take bold risks was still low, especially in the wake of what I'd seen at Gullet Quarry. However, it seemed that Roger's determination to get across this deep, beautiful harbour had inspired some fellow swimmers to do something a bit more organised. A week before mine and Molly's arrival the locals had held their sixth annual Fowey Harbour Swim, tacking out from the Town Quay to Whitehouse, a kilometre swim in the Deakin tradition.

To be honest, I was relieved at the thought of not undertaking such a long swim, even though I could now add Fowey to Jura and the Medway to my growing list of *Waterlog* swims I hadn't faithfully recreated. It was late afternoon, and I consoled myself with the fact that even if we had attempted a return trip to Polruan, it would have been dark by the time we got back.

As we reached the water I began to realise what Roger meant when he said of Fowey, 'The moment you go on, or in, the water, you're on stage.' Houses, hotels, pubs and flats were piled on top of each other, reaching high up into the narrow valley and turning the harbour into a watery amphitheatre. I thought of the coastguard, my usual fears of offending authority whipping up my anxiety, despite my boldness in Winchester. I kept these worries to myself. Molly and I peered over the wall by the yacht club and realised that we were going to have to look for a more secluded spot to swim, away from the watchful gaze of tourists and locals.

We didn't have to go far. Walking down a high-walled, narrow lane, we emerged round the back of the club, finding a public landing place nestled into the rocks down a steep set of steps. It shelved quickly into the inviting azure waters. Best of all, only those in boats, or staring at us through binoculars far off in Polruan, could see us. The windows of the adjacent houses all seemed to point in different directions as we scrambled out of our clothes and into our swimming kit.

The barnacle-encrusted rocks dug deep into the balls of my feet, and I let out a small, pathetic series of 'ows' as I tiptoed towards the water and lowered myself in. It was deliciously cold and so clear that I could see shoals of small fish swim deep below me as I floated out into the harbour.

We stuck close to the shore and watched as RIBs zipped in from the Atlantic, before swimming as far as the nearest boat, *Dell Buoy*, moored fifty metres or so from where we'd got into the water. Despite the easy, shelving entrance, the harbour appeared to deepen suddenly and I felt lifted by the cool, salty water. It was a pleasing change from the murk of the Severn a week earlier.

I took the lazy honk of the Polruan ferry as my cue to get out, scratching my legs on the rocks as I made an ungainly exit, all the while watched by Pop, a black Labrador who had come with her owner to the public landing place to watch the sunset. She sniffed around my wet shorts as they flopped from beneath my towel, watching intently as I pulled on my underpants back to front.

Any pangs of guilt for not following Roger's movements to the letter had been swept away with the outgoing tide. I had to remind myself that this was not about emulation, but experience, as happy thoughts of wild swimming replaced the darker ones of the week before at Gullet Quarry. Breaking my daydream, Molly chivvied me along. We were now in a race against the setting sun, a second swim in the nearby Helford Passage pencilled in before dark.

We ran back up to the high car park, licking ice creams for sustenance, cramming our bags onto the back seat before tearing off on Roger's trail. The tone for the next few days had been set. Drive, swim, run; drive, swim, relax. I wasn't quite sure this was how Roger would have gone about it, but time was precious, the weather clearly enjoying its last burst of sunny abandon before packing up for the winter.

The sun was squeezing its final rays of the day through low, greying cloud as we reached the village of Durgan, the Helford River placid below us. It felt like a scene out of Hardy, albeit a lot further west: stone cottages, a small beach, a young family playing in the sand. The day had started with us battling through traffic on the clogged streets of south London, so it was apt to end it here, the complete antithesis of the capital's relentless buzz.

I could pick out every sound and count them on one hand: our heavy footsteps on the little road; the yapping bark of a dog; the puttering of a boat's engine as it inched out over the river. The river itself was silent. It didn't lap on the beach or create waves. I thought of the crash and churn of Bamburgh and the galumphing rollers at Dungeness. Swimming around Britain was a way of witnessing these islands' continual change. No two swims were ever the same.

The fading sun was pushing the temperature down fast, so there was no time to waste. We squirmed back into our now wet swimming things and strode out into the river, the deep green of the oaks and Scots pines which lined the high banks reflecting far out into the channel. Roger spoke of this being an almost tropical swim, like breaststroking through the Limpopo, and it was easy to see why. I had never seen a body of water in this country look so tantalising or foreign.

The dark sand gave way beneath my feet and I was soon swimming hard out to the nearest boat, the large pink orange buoy beneath its prow seeming like the ideal place for a mid-swim breather. I clung on, let my legs fall and looked upstream. Huge Scots pines hung suspended from the cliffs, ripped up roots and all, tumbling down towards the beach. At high tide the water would have touched the tendrils of their tops. I imagined swimming through them, the scratch of the pines on my back as the water rose and fell around me.

I was brought back to the present by the chill of the Helford nipping at my fingers, breaking my reverie and sending me off on an aimless, final swim of the day, around boats and over onto my back for a long look at the setting sun and the river's wide opening, away and out into the Atlantic.

The waft of cooking burgers reached my nose from the beach, the same family from earlier having a barbecue in the shelter of the high wall which ran along the back of the sand. Aside from the ice cream at Fowey, I hadn't eaten since scoffing a disappointing service station sandwich at midday. I was ravenous.

Molly and I eased our way back to shore, stroking the water as we stood and waded towards our pile of clothes and bags. On his long swim here, Roger spoke of the same far-away feel which I had experienced as I dived in, and I was pleased that aside from the fallen trees, little had seemed to change in this remote place. The real world and its attendant problems seemed a long way off as my endorphin rush set in, quickly followed by some pleasant post-swim shivers.

As we put on layers and rubbed our arms for warmth, talking about dinner and our route for the next day, a hand appeared between us, proffering half a burger each.

'We had a spare one.'

As after-swim treats go, a freshly cooked, handmade burger is up there with a hot cup of tea and a nap on a riverbank. I watched as Molly wavered, hunger flashing in her eyes, her vegetarianism all set to be broken before she demurred. Shaking with cold and grinning in elation, I took both halves and offered greedy thanks as I scarfed them one after the other, watching the chef of our impromptu meal wander back to the barbecue, from where her partner gave us a thumbs up. Their daughter ran across the sand, followed by their Jack Russell at her heels. I felt a rising sense of contentment as I sat down and watched the sun drop over the Helford River, a perfect swimming afternoon complete.

I had read much about the tidal pool at Treyarnon, sitting high above Constantine Bay, a natural swimming pool so clear and soothing that its fans never wanted to go back to the chlorinated lanes of their local pool. Roger had visited on a wet summer afternoon, the rain teeming down as he clambered towards the water and peeled off Gore-Tex before swimming with a black Labrador called Moll.

For us, though, rested after our long drive and double dip at Fowey and Durgan, the temperature was comfortably in the mid-twenties, the sound of The Beach Boys' 'Feel Flows' catching the wind as it played out over the youth hostel café's outdoor speakers. All felt breezy and chilled, surfers making their way out from the beach while families set up for the day, busting out windbreaks and industrial-sized cool boxes. Despite the school holidays being over, there was a distinct midsummer atmosphere that slowed our pace as we followed the coastal path north.

We were worried we might miss the pool, but as we climbed higher and turned the corner it reared up, perched above the lapping waves of the Atlantic, a perfect swimming hole. Snorkellers swam in random patterns across its glassy surface, while a man in garish orange trunks stood poised on a low rock, readying himself for a shallow dive. I heard a light splash and saw his feet disappear as we began to pick our way down the cliffs.

The tide was on the turn and we knew that if we didn't get in immediately, the pool would soon be overwhelmed, our chance of losing our tidal pool virginity gone for another twelve hours. By then it would be dark and we would be on the other side of the county, seeking out more of Roger's swims.

The long summer had worked its magic here and the water was warm, far more so than the nippy Helford River and even the estuary at Fowey. As Roger says, the fact that tidal pools are 'renewed by the moon twice a day' means they are able to heat up far more than the sea, away as they are from the attentions of crashing waves for hours at a time.

After a day spent sitting in the car followed by two relaxing swims, I felt in need of some more strenuous exercise, and swam a few hard lengths of the forty-foot pool, its depth and the occasional sway of the encroaching tide meaning there was nowhere for me to stop and rest. My limbs screamed before I stopped dead in the middle of the pool, put on my snorkel and lay face down, star-fish fashion, the only sound my Darth Vader-like breath echoing around the mask. I kept a keen eye out for shellfish and starfish proper, but saw nothing. I didn't really care. I had found what was surely one of Cornwall's finest swimming spots and was happy to let it soak deep into me.

I looked up to find Molly sitting on the pool's edge, speaking with two fellow swimmers, decked out in wetsuits and peering with great concern into the clear water.

'Joe, have you seen a wedding ring?'

I felt instinctively for my own, found it there and shook my head.

'It's just this guy's lost his.'

He looked stricken, his wife behind him.

Even in a pool this clear, the chances of finding a wedding ring were about as likely as a warm wild swim in December. It deepened fast, large pebbles and seaweed obscuring the bottom. By now the waves were beginning to crash over the rocks which protected the pool at low tide, the tilt and sway of the ocean causing swimmers to bob noticeably. Staying afloat was going to be hard enough without looking for lost jewellery.

I thought back to my own panic about losing my wedding ring on the Great Ouse. I could understand the poor man's devastation, especially as finding his was going to prove an impossible task. I didn't tell him it would be OK. It wasn't my place to make such assumptions.

The man, his wife and children left, disconsolate and empty-handed, while Molly and I made a cursory attempt to find his ring. It soon became apparent it was never going to happen, and so we set off on a last guilty lap of the pool. I clenched the fingers of my left hand together tightly, pushed my wedding ring hard onto my knuckle and thought of Keeley. I hadn't taken it off since I thought I had lost it and I dreaded the idea of losing it here.

The rising tide was starting to inch closer to our dry clothes, so we swam to the water's edge, pulling out and changing as we clambered up towards the clifftop. A pair of swimmers passed us in the opposite direction, a father and son. By now the waves had taken over the entire pool, but still the dad dived in, egging his son on as we looked back in horror.

Despite this being my first tidal pool, I knew the basic rule was to bail once the waves breached its walls. But the young lad bellyflopped in and the pair of them swam against the waves. They struggled to get out, high-fiving when they did so and allaying my anxiety.

But I felt it was foolish for them to have been so cavalier, even if the weather was good and there were plenty of people around. I bemoaned their behaviour to Molly as we sat on a bench and drank tea, more Beach Boys tunes drifting out from the café behind us. Perhaps I should have enjoyed the relaxed vibe a little more, but I was becoming increasingly conscious of the needless risks some swimmers seemed to take.

After Roger had swum in the pool at Treyarnon he had met the lifeguards on the nearby beach, who'd told him about a group of drunken swimmers getting into difficulty during a midnight dip. Those who had saved them 'blamed ... indoor swimming and warm-water "fun pools" for preventing young swimmers from learning a proper respect for the sea.' Roger said they swam 'with no thought of self-reliance', thinking the lifeguards would always be on hand to save them from the 'giant fun pool' that was the Atlantic Ocean.

I looked up this passage while I sat fuming. I had seen and heard of the same behaviour throughout my trip. The line between derring-do and stupidity is a thin one, one which Roger himself doubtless crossed a few times and which had often led to overcautious signage and rules, as I'd seen first hand at Beezley Falls. But I still marvelled at those who didn't seem to think before they got in, as if nothing could possibly go wrong.

I managed to calm myself after a few minutes of mindless chatter, remembering that it wasn't my concern, and took a last look down at our pool before we left. By now it no longer existed; rather it was hidden beneath the ocean and replenishing itself, getting ready for the next influx of swimmers.

After a lunch of cheese and onion pasties and overpriced lemonade on the harbour wall in Padstow, we drove an hour west to Godrevy Point, where the Red River slips into the Atlantic Ocean. The place was full of surfers catching the last waves of the late afternoon, wading through the polluted river, trailing their longboards with them through the shallow, nominally fresh water.

I was all ready to double-dip here, to wade into the wide pool which sits high above the back of the beach, a neat lip providing a handy resting place to perch and stare out to sea. But as we passed the old stone chimney stack of the disused tin mine and crossed a small wooden bridge, the water looked less than inviting. It wasn't quite the bright red of old, and I had heard second hand that the quality had improved in recent years, with insects and fish returning to a river that was once polluted with dilute arsenic. But to my eyes it still looked fetid and grim. A yellowish scum licked the orange sandy banks, the water tinged an unwelcoming shade of terracotta.

Molly wasn't keen, and after soaking in the clean salty pool at Treyarnon, the thought of sinking into this grimy river didn't appeal to me much either. We left the river behind and walked down to the beach where, despite the lifeguards packing up for the day, surfers were piling in, a series of high white breakers making for perfect conditions to go out on the board.

We waded in, the gradual entry tough after the swift baptism in the tidal pool earlier in the day. We were the only swimmers, and dived under waves, swimming fast to get amongst the neoprene-clad surfers. One cursed his luck as he fell off the back of a wave, while I kept a close watch so as not to be taken out by any of the more professional bunch who stood up with imperious ease and shot back to shore.

The soporific drive along the coast from Padstow was soon worked out of my system and I swam in long back and forths, battling to get to the rear of waves before trying to ride them back to calmer water. I could feel the strong pull of the tide beneath me and was careful to stay within my depth. Caution was beginning to override everything I did in the water, a slight swell of worry flaring up after what I'd seen at Treyarnon. I tried to push these feelings down and enjoy the grey waves on my skin, instead focusing on how they made me happy and cold at the same time.

We were both verging on hysterical when we came out, taking an age to get dressed and finding ourselves chatting unmemorable nonsense, the witterings of two swimmers who'd overindulged for two days running.

I felt no regret at not bathing in the Red River as we recrossed it and walked back to the car; it looked even less appealing now the light was beginning to fade. Vindication came when we got back to Molly's parents' house in Falmouth and read up further. It turned out that two storm water overflows emptied into the Red River's catchment area. The sewage treatment works at nearby Hayle emptied out into the ocean west of Godrevy Head just up the coast. What's more, two months before our visit the beach had been closed three times by the council, after the sewer overflows spilled into the Red River and across the beach into the sea following heavy rainfall. It seemed that despite talk of the river being cleaner than it had ever been, it was still not somewhere worth swimming.

The thing is, the swim off the beach had been first class, a proper sea dip to help blitz the mind of any worries about swimmers not taking precautions and the increasingly nagging thoughts about how I would cope once this retracing of Roger's journey was complete. But that didn't stop me from standing under a hot shower for fifteen minutes following our sewage discovery, skin red under the scalding water, in an attempt to wash off any pesky poison.

The following morning, skin seemingly free of any sewage-borne diseases, we drove from Falmouth to Porthcurno in the far west of Cornwall. It was still scorching, summer refusing to quit as we walked down to the beach along a vertiginous path, past the old telegraph hut where communications cables from North America had made landfall.

It was a Sunday and the white sandy cove was rammed with revellers, all determined to toast themselves to a crisp on what could easily have been the last hot day of the year. As at Mothecombe back in June, windbreaks provided homey privacy for families and solo sun worshippers. These little beach bothies looked the ideal place to idle away a few lazy hours.

We laid our towels just out of reach of the waves and looked out to see swimmers far off, tacking out to distant rocks or face down with snorkels, searching for marine life.

Roger swam out to a sandbar just off nearby Logan's Rock, and I fancied something long and soothing myself, so strode in with purpose, the water shelving to shoulder deep within a couple of strides. An extra push and my feet dangled beneath me. Only swimming could save me now.

Molly made for the edge of the cove and the cliffs where walkers were scaling the heights and peering into the depths. I went for a more straightforward option, swimming hard against the strong tide to see how far I could dare myself to go. This wasn't quite in keeping with the safety-first approach I'd taken at Godrevy and somewhat flew in the face of my complaints about swimmers taking too many risks. Still, there were others beyond me, taking long strokes or just lying on their backs, borne up by the heave of the Atlantic.

I was a few hundred metres out from the beach when my bottle went and I decided to turn back. The sandy bottom was visible but far off, the water a bright turquoise such as I'd never seen in the UK. I looked back towards the beach to see a group of teenagers flouting the 'No Inflatables' rule spelt out on the big board by the lifeguards' hut. Despite being so far away, I could hear their happy screams of laughter as they splashed in the shallows. The lifeguards didn't seem to mind.

I staggered out, the waves pulling at my ankles, and collapsed onto my towel, deciding to attempt a bit of late-summer bronzing myself. If it was good enough for my fellow beachgoers it was good enough for me. I slipped into a doze to the natter of kids daring each other to perform underwater handstands and other watery tricks. The only other sound was the quiet slump of the waves.

I could have spent the whole day alternately getting soaked and drying off at Porthcurno. But we only had one afternoon left before setting sail for the Scilly Isles, and another of Roger's swims to investigate first. I had enjoyed how varied his Cornish choices were, how they were spread right across the county and in such different places too: the dirty duet on the Red River, the busy harbour at Fowey, the refreshing pool at Treyarnon. Each one was a testament to the variety of wild swimming, capturing his long journey in microcosm.

Our next stop was another sea swim: one with a stunning view, but in a more open setting. Marazion, just along the coast from Penzance, was where Roger had come to revel in childhood fantasies, exploring the knackered old Pullman carriages, parked near the disused train station, which had doubled up as holiday homes back in the 1950s. He had longed to stay in them as a child, but had never done so, bemoaning their sorry, dilapidated state on his visit.

Before setting off to Porthcurno from Molly's parents' home in Falmouth, I'd asked Molly's dad about these old coaches, but was told they were no longer there. A quick search on the web showed that the remaining carriages had been broken up in 2006 and replaced with holiday cottages, the old Marazion train station now converted into a private home.

St Michael's Mount looked like a mirage in the afternoon heat, quivering green on the horizon. Molly wanted to do as Roger had done and swim all the way across, half a mile there, half a mile back. To me it looked an awful lot further. It was all part of her new 'go big' swimming strategy, one which I had been keen to indulge, but was less fussed about as I settled myself into a deckchair on the beach, breathing big gulps of salty air.

Molly waded in, trailing seaweed behind her, and scooted off towards the distant castle walls while I took my time taking in the scene. I decided to ape Roger and go for a long walk before getting in. I stomped off in the direction of Penzance, Molly now a dot on the green-blue sea. A few hundred metres along the coast, I slid in and immediately felt cold as my shoulders dropped and my feet struggled with the rocky bottom. Three days of swimming still hadn't helped me fully acclimatise, but I refused to listen to my body's pleas for mercy and swam in Molly's wake. She had made it about halfway across before turning back, and now she was heading straight for shore, swimming against the angle of the waves. I watched as she pulled herself free while I swam on, eyeing canoeists and speedboats.

I had to admire Roger's fearlessness in taking on such huge swims at great personal risk. But as I had learnt over the course of this two-year journey, we were very different swimmers. Maybe not in style or technique, but certainly in approach. Perhaps my predisposition for anxiety meant I could never do as he did, swimming hard, far and fast. But I could at least see where he'd done it and remind myself that it was he who set the standard for all wild-swimming adventures.

Parked in my creaking deckchair, wrapped in a towel, I sat drinking tea with Molly, watching boats come and go from faraway Penzance harbour. One of them was the *Scillonian III*. As we stared at its slow approach, Molly told me all about her trip to the isle of St Mary's the previous year: the pretty gardens, empty beaches, quiet lanes. I drank the last dregs from my travel mug and tried to imagine Bryher, the little island where we would be staying. The most distant destination in *Waterlog* was within reach.

Firethorn was bobbing at the bottom of the stone steps in St Mary's harbour. We inched down and wedged ourselves onto the hard wooden benches at the back of the boat, the youngest members of the Bryher-bound crew. We were early, having almost missed the *Scillonian* in Penzance thanks to a mixture of our own incompetence and a nonsensical parking app.

Molly had left the car opposite the Jubilee Pool, the town's stunning lido, shuttered for the summer following the massive storms of the previous winter. This classic, triangular pool, so nearly tarmacked over in the 1980s, had borne the brunt of some of the worst winds this town had seen in living memory.

As we rushed to make the ferry, I glanced through the metal gates to see it drained and destroyed. Local swimmers were campaigning hard to raise the funds to get it reopened as soon as possible, but this was going to be a huge undertaking. Thankfully, funding had been secured, with bold plans to offer kayaking and water polo alongside swimming when the gates swung open. But for now it meant I would have miss one of the key sites from Roger's Cornwall itinerary. Had I lingered any longer we would have been stranded on the mainland. The *Scillonian*'s gangplank was pulled away just as Molly and I stepped aboard.

Such intense weather was impossible to imagine as our little vessel chugged out of St Mary's harbour and over Tresco Flats. The sky was cloudless, a light breeze causing me to reach for a jumper as we stood up and peered over starboard into glassy, electric-blue seas, white sand clearly visible on the bottom. The captain swerved firethorn wildly as we entered the narrow strait, Tresco to our right, avoiding shallow sandbars and rocks, before we gently kissed the little jetty which stuck out from Bryher's sandy eastern reaches.

Roger made swimming here sound like the apotheosis of his Arcadian dream, an island of dozens of little coves and bays all within easy walking distance of each other. Having found some places to be somewhat dissimilar to his descriptions over the previous two years, I had a certain scepticism about what we would find as we threw our tents and bags into a farm vehicle and followed its slow chug up to the campsite.

My pessimism was punctured as soon as we crested the hill which the campsite clung to, views down to Stinking Porth and Great Popplestones Bay opening out and inviting us to choose which one we'd like to swim in first. Still high from three days of Cornish swimming excess, Molly and I ran screaming like excitable toddlers down the sandy tracks, turning off at the now swanky Hell Bay Hotel and onto Stinking Porth. It had taken us ten minutes to cross the island. The whole of Bryher was ours to explore and, although we had just a day to do so, we felt unhurried, relaxed – feelings I usually struggled to tap into when life moves at a fast pace.

Stinking Porth lived up to its name. The piles of bladderwrack at the back of the beach gave off a heavy, damp stench as we walked over them and onto the sand. Back in Falmouth, Molly's parents had told me about how cold the water was on the Scilly Isles, no matter the time of year. Roger came in April in the hope that it would help him ease his way into his long summer trip. He wound up clad in his wetsuit to stave off the biting cold of the Atlantic after one skin-tingling dip.

Despite being forewarned, I struggled to believe that after spending a summer under the sun the sheltered water of this little bay would be much colder than that of Porthcurno or Godrevy. But as my feet sank into the wet sand and the water reached my calves, my thighs, my unmentionables, I was close to screaming, and not in joy. The cold was absurd, pinching at every sinew and causing me to gasp hard for breath. I battled against the urge to run out and forced myself to dive. Total immersion brought with it a burst of adrenalin, but I knew as soon as I surfaced that I'd be swimming without protection for no more than a few minutes. Molly was next to me, head out, breathing like a golden retriever, all air seemingly shoved from her lungs the moment she'd joined me in the water. Being a toughened Cornish swimmer, she powered on when I told her I was retreating to the beach to get togged up in full neoprene. Usually the first to berate me for my willingness to rubber up, she nodded her approval and swam off into the deep cove.

Dressed in wetsuit and boots, snorkel clamped across my face, I strode back in and slid under without the chill nipping at my toes. Flippers would have come in handy as I set out for distant rocks, face down and swimming a speedy freestyle. I marvelled at the clarity of it all as I got deeper and deeper: the clearness of the water, the ridges of white sand visible despite the depth, the gentle sway of long tresses of seaweed.

I soon found myself above a kelp forest, its long strands stretching away thirty feet below. I lengthened my stroke and pushed my arms deeper to touch their tendrils. Normally I would have headed for shore at the uncertainty of what was beneath me, but I felt part of this little corner of the Scillies, just another creature in its waters. The snorkel aided this sense of being at one with it all. There was no need to pull my head from the icy water, so I stared down and let the incoming tide push me and pull me in whichever direction it fancied.

Molly had gone climbing on the rocks which burst up from the beach, pushing herself through a tiny arch as I took a slow walk back along the beach to where we'd left our bags. I felt stoned, unable to imagine a world beyond Bryher, its *Tempest*-like beaches and bays. If Cornwall had felt distant from London, the Scilly Isles were truly otherworldly.

Dried off but ready for more, we took the short walk around the coast to Great Popplestones Bay, past the freshwater Great Pool, where huge shoals of fish created havoc on the surface, splashing hard as if the water beneath them was evaporating, their life force being sucked up by the sky. Strange stone sculptures marked our way, pebbles balanced atop one another every metre or so, leading to a little maze which swirled in on itself as the path turned from grass to open sand.

Roger came across these intricate pebble creations further south at Rushy Bay, and it pleased me that this fresh effort stood here all these years later. It added to the ethereal nature of the place, a mystical set of islands detached from the average daily realities of mainland Britain. I enjoyed the fact that someone would need to come and lay out these little mazes and precarious sculptures every time a heavy storm blew in. There was a commitment to it that made me happy, a sign that people on Bryher cared about more than tourists and making money.

Molly slumped down on her towel, drowsy following her wetsuit-free swim, closing her eyes to the still-high sun. It was late afternoon and there was still plenty of warmth in its glow, but I struggled back into the neoprene, caked in sand from Stinking Porth, desperate to ensure this second swim of the day lasted more than a few delicious moments. The beach here slipped into the ocean quicker than around the coast, the entry to the bay feeling the full force of the Atlantic from the west. Waves tore over high boulders and smashed into cliffs, but in our sheltered spot deep in the cove all was calm, a slight lap on the shore as I snapped on my goggles and nestled the snorkel's mouthpiece around my gums.

My earlier swim had been a resounding success, so I set off in the same fashion, head down and swimming hard for deep water. The seaweed here was thicker and rose higher, skirting the surface and wrapping itself around my arms and legs the further I pushed on into the bay. The dark closed in as more seaweed covered the sandy surface, and all I could see was a deep brown wave of underwater plant life, as if beckoning me to swim further. I surfaced in a thick soup of tendrils and realised I had swum 300 metres out to the nearest rocks, weeds skirting its edges.

Swimming without getting into a tangle was becoming impossible, so I turned and made for clearer waters, where things were rougher. The salty slap of the sea on my face told me that the glassy stillness I'd enjoyed earlier was over, so I turned and powered back to shore, beaching myself and clawing at the wetsuit, desperate to dry off in the sun before it slipped too low for sunbathing.

That evening we ate bread and cheese bought from the surprisingly well-stocked Town Shop, from where we also procured a more than decent bottle of Argentinian Malbec. The 'Whole Earth Catalogue' vibe my predecessor found on the island did still exist, but now it had a top-notch wine supplier to go alongside the honesty boxes dotted outside people's homes offering up local honey, fudge and lobster, sellers unconcerned about anyone making off without paying.

We had planned to eat at the Hell Bay Hotel, but found the modest establishment of Roger's time far fancier than we had first thought. The restaurant was fully booked, but our lo-fi meal, eaten while sitting in a pair of broken deckchairs left opposite our tents, was less expensive and far more enjoyable. To be honest, the hotel was anathema to the atmosphere on Bryher, an overly luxurious spot not in keeping with the rough-and-ready vibe I had fallen for earlier in the day. Its heated pool and spa treatments would never be able to top the icy cold of the sea just a few metres from its imposing front entrance.

We polished off the bottle, tipsy now, and decided to run to the top of Shipman Head Down, which rose north of where we were camping. I was fully aware of Roger having raved about the sunset as seen from the top of this high point, and we reached the mossy summit just as it began to touch the horizon, far off out into the Atlantic. We took lunar-like steps over the sea pinks which carpeted the top of the hill, the wine now working its magic and sending us off in different directions, hollering to no one, the Atlantic's gusts catching and carrying our shouts. I stood stock still as the sun made its final drop into the sea and turned to see the moon rising in the opposite direction. At that moment I felt as if Bryher was the centre of the universe, the axis on which the whole thing turned. I revelled in this drunken thought as we crashed back through bracken and gorse into our tents, where I passed a fitful night, dreaming of swims and being woken by the crack of canvas in the wind.

Early the next morning, after dropping £3 in the honesty box at Veronica's Farm for some large chunks of fudge, we walked the sandy paths down to Green Bay on the island's east coast, looking over to Tresco. The tide was racing out and soon walkers would begin to carefully pick their way across the flats, crossing from island to island without having to jump aboard a boat. The wetsuit was damp with dew where

I had left it out overnight, sand drying in the crotch and armpits. I pulled it on, cringing, and jogged out towards the water, in the hope I might see the submerged ancient farm walls and boundaries which Roger had seen on his visit.

As soon as I hit the water I knew my luck was out. I waded out a hundred metres, but was still only knee deep, so settled into a crawling motion, sticking my head under and pulling myself along using my hands on the seabed. My amateur archaeology skills yielded no results, and after half an hour all I could see was my frozen fingers pawing at mud.

My disappointment at failing to find the old ruins which Roger had written about so excitedly was soon tempered as we walked south, Rushy Bay opening up before us, the uninhabited island of Samson a seemingly tropical paradise across the water. My swims the day before had perhaps been my favourites of the entire *Waterlog* journey, in the most beautiful of places, but this beach was perfect, a level up from those marvellous bays. I knew as soon as I saw Rushy Bay that I would have to swim in it without the wetsuit for protection. It was now mid-September, and there was little chance that the weather would be this warm again.

To my surprise, Molly said she wanted to get done up in the wetsuit, so while she yanked it on and made faces as its damp confines wrapped themselves around her skin, I stripped down to my shorts and made for the water. I knew what to expect, so the killer cold didn't knock me sideways like it had done the day before. I stayed focused on my breath and looked all around me, at the Northern Rocks, the gulls wheeling in the sky, the wisp of stratus clouds high and untroubling. In this place I felt a profound sense of calm.

It was the physical distance from the everyday, yes, but also the strong, cold touch of the water, setting my skin alight and directing my focus onto nothing but the present. This was the best anti-anxiety drug I could ever find, but I knew that it was one which was not readily available, and that scared me like it hadn't done for a long time. As I continued to swim, I realised that it was now a year since I had broken my wrist. A year since I had first sought Mark's help and begun to tackle my problems with anxiety and self-hatred. And, by and large, I knew that I had started to make things better. For the most part, I had managed to stop swimming being the sole panacea for my endless worrying. I was talking more openly about it, recognising that ultimately worry couldn't fix anything, and in the previous twelve months had felt lighter, less stressed, as a result. I was finding ways to heal myself by seeing the joy in spending time with people I loved and sharing what I loved with them. I was worrying less about work than I had ever done. In that respect, I was much better.

I breathed deeply and tried to enjoy the slap of cold waves on my face, trying to bring my attention to the here and now. But I could feel a groundswell of worry surge within me as this sense of calm began to dissipate. I had felt it nudging at my consciousness as this Cornish leg of my journey moved on, but pushed it down. I knew that there were only a few swims left before I completed Roger's journey, and the fact that I had been swimming so much over the summer meant that losing its routine, and the new experiences which my predecessor revealed to me on each and every swim of his, was of increasing concern. What would I do without it? Once again I could see I was beginning to pin all of my hopes, my needs to fix my anxiety, on this journey. I worried about it in the same way I used to worry about work, concerned I hadn't 'done it right'. Concerned about what others thought of it. Concerned, too, that I was letting Roger down. The things I had stopped worrying about over the preceding few months appeared to be back.

I had done so well, but was forgetting the bigger picture: the release that swimming in Roger's wake afforded me, the fact that it was meant to be joyous and not a chore, that I didn't need it to make me feel better and that I could take the good things from it – the therapy, the strong love of my marriage, the new and rekindled friendships – along with me whatever happened. Instead of seeing all of this in a calm and orderly way, my mind began playing out scenarios, rapidly trying to work out when I would be finished and what I could do to replace this journey with something new, something exciting, anything to stop me from worrying that I wasn't going to lose all the good things that had come from it.

I went and lay on my towel and slept a while, trying to eke out that feeling of calm I'd enjoyed a few moments before. I was woken by the sound of oystercatchers piping on their way out to sea, Molly waving and shouting about how much she loved the wetsuit.

For a brief few moments I managed to push those worries down, but it was no use. I tried not to feel sad about our trip to these islands soon being over and my *Waterlog* trip racing towards its end, but I couldn't shake that melancholy even as the sun beat down and we took a slow stroll back to the campsite.

Our twenty-four hours in Bryher were up. We collapsed our tents, stuffed our rucksacks and took a sad walk back to the jetty. I could see why Roger had opted to come here first, but for me this was the ideal place to come towards the end of the journey. I contemplated whether to end it now. I couldn't see how any other swim of Roger's could live up to this. I would have to be convinced that even just one could match those on Bryher, otherwise there was no point in going on.

Later that night, as my sleeper train trundled out of Penzance and passed the old Marazion station, I pulled up the covers in my cabin and drank whisky from a miniature bottle snaffled from the restaurant car, looking back at photos of the summer's swims on my camera. A creeping sadness came over me as the carriage rocked me to sleep and I thought of the passing of another year and the impending end of my trip.

Back in London, snuggled up with Keeley, I remembered the beauty of Bryher's sandy bays and the need to make myself better, with or without swimming. The following morning I dropped Mark an email:

'OK if I come in and see you?'

I eased myself into the same armchair, the tissues pulled just so from their box on the nest of tables beside it, a glass of water poised for when my talking left me dry and thirsty.

Mark pushed the door to with his feet and slurped on a cup of tea as he took his seat opposite me.

'Good to see you. How long's it been? And how are you feeling?'

I told Mark what had been going through my mind during that last swim in the Scilly Isles. How I was worried about my trip coming to an end and what I was going to do afterwards. That it was making me feel stressed and anxious in the same way work had done when I had first seen him. I explained that after our sessions had finished, I had got good at learning to say 'fuck it', at recognising when I was worrying about fleeting moments, like broken mugs or missed trains, compartmentalising them and seeing them for what they were: brief worries to float past, things that would be forgotten in an hour, a day, a week.

But I also told him I was once again starting to invest too much hope in swimming and the water again, the belief that it could fix my ills. I still loved it, but looked to it too much as a catch-all cure. I explained that I had seemed to forget how to catch myself when I began stressing out, not stopping to breathe and see things as they really were, meaning swimming took on greater significance. I mentioned the wedding ring incident with Tim. I told him about Tim's advice – to look at the bigger picture, to suss out a logical approach to what felt an illogical worry. Mark nodded and motioned for me to keep talking, taking another loud slurp from his mug.

I could feel the fug of anxiety snapping at the edges of my consciousness again, dominating every thought process as it had done in the run-up to my wrist break and in the weeks after, when I had first come to see him. Everything I did aside from swimming in Roger's wake now made me feel guilty, as if I wasn't tending properly to this beast that I had created. If I did a non-*Waterlog* swim, like going to Brockwell for a pre-work paddle, I felt bad, as if I wasn't being faithful. It was just how I used to feel when I wasn't working but swimming instead. The hobby had become the job, and I felt I wasn't being productive enough. It was nothing I hadn't told Keeley between getting back from Cornwall and pressing the buzzer at Mark's clinic door, but it felt more real telling it to a professional. It felt like an admission.

'Wasn't this supposed to be a way of getting away from work? Of doing something different?'

I nodded.

'I seem to remember you worrying about the same thing last year. You're turning this into work again when it's supposed to be fun. What exactly do you get from this journey?'

I told him that it was about that feeling of nowness when I was in the water. But, as I had realised in Jura and on the Wissey, it was just as much about seeing friends, being around people I cared for.

Saying all of this out loud gave me a sudden jolt of objectivity. I was forgetting to float and look around at the good things this project had created. Thinking only about the end of the trip was another way of lining my ducks up in a row, of setting arbitrary goals that only caused stress.

I was worried about not seeing everyone as much. Of going back into the lonely shell I had lived in before I had begun the journey, spending too much time at home alone.

'But it's entirely in your power to ensure it doesn't happen,' said Mark. 'You just need to keep making the effort. You're worrying about something that hasn't happened yet.'

I realised that this was another case of my allowing my thoughts to run away with themselves, of not applying the techniques I had learnt from Mark the first time around. This tune-up, with Mark lending an ear and letting out the occasional guffaw to make me feel better about the ridiculousness of the state I had got myself into, was just what I needed before getting back out there again.

I was probably never going to be free of worry and anxiety, so I may as well go out and enjoy this thing I had started, with the people who had come along with me for the ride. We talked through the concept of letting everything float by, of breathing, of recognising thought processes in order to change them, of saying 'fuck it' and doing it anyway. It was as invigorating and helpful as a bracing sea swim.

I crossed the stony beach opposite Bolton Abbey and dropped my bag by the water's edge. It was a dank September afternoon, the warm sun of the Scilly Isles a distant memory up on the edge of the Yorkshire Dales.

After seeing Mark, things had begun to get better and I was glad to be back following Roger, looking forward to an autumn of swims and the water touching my skin. Keeley encouraged me to get back out there and make the most of it before it grew too cold.

Dave had driven over from his home near Huddersfield and collected me from Skipton station, a willing taxi driver who had taken a keen interest in my last swims. His knowledge had proved invaluable at Kirkby Lonsdale and in the Dales during the summer, and I was happy to have him with me, driving me across this largest of counties in search of far-off swimming spots.

Roger had found this water hole packed with swimmers treating the river bend like a beach in Cornwall. He had come in high summer, though, while I was here on a wet weekday afternoon a fortnight after the schools had gone back.

There were no swimmers today, although a gaggle of walkers stood egging each other on at the stepping stones downstream. A large sign posted by the estate's owners warned them to take care on the loose cobbles, but one by one they trod out, some showing caution, others striding with reckless abandon towards the other side. A cheer went up each time one of them made it safely back to dry land.

I couldn't have picked a more picturesque place for my first swim since Bryher. My worries about not being able to top that almost tropical spot had proved unfounded. It was an important lesson for me to learn and keep in mind. The shattered abbey stood high on the opposite bank, standing so tall that if I stared at it hard enough its vertiginous walls seemed to fall towards the River Wharfe below.

I had come north not just to take the water at Bolton Abbey, but to also attempt Roger's most notorious swim, one which I had been dreading since day one: the descent into Hell Gill. I really should have visited this notorious cavern when I had last been here in the summer, but other swims had got in the way. Having not 'gone big' so far, as Molly would have put it, I was determined to finally do so in the one place where my predecessor had almost taken a risk too far. A dip at Bolton Abbey seemed to be the ideal way to ease myself into proceedings.

I was enjoying the thought of an autumn dip, especially as my broken wrist had denied me the pleasure twelve months earlier. To that end, I opened my bag and ignored the wetsuit packed at the top, grabbing my towel, shorts and swimming shoes. The freezing water around the Scillies had steeled me for what I knew would be a tough session, and I wasn't disappointed as I waded in. The water rushing down from the hills into this beautiful river was extremely chilly, and I made sure to keep my head up and out to avoid any nasty shivers as I pushed off into the deep meander. The Wharfe here was a deep peaty orange, just like the burn I had looked at with longing on Jura and the fast-flowing West Dart at Hexworthy Bridge. It couldn't have been less like the muddy brown murk of my last Yorkshire swim, in the shallow Leeds to Liverpool Canal just a few miles away in Gargrave.

My head snapped back as I heard a collective hooray from the bank. I thought it was for my swimming endeavours until I spotted an unfortunate soul wading across the Wharfe by the stepping stones, using the submerged cobbles for balance after he'd slipped and fallen in. Even from this far off I could see he looked thoroughly miserable. He may as well have stripped down to his undies and joined me for a swim, although I didn't fancy my chances of convincing him, despite the fact that he was already half soaked. His pals laughed and called out encouragement as he scrambled out and made his way back across the wooden bridge, doubtless wishing he'd taken the easier route in the first place.

I pushed on upstream, the riverbed dropping deep, its rocky bottom putting me in mind of the refreshing dips in the Dart when summer was still all glinting promise and long evenings. I was glad to be here alone in the water, without the intrusion of other swimmers. After sharing so much water in the past few weeks, it felt good to have the Wharfe to myself, even if Dave stood watching on the bank, snapping pictures and voicing his growing concerns that I might succumb to hypothermia if I stayed in much longer. I heeded his warnings, thoughts of Hell Gill flashing through my mind and the realisation that that swim, not this one, was the big reason for coming all this way so soon after spending time down in Cornwall.

Roger had attempted Hell Gill in a skimpy pair of speedos and wetsuit boots, with only a rope to aid his attempts to crawl back out. It was as foolhardy as it was dangerous, but it remains the most exciting passage in *Waterlog*, where he realises that if he can emerge from the underworld unscathed, he can achieve anything. 'I had never delved so far into the earth before, so alone, or so naked. It could have swallowed me up, but here I was, the other side of it.'

The cold of the river sat heavy on my chest, and I slowed my breathing and tried to meditate and stay focused on the moment, eking out this feeling of quiet bliss while remembering that, like everything, it was only fleeting. I held on to this peaceful feeling as we left the broken abbey and drove up through Wharfedale, tracing the river's upper reaches as it grew narrower and flowed faster, tumbling white over massive boulders, creating tantalising little pools at the bottom of every waterfall.

In the village of Hubberholme we stopped at the strange little church of St Michael and All Angels. Its thick, twelfth-century walls provided a tranquil haven at the end of a long day of train travel and swimming, and I padded along its cold flagstones, touching the odd little wooden mouse sculptures cut into the pews, carved by the artist Robert Thompson.

Despite being a long-lapsed Catholic, I offered up a short prayer for tomorrow's descent into the Dales. My nerves were fraying and I began to worry about what to expect from Hell Gill as I returned to the car and sat staring out at the end of Wharfedale in silence, contemplating what was sure to be the biggest challenge of the entire journey so far. I deepened my breath and remembered that ultimately, it didn't matter. Being here with Dave, enjoying the moment, was all that was important right now.

The main thing was that I had a plan. Roger had tackled Hell Gill alone, drawn to the 'roofless cave' after hearing it discussed by potholing fanatics at the climbers' café in Ingleton. He slid into it in just a pair of swimming shorts, with a rope for company. But there was no way I was going to be that cavalier, especially as autumn had arrived in this corner of the country.

There was a claggy mist clinging to the hills around Hawes when we woke the next morning. We had spent the evening before studying a beaten-up OS map and a thirty-year-old copy of Tony Waltham's *Yorkshire Dales: Limestone Country*, an indispensable guide to going underground in God's own country which had been on Dave's bookshelves for as long as I could remember. Compared to Roger's poetic prose, Waltham gave a more practical explanation of the Gill, which sits bang on the border between Yorkshire and Cumbria. He talked of the enveloping darkness at the heart of the narrow gorge, trees crowding its high opening to prevent any light from entering. He also spoke of entering it from the bottom, rather than sliding down from the top, as Roger had done with almost disastrous consequences. For this, I'd need Wellington boots and a strong dose of gumption. I could get the former at the farm shop in town.

At the county border I popped on my uncomfortable new footwear and checked over the contents of my rucksack: swimming cap, neoprene boots, wetsuit, flask, a change of clothes. I was not going to slide into this thing without a care in the world. This, I knew after so long following his trail, was where Roger and I really differed. He was bold, sometimes to the point of recklessness. I was cautious, often to the point of inertia. I had felt it at the Medway and down at Fowey and numerous other times on this two-year odyssey, but never as keenly as I did as we walked up towards Hell Gill. I tried to recognise it for what it was, but right then I could have done with this last of the great English eccentrics being there in person to lead me onwards and down into the underworld.

The weather was miserable, a steady drizzle settling on my waterproof jacket and soaking into my trousers as we followed the hidden stream up towards the farm where the gill itself opened out. A shepherd screamed at his dog from atop a quad bike, its high-pitched engine soaring and fading as he traversed the low hills. His sheep were being penned in right next to where the gill spread itself out into open ground, and with a high fence around it, there was no way Waltham's suggestion of going in from the bottom was going to work. If I wanted to do this, I was going to have to do it Roger's way. I imagined him beaming with pride and tramped on.

We carried on by the path upstream, the gurgle of the gill deep below us to our right. The sound calmed my fears. But as we reached the stone bridge which crossed the deep-cut stream, we saw that everything had changed.

The upper left-hand bank of Hell Gill had had a severe haircut, the pines which once crowded up and over its lip shorn back to nothing, creating a ten-foot space between tree line and cliff. Light poured in and we were able to lean over and see the white rush of water as it hurtled downstream through the narrow cleave in the rock.

Trepidation was replaced by excitement, and I was now beginning to think that I could not only get into Hell Gill as Roger had done, but also go one better and slide all the way down. I turned and stomped up the hill, around the denuded pine forest and past stacks of logs, sap dripping from their freshly cut ends. The changes were recent and favourable, and I could sense Roger's hand at my back, egging me on.

We hopped over a low drystone wall and saw Hell Gill's entrance beneath us. The series of plunge pools were just as Roger described, each one deeper and wider than the last. I remembered that Waltham had called this descent a one-way trip if tackled from the top, and even with the extra light it looked like a dangerous expedition. Beyond the final pool, all was dark and gloomy, the only thing visible the brightness of the rushing water.

Before making my attempt, I walked downstream along the stripped-back bank, lay on my front and crawled to the edge of the cliff. I could see the narrow natural alleyway down below, but could not tell how deep it was. If I was to get there, I would surely have to go without wellies.

Upstream, where the water slipped past shallow banks, I tugged on my wetsuit and decided to try the wellies anyhow. I looked ridiculous, but I knew I would rather wear this idiosyncratic outfit than a pair of speedos, Roger-style, especially as the drizzle had by now turned to persistent rain. I dropped in and half walked, half slid into the pool in front of me. The limestone was slippery and impossible to stand up on, so I climbed back out and swapped into my neoprene shoes, which were warmer, but afforded even less grip.

I didn't wear gloves and immediately regretted it as I stuck my hands into the stream. The water fell straight from the hills and was bitterly cold, turning my fingers first red, then blue. I couldn't imagine it would have been much warmer when Roger came, and it made his exploits here seem all the more foolhardy and, I'll admit, impressive.

I swam in the first pool to acclimatise, then let myself slide over the narrow lip and into the next one. It was deeper and cooler, with a high overhang under which I could swim easily against a fast-flowing eddy. I stayed here for a while and began to wonder just what I was doing. How had I, a person who had a visceral fear of water as a schoolboy, wound up standing in a narrow gorge in one of the most isolated corners of northern England? I enjoyed the stupidity of it all, realised it made me feel happy and alive, and decided to drop down to the next pool. And then the next.

All this time, Dave stood high up on the bank, shouting down dark portents about what would happen if I carried on. I knew he was right, but I could feel the water pushing me on, further into the underworld. There was a dark, mysterious pull too, the gorge coaxing me on to find out what was hidden further down in its bowels. Perhaps I could go all the way.

At last I reached the point of no return. Here the gill took a sharp right and thundered off deep into nothingness. I didn't have a rope and knew from both Roger and Tony Waltham's advice that once I committed there was no coming back. My predecessor had somehow managed to scramble clear, but he had a bungee rope with him and the cold water smashing into his bare skin to urge him to get a move on. My climbing skills were non-existent. If I went down this last visible lip, I didn't know what I'd find and Dave would have to fish me out at the far end.

I had thought I had come prepared, but as well as my lack of a rope, I had no helmet or head torch either. I swam and pondered for a few minutes and then realised that this was far further than I had ever hoped to get. Just an hour ago I had been thinking that I would splash around in the gill's lower reaches. But I had come almost as far as Roger and seen a place that had only recently been transformed. I turned and began an unseemly swim and scramble back through the pools, stopping in each one to paddle a few strokes and splash my face. I took a little sip and tasted heather and happiness.

There was no chance of a sunbathe on the upper reaches of the stream, even if the rain had stopped and the sun was doing its best to burn off the low cloud. Instead I tramped back into the pine wood and stared downstream. I had no regrets about coming out when I did. All my fears about failing to find a swim to match Bryher had been blown away by the sharp falls and little pools of Hell Gill. It was so different and yet equally beautiful. Finally, I had 'gone big' in the one place that it mattered most. I felt a surge of relief, knowing that I hadn't needed to worry about the future of the trip after all. Finishing didn't worry me anymore; it felt exciting now. It would be an achievement, not an ending.

I couldn't bring myself to come all this way and not go in search of the tufa pool on Cowside Beck one last time. I felt transformed after Hell Gill, much like Roger says he had been, and was ready to take on one final challenge for the day before falling into a post-swim snooze on the drive home.

I was also armed with some new information, handed to me by a fellow Deakin acolyte. It offered a specific place to aim for on the high road opposite Yew Cogar Scar, so I could stride directly over right-to-roam land and into the pool.

My last time here I had bounded down the high-sided valley in shorts and T-shirt, sinking naked into the shallows when I realised I was lost and would not find the pool before the sun went down. But on this September afternoon all was grey, although the rain had at least cleared up, offering dry passage down to the water.

I put on my walking boots, Dave choosing to rest his legs in the car and listen to the latest news about the Scottish independence referendum. The noise of an angry radio debate dissipated as I set off.

I held the OS map and a printout of the directions, determined not to go wrong this time. I vaulted a low fence with a 'No Access' sign, staggered to my knees and stood up to see the most perfect natural swimming pool a hundred feet below. I could hear its light burbling as it tickled the low rocks and skirted the moss which surrounded its banks. There was the spinney of ash Roger had spoken about, one of the trees lying prone across the stream.

In that moment I had the most intense childhood flashback. I was clambering the solitary ash tree at the bottom of my parents' garden, peering over the wooden fence and beyond the nettle beds to the narrow path cutting through the copse which marked a border between our estate and the next. Older kids rode dirt bikes along the track, their engines whining like wasps.

That sound buzzed in my ears as I ran down to the tufa pool. I had stuffed my damp wetsuit in my bag, but there was no way I was getting in with 'the condom' on. I lay my towel, jacket and flask within easy reach on the high mossy banks and stuck a hand into the water to check just how cold it was. Extremely.

The natural moss steps made getting in a breeze, but pushing off I was immediately out of my depth. I could see the bottom of the pool beneath the eddying rush, limestone slick with weed, and stuck my head under. It sent a huge shiver along my spine, but I resolved to stay in for as long as my body could take it. I had missed out last time and I wanted to enjoy the cold water here for as long as possible.

I swam in short circles around the pool, laying across a submerged rock at its edge to stare off downstream. Looking in the direction of Arncliffe, I could see just where I had gone wrong a couple of months before. If I had explored another hundred metres further upstream, rather than turning the other way in frustration, I would have found this place then and been able to skinny-dip and sunbathe in the opening of the little cave which stood next to the top of the pool.

Any regrets were short lived as I jumped out on the far bank and went for a quick explore around the cave. If it had been warmer I would have drifted off here for a few minutes. But by now I was aware of my skin turning bright pink. I slipped back in and swam a few more laps, before realising that I needed to get out before the shakes really set in.

I got dressed methodically, taking my time to enjoy the solitude of this special swimming hole, nestled so deep in the valley that it remained a happy secret to those who ventured this far off the path towards Malham Cove.

I knew Dave would be waiting, wondering where I was, but I poured myself a cup of tea and sipped at it for what felt like an eternity. I offered up thanks to the water gods, the local geology and those handy instructions from a fellow *Waterlog* aficionado for bringing me to this place.

Taking one final look, I turned and ran up the hill, my heart pounding in my ears, the most powerful endorphin rush gripping my system and sending me into an ecstatic high. I crested the hill, took a deep breath and felt the cold beck water tingle on my skin as I walked towards the car.

I went to Hampstead mixed pond for one final 'moat swim' before it closed its rickety wooden gate for the last time for the summer. It was a late September morning and the water had dropped below the magical 20°C mark. There was only one other swimmer in, a marked change from the balmy, midsummer chaos I'd enjoyed a few weeks previously. The sun was hidden behind thick cloud on this last trip of the season, and there was no chatter on the banks. The only sound came from a single moorhen pottering in the waterside shrubs.

I swam out to the far rope and took a look back at the little black wooden shed that doubled up as the lifeguard station. It was four years since my first ever trip here with Keeley, and I was hoping this would be my last before finishing up my *Waterlog* mission. Winter was on the horizon and I wanted to get everything done before it got to ice-breaking levels of cold, making me beat a tactical retreat to the warm embrace of the nearest heated lido. The sense of achievement and contentment I'd enjoyed up in the Yorkshire Dales had travelled back south with me and I was enjoying being on an even keel again after the low following Cornwall. I'd even started going to yoga classes, stretching out in ungainly fashion, but finding a stillness in the breathing and meditation that came with it. I was beginning to make peace with the end of my journey in Roger's wake and seeing life beyond it, excited about what life held for me, rather than being nervous. I was, 'Loving everything that increases me', as Raymond Carver's poem put it.

The lifeguards were holding a 'come rain or shine closing party' at the mixed pond the day after my dip, but I needed to get out of London once again and get back on Roger's trail. I had booked train tickets down to Poole and planned a day trip to Bryanston and the Dorset Stour. It was a swim that had somehow fallen off my itinerary, despite having swum all over the south-west at various times in the previous two years.

It had been almost six weeks since my last proper solo attempt, without a support vehicle or someone holding the towels: the failure to as much as get into the water of the Medway. And while I did feel unsure about heading out alone, I made sure to imbue myself with that sense of feeling the water as I left town, listening to a new swimming playlist I'd made, getting myself ready for a languid dip in the autumn sunshine. Hope shot me through me as the fiddle of 'Swimming Song' came through my headphones. Hearing it was almost as good as sliding into the current on a hot day.

This wasn't a swim that I had given too much thought to, but I could feel my predecessor guiding me now more than ever, pushing me on to see the country as he had, to swim its rivers and to find joy and happiness in the water and all the other things that it had afforded me since I had started following him.

There was a last whiff of summer blowing in off the harbour as the train departed Poole and I walked through town to the bus station. The place smelt of salt and boat fuel and I felt at peace as I took a seat on the top deck and watched the coastline recede.

I had plotted a route to Blandford St Mary, following a footpath through the woods and into the grounds of Bryanston School, where I could drop into the Stour unnoticed. From my high seat on the bus, I could see the wide river meandering away towards the sea, and felt ready to feel its force behind me further upstream. Families clung to the verges of the A road, filling Tupperware with the last of the season's blackberries. All was well in the West Country.

On foot, I followed a wide road up towards the little village of Bryanston, frogs flattened and baked into the tarmac. Conkers showered down from crisp, brown horse chestnuts, their unpredictable 'thunk' making me jump and stick my hands above my head for protection.

After getting lost in the grounds of this fancy private school, I dropped down through a dense wood, carpeted with the first fallen leaves of autumn, and emerged onto a private road. A group of workmen were busy talking while a pneumatic drill idled on the ground, ready to make an almighty racket. The path here swung back up into the trees, but I crossed the road and darted down towards the banks of the Stour, sending mud, bracken and pebbles skittering down to the water's edge.

This was a very different river to the one I had seen from the bus and the one which Roger had swum in by the school's boat sheds, which sat further downstream. It moved at a ponderous rate and was narrow too, reminding me of the secluded spot on the Wensum where Tim, Molly and I had swum at the start of the spring. Two fallen trees marked out a 200-metre stretch, ideal for swimming.

I was hidden from the workmen, so stripped off and slipped in down the bank, my feet crashing through the surface and landing hard on the shallow, stony surface. Everything was in shade here and the river was a good few degrees colder than Hampstead mixed pond. I hadn't put my wetsuit on, so made sure I didn't dawdle, wading into the middle and then swimming briskly up and down this natural lido.

I thought of the sharp nip of the Blandford Bomber, the blackfly which was unique to these parts and which Roger had come here looking for. My predecessor seemed obsessed with this little creature but hadn't come across it and, thankfully, neither had I. I didn't much fancy a nasty insect bite on my chin.

I swam a few lengths and felt the strong push of the current against my chest as I stroked my way upstream. Roger said he didn't detect a current on the Stour, but almost twenty years on there was most definitely one to contend with.

Back in Blandford St Mary, I sat beside the Stour as it widened into the village under a long stone bridge, its water covered in blanket weed. This hadn't been the most memorable of Roger's swims, but it had been one of the most instructive. It reminded me that I could be bold and do this by myself. This final stretch was set to be one I'd have to tackle largely on my own, and I was beginning to feel fearless.

I had swum in nearly all of Roger's chosen spots in the capital: Highgate men's pond, the Oasis, the private pool at the RAC on Pall Mall, the sauna and steam at Ironmonger Row, Marshall Street Baths and my first ever *Waterlog* swim, Tooting Bec Lido. But there was one which still eluded me.

Berthold Lubetkin's Highpoint apartment complex in Highgate has its own heated outdoor pool, tucked away in the corner of its neatly manicured gardens. I had been trying to manoeuvre my way into this private water ever since I'd first set out on this journey, but my attempts had proven fruitless. I needed a resident to let me in and I was struggling to find a willing sponsor.

My luck turned after I got back from Bryanston, when I found a contact for the building's residents' association. After some toing and froing I was put in touch with Lucy, who lived on the fourth floor and was willing to indulge my whim.

When I explained about my *Waterlog* mission, it transpired that she was the same Lucy who had swum with Roger at Highpoint after moving there from Walberswick. Not only would this be a chance to swim in a place I thought I'd never get to, it would also be a good opportunity to get the inside line about Roger's original adventure from someone who'd been there.

As it turned out, my timing was fortuitous. Lucy emailed to say that the only date which both of us could do happened to be the last day of the year that the pool would be open. At the end of September the heating was switched off and the pool left to lie dormant during autumn and winter.

It was a typical smudgy London morning when I walked up North Hill from Highgate Tube station and was shown into the most stunning art deco lobby. An open lift shaft soared away to the top floor, and I entered the cage feeling like James Bond in *Diamonds Are Forever*. I loved how this journey had sent me to so many strange and different places, Roger's taste once again proving first rate.

I emerged on the fourth floor to be greeted by a pair of double doors being swung open, a lady emerging and proffering her hand. This was Lucy. Fit and healthy with luxuriant grey hair, I could imagine her being exactly the kind of swimmer Roger had described. Someone who thought nothing of striking out across the high waves off the Suffolk coast, as he described her in *Waterlog*, and powering on without a care in the world.

Lucy showed me in and made tea as I stared out into the garden, the pool a tiny dash of blue far below. Lubetkin was clearly a fan of natural light. The windows curved around the corner of the building, making the room bright and airy despite the autumn gloom outside.

Lucy explained that she used the pool every day, and had done so since moving down to London in the late nineties. I couldn't help but ask her what she thought of *Waterlog*, especially as she was the first of Roger's cohorts I had met.

'Well, it's a vanity project, isn't it?'

I slurped my tea and fixed my gaze on the carpet.

'Oh,' I said. 'Well, I shan't quote you on that. I'll make sure that's off the record.'

'No, that's quite OK,' she replied. 'That's not to say your project is vain.'

We maintained a studied silence before switching to small talk of other things. Work, books, art deco buildings. I gradually brought up swimming again. Lucy told me about how much she loved swimming far out to sea, feeling the swell lift her up off the coast of Suffolk. I explained that I never had the nerve for such an approach and preferred getting buffeted by the white water, as I had done at Walberswick almost a year earlier.

Silence fell and I drained the last of my now lukewarm brew and asked if I could take a dip. Lucy had to accompany me, as non-residents weren't allowed to swim alone. The rain began falling in mizzly waves as we walked across the gardens and through a locked gate, there to keep out any interlopers.

Herbaceous borders and shrubs kept the pool hidden until the last possible second, when it appeared like a summery blue dream on this most miserable of London lunchtimes. Short, narrow and just twenty metres long, it was the kind of pool I dreamt of having all to myself, a trade-up on a grimy indoor bath if ever there was one.

Lucy pointed me to the neat, whitewashed changing block at the far end of the water while she parked herself under a yew tree with her book, instructing me to take my time.

The flagstones were cold and slippery as I emerged in my shorts and goggles and slipped in. The rain was splashing off the surface, and I wasted no time in powering away into a fast front crawl to warm up. As ever, swimming in the rain was far preferable to standing in it, and I fell into a reverie as length after length elapsed, falling back on the deep-breathing skills I'd picked up in yoga class.

Occasionally I caught a glimpse of Lucy as I turned to breathe, ensconced in her book and unperturbed by the intensifying downpour. My mind turned to all the other London swims I had enjoyed on my journey and how each one was so different. Swimming in a heated private pool on a wet September afternoon was very far removed from marking out my own laps in the icy water of Highgate men's pond, just down the road from here, on a cold March morning.

It also reminded me just how much London outdoor swimming had changed since Roger's visit to Lucy's home. The reopening of Brockwell Lido, the rebirth of Marshall Street Baths, even a monthly 'swim marathon' which started in Hampstead Ponds and worked its way across the capital via the Serpentine to finish at Tooting Bec, were all evidence of this happy development. Swimming outside was now something of a mainstream concern, albeit one that many thought you required a large dose of insanity to enjoy. Attitudes had changed, even if this private corner of Highgate appeared to have stayed very much the same.

I pushed myself out and walked back to my bag, changing fast in order not to put Lucy out any more than I already had. The rain had let up somewhat as I emerged, and she walked me to the main building, taking the spiral staircase around the lift shaft and back into that magnificent lobby once again. We exchanged goodbyes and I tried not to think about our awkward conversation. Vanity project or not, Roger's journey was now mine. Rather than ponder and worry about our chat, as I might once have done, I focused instead on the delightful surroundings, the perfect water and the glow it had given me despite the autumn chill.

My running shoes were already full of dewy water as I untied their laces, took off my shorts in full view of the southbound platform of Waterbeach station and struggled into a pair of trousers. The path ahead was a mess of off-green stinging nettles and tall grass, soaked from the previous night's rain and the morning's mist.

I had brought my bike back to the Cambridgeshire Fens, fifteen months after my first visit here, when I had swum alone in the River Lark. But the path I had chosen on the map to get from high, isolated Waterbeach to the banks of the Cam was overgrown and impassable on two wheels. It was mild, and I cursed and sweated as I pushed my bike on through the mud and wet, my thin trainers acting like a sponge, my sopping socks making me miserable. Just like when I had come here before, I felt like an insignificant brushstroke under the vast, grey canvas of a sky.

Cycling was bumpy and tough going once I finally reached the river, the towpath grassy and awkward to ride on. Despite being the last day of September, the sun was beginning to burn off the low cloud and send the temperature soaring. I began to glow red as I struggled against the difficult terrain, my clothes sticky, my skin calling out for a proper swim, minus the wetsuit. It was going to get its wish. The neoprene was stashed in my wardrobe back in south London.

My destination was a triangular pool where Burwell Lode and Reach Lode met on their way to the Cam before going on into the Great Ouse and away into the Wash. I wasn't going eel hunting like Roger had done on his trip here, but those slippery characters preyed on my mind as I thought about the day's swimming. I remembered catching one while out fishing as a teenager, its razor-sharp teeth and slithering body wrapping itself around my line as a friend and I tried to set it free. The thought of one latching on to one of my toes, or worse, sent a shudder up my spine as I continued juddering along the high path, the Fens opening out into a hazy horizon to the east.

Crossing a drained lock, I arrived in the village of Upware, taking a right turn down the long, straight path along the side of Reach Lode. This narrow, straight drainage channel looked dark and tempting as my bike skidded through old tyre tracks. I hopped off and began to push it instead, keeping a keen eye out for the pool.

I passed the turn-off for Wicken Lode and continued on for another half a mile before the river split, Burwell Lode flowing in. The pool sat at its confluence, reachable only to those willing to swim there.

I found an opening between the reeds and looked around to see if anyone would see if I dropped my kecks and got changed without the cover of a towel. The closest person was a farmer in a tractor, ploughing a field about a mile distant, gulls in his wake. The only other spectators were a bunch of cawing ravens. I was safe.

I strode in and immediately lost my feet in deep, silky mud. It clouded around me, sending up an almighty sulphuric stink as I ducked my shoulders under and swam fast to the far bank, a distance of no more than twenty feet. I scrambled out, grabbing at tall grass as cut reeds scratched at my legs beneath the surface. I remembered that eel I'd caught all those years before and pulled myself clear, legs coated in black mud, and took another two strides before sinking into the vast pool.

It was much bigger than I had expected, perhaps a hundred metres across. Very few people would have come to these waters, and it felt isolated, with a delicious cold edge. I made sure not to swim too far into the middle, aware that I was alone and far away from anyone. By now it was really warm, the sun high and doing a last impression of summer. I dropped my feet and found it deep, far more than the five feet Roger claimed. I kicked in furious fashion to stay afloat and felt the coolness of the water against my chest and arms, the sign that it was time to think about getting back to my clothes. There was Reach Lode to renegotiate after all.

I sunbathed by my bike, eating sandwiches and keeping a watchful eye on an armada of swans and their young heading downstream. They stopped and took a long look at the detritus of my lunch – orange peel, crumb-filled cereal bar wrappers and empty foil – before heading off to terrorise other river-goers.

Roger's swim here was a long one. After taking in the pool he had headed along Reach Lode and turned down Wicken Lode and on to the crystal-clear New River, a distance, by my calculation, of some two and a half kilometres, one and a half miles in old money. I could hardly swim that distance in an indoor pool, let alone in a cold Fenland river in autumn. How he had managed it on a May morning remained a source of fascination to me. As I'd already established, my swimming stamina was nowhere near as impressive as his, so I got back on the bike and rode around to the bridge which led over Reach Lode and away up Wicken Lode. Riding felt less like hard work than battling the cold water. I already knew how it felt on my skin, and that was enough for me.

The water did indeed look clearer here, just as Roger had said, and I gave plenty of thought to putting on my wet, muddy shorts and going for another dip. But as I pedalled on I came across the towering bird hide of Wicken Fen Nature Reserve, keen birders waving at me as I cycled past. Roger had managed to avoid the gaze of avid twitchers by hiding in the reeds on his swim here, and there was no way I was going to hop in with an audience. Instead, I satisfied myself with a ride along this winding, beautiful river, where the English summer was having a final hurrah. The path opened out and walkers and barge-dwellers shouted hello as I pushed on. I felt a warm sense of elation on top of the burn of my adrenalin rush from the earlier swim, of Roger's journey once again giving me memories to treasure.

I parked my bike behind a bench where Wicken Lode and the New River met. It was here that Roger had clambered out and walked back to his things, hidden deep in a reed bed. I closed my eyes and dozed for a few minutes, the reeds singing. I opened them and caught sight of a kestrel directly overhead, head still, wings flapping at speed. I stared at it for what felt like minutes before it swooped towards the ground and flew up high once more, this time further upstream. I put on my helmet, straddled my bike and set course for Ely.

CHAPTER NINE

October

~~~

Jaywick Sands, Essex – River Doe,
Suffolk – Heveningham Hall, Suffolk

After my Fenland adventure, I decided to stay focused on East Anglia, heading to the Essex coast. Jaywick and neighbouring Clacton were in the grip of election fever, a by-election having been triggered by the local Conservative MP, Douglas Carswell, resigning and switching allegiance to UKIP. It was polling day, and Carswell's sheepish, lopsided grin loomed up on the side of a bus as we arrived into town, the nation's media already setting up camp by the seafront and awaiting the verbose party leader's arrival.

Jaywick had been in the headlines for weeks and I wanted to come at this critical time to see it for myself. Every news report and article was filled with doom and gloom. The one time self-sufficient seaside town was now the most deprived place in England according to the Office for National Statistics, ripe pickings for those preaching an anti-immigration message.

That image jarred with everything Roger says about Jaywick in *Waterlog*. He comes across as a hopeless romantic as he reminisces about his first holidays here in the late 1940s. Even though what he saw was rundown and tired, he found joy in the unpaved roads, the jaunty names of the chalets and the 'defiantly anachronistic' spirit of the place.

I had cadged a lift off my parents, sitting in the back of their Volkswagen as if the past twenty-five years had never happened. They had been keen to come on one of my *Waterlog* swims and were particularly curious about Jaywick because, like Roger, this was the first place my mum saw the seaside. My great-granddad owned a static home which he kept at the Martello Caravan Park and my uncle Dave had told me more than once about going to the arcade and hearing 'Whiter Shade of Pale' by Procol Harum for the first time. It seemed like an epochal moment for him.

We pulled up into a potholed car park where the last remnants of a car boot sale were being packed up. Three men sat in the front seat of a blue transit van, reading the paper and blowing cigarette smoke out of the windows. There was a very real sense of being at the end of the world here, and not in the same way as on Bryher. It felt like a place that the world had forgotten and left to its own devices. A dead end rather than a destination.

We passed a polling station, a nervous-looking Labour supporter tugging on a cigarette and fingering his rosette as if trying to put off the inevitability of defeat. Young families pushed prams along the water-logged promenade, the beach hidden from view by a high concrete wall. The chalets here were either dilapidated beyond repair or smart and tidy to a fault. There didn't seem to be much in between. It may have been forgotten by the rest of the country, but that wasn't to say Jaywick wasn't still proud.

My dad and I scaled the sea wall and walked along the low dunes, the grey waves smashing into the beach away to our left. Dad pulled a cap out from his coat pocket and tugged it onto his bald head. Far out to sea, the turbines of an offshore wind farm twirled in the face of the North Sea's breezy assault. There was no one swimming, just the odd dog walker hunkered deep inside a windproof coat.

We reached the far end of the beach, where large riprap boulders protected the coast north towards Clacton from being inundated by the sea. I didn't think it possible, but the North Sea here felt wilder than further up the coast in Suffolk and Norfolk, more akin to Bamburgh. Even if I managed to get past the initial white-tipped waves, settling into anything like a swimming rhythm was going to be impossible.

The beach arced away to the south and offered a marginally more sheltered place to enjoy a quick dip. Despite it now being October, I had left the neoprene at home again. It was a sunny day, even if some encroaching grey cloud began to spit its contents over us as I slung my bag down and began to get changed. Dad held my clothes while my mum, her tiny five-foot frame wrapped up in a purple down coat, took pictures on her iPad. It was great to be spending time with my folks.

By now the rain was starting to come down more heavily, so I ran in and let the waves take me. Either the chill of autumn hadn't yet reached this stretch of Essex coastline or I was getting used to cold water, but there was no breathless punch, just the cold tingle of salt water.

This was my first time in the North Sea since visiting Bamburgh and I enjoyed its unpredictable nature, the waves rearing up from all directions and the fact that if I kept my head low and looked out to sea, it felt like I was way out by the Dogger Bank rather than twenty feet from dry land, a towel and a flask of hot chocolate.

I stayed in for longer than expected and emerged red, Mum fussing around me as I got dressed. She fretted about hypothermia and the need for me to get somewhere warm, but all I wanted was to stand for a few moments and enjoy the afterglow of the swim. I looked around the coast to the old Martello tower and realised that Jaywick was forever in a time warp, its otherness drawing in anyone who came here without preconceptions, or with a willingness to have them busted.

We took a short walk around to the caravan site. We crossed a deep ditch which my mum said led all the way around to nearby St Osyth. In the 1960s, the campsite used to put on horse rides for holidaying kids, taking them around this now overgrown route and back, an adventure that still held strong memories fifty years on.

The site was much as Mum remembered it. The shop in the same place, the caravans in neat rows and beautifully kept. The only difference was a large 'fun pool' at the centre of the park. Swimming in the sea probably wasn't high on the agenda of those coming here with children in the twenty-first century. It was a shame, but I could see why. The North Sea is unforgiving and does not allow for casual frolicking in the shallows.

We walked back along the promenade, across Sunbeam Avenue, the large windows of the wooden chalets affording huge views out to sea. It was good to be disabused of any notions of decay about this place and share in some happy family memories too.

In Clacton, we ate egg and chips by the pier, the sea churned up and smashing into the high wall at the back of the beach. The purple and yellow bunting was out in force in preparation for the inevitable success of UKIP that evening. But my swim had shown me that this town and area were far more than a political football. The Essex coast had a proud history that was more important than any political ideology, its sea providing happiness even if it looked bleak on the surface.

My dwindling list of Roger's swims still contained a few more dips in East Anglia, all drawn from the final chapter of *Waterlog*. These last efforts of my predecessor traced 'a sort of ley line' from his farmhouse moat in Mellis to the sea at Walberswick, but having already swum in the latter, and with other swims further afield to attempt too, I decided to pick off the remaining rivers and lakes one by one, in a more haphazard re-creation.

A week after visiting Jaywick I took the train to Diss and met Luke, with whom I'd swum at Mendham Mill the previous summer. I rarely saw Luke without Tim and Molly, despite us having been friends for far longer, since our earliest days at university. With two kids and a life as a touring performance poet he was always busy, so to catch him like this was as much a treat as going for a swim in this pretty corner of England. It was damp and cool as we drove along country lanes with the windows down, Luke singing along to his favourite Pete Doherty tracks as we headed east from where Roger had once lived at Mellis, towards the village of Eye.

Roger had undertaken this final journey of his in late September, so I had a rough idea of what to expect from our impending paddle. We were heading for the Abbey Bridge, a hump-backed affair which traverses the River Dove on the eastern side of this pretty village. Roger talks of being shocked into going in by the sight of two duelling kingfishers and shocked into getting out by the sheer cold. But despite the nip of the water, the picture he paints is of a bucolic swimming hole, frayed ropes hanging from a Scots pine, mist rising as he clambered out and rode his bike on towards the sea.

Unfortunately for Luke and me, this didn't quite tally with the view we were greeted with as we stared over the parapet and into the Dove. The water was covered with a film of scum, while Fruit Shoot bottles bobbed in the reeds. These were, of course, temporary abominations, but I cursed Roger's sometimes one-eyed view of the countryside. I'd seen it in the filthy mess I'd found along the River Lark and his failure to mention that Beezley Falls was a paying attraction. To me it felt like a need to see Arcadia where sometimes riverbanks could be more like Perfidious Albion.

It would be fair to say that over two years of trailing Roger had left me sometimes cynical and frustrated, as well as feeling elated and relaxed. As I slung my leg over the rusting fence and onto the steep conglomerate bank, I had to remind myself that *Waterlog* was not a guidebook and that I had turned it into one for my own purposes. That I was seeing the countryside from my point of view, and Roger had seen it from his.

Things did at least look more promising at the water's edge. It was raining, but we were able to duck under the arch of the bridge and get changed in the dry. The Dove slipped over a low wall and ruffled around the pool we had seen from the road. I could imagine it being the ideal swimming spot on a warmer day.

Luke was wavering about getting in, and I can't say I blamed him. He only had a pair of very snug swimming trunks for protection, while I had brought the full works with me: wetsuit, cap, boots, gloves. I walked out into the wet afternoon and dangled my feet over the edge. I could feel the cold of the Dove trying to bite at my toes through the outer layer of rubber.

'Is it jumpable?' asked Luke, holding his bare arms to his chest as he stood behind me.

I slipped deeper and found myself standing waist deep.

'That's a no, then,' he said, as he took a step back and assessed his options.

I swam into the fast eddying pool, keeping my head above water. Luke followed, huffing as he swam a cursory few strokes and then scurried out, punching the air as if he'd just won an Olympic race.

I stayed in for a few minutes longer. The frog's-eye view of the Dove was pleasant, if not delightful. If you ignored the floating fizzy drink bottles and discarded crisp packets, not to mention the rumbling of cars passing over the bridge, it was a handy place for anyone desperate for an outdoor swim.

Desperation was fast becoming the watchword of this adventure. I really wanted to get the trip done and dusted before swimming outside began to resemble a military operation when it came to getting changed. That or taking swims so short they could only really be classified as ice baths.

We left the bridge behind and spent a pleasant afternoon driving about the Suffolk borders, reminiscing about old times, talking about how my journey had gone, his plans for his next show, based on coming of age at university. It was nice to know that over a decade since we had graduated we were all doing well, all living lives that could be considered a success. Swimming had helped me see that I didn't need to judge myself through the prism of work. I was still doing many of the same jobs I always had, but realised that they did not define me and were nothing to be embarrassed about. To spend time with an old friend meant a lot at that moment. I was proud of him and him me. We picked up Luke's kids from school and went and ate fish and chips in Diss, sitting opposite the town's Corn Hall, a happy foursome. Roger's bucolic notions about the River Dove couldn't have been further from my mind.

*   *   *

A few days after our Abbey Bridge swim, I returned to Suffolk for a very different kind of dip. It had been a while since I had stretched my arms in any kind of lake, let alone one which formed the centrepiece of a Capability Brown-designed garden.

Heveningham Hall, a few miles from the town of Halesworth, was where I would be doing just that. I had lugged my bike up from London and followed the rolling road which Roger had cycled along on his final ley-line adventure, although I was going in the opposite direction.

I had been given permission by the stately home's owners to 'enjoy' the water and had arranged to meet Graham, the estate manager, on a bridge which crossed the lake close to the road. At the designated spot, about a hundred metres from the road, I spotted a vintage Land Rover. The gravel track which led up to the bridge was blocked by a scalable fence, over which I heaved my bike, before gracelessly chucking myself over.

As I approached the bridge I shouted a quick hello.

'Graham? Nice to meet you.'

'Er, no, I'm Lynton. Can I help?' replied the man in front of me. Clad in a navy jumper, cream trousers and tassled loafers, he didn't look much like an estate manager who spent every hour outdoors.

I explained that I had agreed to meet Graham here, who I was and what I wanted on his land. Lynton – the general manager, as it turned out – relaxed and laughed as I told him about my *Waterlog* journey and how Roger had swum here as the gardens were finally being finished to Brown's designs, two hundred years after he had first laid them out. The home and gardens had fallen into disrepair under its previous owners and the current residents had spent a great deal of money to bring it back to its present condition. The spoil from the lakes, which had been re-excavated in the late 1990s, now formed a high hill on the far side of the lake, where mature trees were glowing orange in the late October light.

Lynton enthused about the water in the lake.

'It's very clear. In the summer people chuck themselves in off this bridge. Mind you, no one swims at this time of year.'

Graham soon arrived and Lynton drove off back towards the stately pile, which peeped just above the trees. I told Graham I'd be swimming in a wetsuit, which he claimed was cheating. I used Roger's defence that an otter never feels the water on its skin, its fur acting like natural neoprene. He laughed and left me to it.

Rubbered up, I made my way down below the bridge and sent a cautious foot towards the water. I plopped in and stood waist deep, both my boots buried deep in the mud on the lake's bed. The swim from the bridge to the eastern end of the lake by the village of Walpole was about half a mile, a manageable distance in a pool or lido, but much harder in autumn-cooled water with weeds poking above the surface.

I set off slowly, finding the same 'submerged skyscrapers' which Roger had struggled through on his swim here. They made settling into any kind of rhythm almost impossible, although as I stared down into the deep I could see them swaying gently, the weak light catching their bright green tendrils as I stroked past them.

This was the first serious bit of open-water swimming I had done since Henleaze, and it turned out that my directional skills, so good on dry land, were utterly hopeless in the water. I swam front crawl, zigzagging from bank to bank, the far end never appearing any closer whenever I swung my head forward to catch my breath.

Before he left me, Graham said that when they excavated the lake twenty years ago it had begun to fill up thanks to the springs which dotted its bed. I could well believe it. My head was throbbing with the cold and my eyes bulged every time I stuck my head under.

Eventually I opted for Roger's favoured head-out breaststroke, which at least allowed me to swim in something approaching a straight line. Soon I was among the thick reed bed in the shallows, where I stuck down a foot to be greeted by an awful stench rising up from the deep. My gloved hands grabbed at the sharp reeds and I dragged myself out, my conquest of Heveningham Hall's lake complete.

Despite being fully kitted out, I felt that happy glow normally reserved for the moments after a 'skin swim' and strolled back towards the bridge with a grin on my face, arms swinging, my silicone cap whipped off to allow the cool breeze to dry my hair. Up ahead I fancied I saw Roger saddling up and heading east towards Bulcamp Marshes, his next stop, and where I planned to go in a few weeks after some other *Waterlog* assignments a bit further afield.

I stuffed my wet things back into my rucksack and ate the by now pancake-flat sandwiches Keeley had made me for the trip, watching over the lake as it settled back to normal following my intrusion. Farm vehicles buzzed around behind me, but I lay back and zoned out, taking a few moments to meditate on this strange swim before getting back on the bike.

I felt an enormous sense of calm, the same way I'd felt after 'going big' at Hell Gill. This was a proper, lengthy effort and I'd survived it unscathed. Back in Halesworth I drank tea and ate cake sitting outside in the last of the day's sun, before perusing the shelves of the local bookshop. *Waterlog* sat proudly in the travel section. I gave the uncracked spine a quick nod.

'Not many left now, Roger,' I thought. 'Not many left now.'

CHAPTER TEN

November

~~~

River Isle, Somerset – Hambridge, Somerset –
Bulcamp Marshes, Suffolk – The Rhinnogs, Wales

I could hear the River Isle deep down to my left, hidden behind a steep, thick wall of nettles. Up ahead the sound of the A303 grew louder with every step. After accompanying me on my ill-fated Malvern swim, Tom had joined me in Somerset for a dual dip close to where his parents live on the edge of the Levels. And as we tramped through wet grass along a beaten-down footpath, it appeared I had once again sold him a dud.

'Are you sure this is right?' he asked, the roar of an HGV drowning his voice out as I caught a glance of the brown, murky river in a break in the stingers.

I consulted the map and then read Roger's description of his visit to this supposedly remote West Country river:

'In a wild stretch of the River Isle, a mile upstream from Ilford bridge, I stumbled on the perfect swimming hole. It was marked as a fishing spot by a little wooden square pegged in the bank.'

Neither of us could see a wooden square pegged into the bank or anything approaching a 'sudden pool ten feet wide'. In fact, the only thing we really noticed, aside from our feet getting damp, was the sound of the arterial road cutting a swathe through the countryside. A road which Roger makes no mention of.

I scanned the OS map again. We had definitely come upstream from Ilford bridge, and were looking at a stretch of river ahead of a small copse, the shade from which Roger surmised was the cause of the water's iciness.

After finding the River Dove not to be quite up to my predecessor's billing, I found this situation infuriating. The A303 was not a new phenomenon. It was once a key route through ancient Wessex and it's been a main road since 1933. It was here in the late 1990s; it's just that Roger didn't mention it.

Once again I had to remind myself that I wasn't dealing with a guide-book. But such an omission left me wondering about his motivations. Did he want to present England as a pastoral idyll whenever a city was miles away? Because that really wasn't the case. Then again, was it my fault for projecting my own visions of a place onto the map without having been there?

I tried to shut out the noise as I ducked into the woods and found a suitable place where I could get in easily. Tom was staying on dry land, wrapped up in a navy Berghaus waterproof with a woolly hat to match, and I was getting fully togged up again, the cold of November not conducive to spending a decent amount of time exploring what I had to admit, now I stood above it, was a wild river, even if it was one that flowed next to one of the UK's busiest roads.

I hung my clothes on a handy alder, its small branches ideal for my T-shirt, jumper and jeans. I turned from my makeshift wardrobe and made tentative steps into the river. It was waist deep and fast moving, shelving quickly and leaving me no choice but to swim against the current. The traffic noise was drowned out by the gurgling sound of the water rushing over a gravel beach about a hundred metres upstream. I swam hard and struck shallow ground, half wading, half crawling my way through the brownness before striding out at this handy rest point.

This could conceivably have been Roger's chosen spot. There was a deep pool and a gravel rill, as he described, although the fishing spot was long gone. The beach was carpeted in crisp brown leaves, the trees still clinging to the last of their adornments despite the attentions of a fast-moving wind.

I stepped back in and allowed myself to be carried downstream to my clothes, the wetsuit keeping me buoyant. I repeated the process, the back and forth reminding me of the natural flume I'd enjoyed on the River Bure at John's Water way back at the start of the year. It was a similarly grey day, although that delightful spot had at least been untroubled by the rumble of traffic.

With the Isle still clinging to my beard, Tom and I drove to nearby Hambridge and a date with a drain. If we had been here eight months earlier, we would have been underwater. The Somerset Levels had taken an absolute battering and been flooded out during the same heavy storms which had destroyed the boardwalks at Burnham in Norfolk, leading to complaints about the Environment Agency failing to adequately dredge the county's rivers.

It wasn't quite at storm levels, but the hefty showers which had streaked across Somerset overnight had left the place sodden. Roads were covered in huge puddles and footpaths were doing their best impressions of bogs. As Roger says, 'water is everywhere' across this landscape.

That was certainly true along the disused Westport canal, now used as drainage and irrigation for the surrounding farm fields. The path was drenched and so were we as a sudden downpour found us pulling hoods from Velcro pouches and standing stock still until it passed.

Roger swam here in a channel which runs parallel to the old canal. The path turned off towards it at right angles, but a low-slung electric fence blocked our way. Undeterred, we busted out our best commando rolls, caking our trousers in thick mud before vaulting a rickety stile and catching the attention of a herd of cattle in the next field.

Although Roger's drain was marked in light blue on the map, on reaching it we found it to be little more than a glorified ditch. If I'd tried to swim in it I'd have been putting in some serious training for the world bog-snorkelling championships rather than enjoying an outdoor swim.

Instead, I headed back to the canal. After my adventures in the Leeds to Liverpool canal at Gargrave, this dip held no fear. I put on the wetsuit and squelched in. The channel was no more than four feet deep and coated on both sides in blue-green algae. I kept my head high and mouth shut as I swam towards a distant bridge.

I thought back to the Fenland channels I had swum in. Those were clean and clear, but with no outlet or stream to flow into and plenty of rainwater, this was a filthy alternative. The low scudding clouds and spots of rain made the juxtaposition even sharper.

Despite this being a scruffy swim, it felt good to have got in. I realised as I pulled myself out and changed in the wet of a Somerset afternoon that I could so easily have chosen to do Roger's most picturesque swims at Porthcurno, Cowside Beck, Jura, and left out these less attractive dips altogether. But as with anything in life, I needed something to throw that beauty into sharp relief, to accept that it was all about balance. If anything, I was now getting quite an affinity for drainage channels and canals. That sense of ticking boxes, of this being a chore, had been confined to the past, even if I was still religiously colouring my spreadsheet green with every swim completed. I was finding pleasure in every swim. Nothing held any fear. The whole trip was becoming ever more ludicrous and enjoyable with each dip.

The smell of irrigation ditch still deep in my nostrils, I returned to Suffolk once more, picking out another swim from Roger's last adventure across his home county. I couldn't help asking myself why I hadn't done the five swims Roger tackled from Mellis to Walberswick in one go, rather than choosing to do them one at a time. The likelihood is, though, I would have been flat on my back after the first two swims with a further three to go. This apparently little journey at the end of *Waterlog* was Roger's wider trip in miniature. A Herculean feat completed in short order.

I arrived at Blythburgh with Tim on a bright, cold autumn afternoon, Bulcamp Marshes looking resplendent as we turned down the road towards Walberswick and parked up in a sandy lay-by. Guttural squeals from the nearby pig farm punctured the calm. I made a mental note to stay away from bacon in future as we walked through the shade of Scots pines and out onto a path which tracked along the edge of the rushes, the water far off and virtually inaccessible to all but the most intrepid and foolhardy of swimmers.

Roger had come here immediately after tackling the long sweep of the lake at Heveningham Hall, arriving to catch high tide and swim in just a pair of shorts, claiming 'there was no need for a wetsuit' owing to the brackish tide being warmed up by the mud over which it flowed. He'd been here in September, and although I found it hard to believe these claims in the cool of November, I knew deep down that I couldn't, in all conscience, get in wearing the wetsuit with the sun beating down as it was.

After hacking through the trees and tramping across flattened reeds, Tim and I emerged on a grassy peninsula which stuck sharply out into the marshes, narrowing to a metre-wide point about a hundred metres from the woods. I splashed my hand into the water and kept any thoughts of the cold to myself. Having been cosseted by neoprene in Somerset and at Heveningham, getting in and staying in was going to be a tall order.

Despite the low sun and total lack of cloud, it was a nippy afternoon. A light breeze ruffled the water as I began to pull off my clothes. I tugged on boots and gloves for some cursory protection as Tim watched behind me. We'd decided to go in one by one. I stepped off the bank into a foot of dark water, Roger's warnings about submerged wooden posts dotted across the marshes fresh in my mind. I could see one just a few feet away. I grasped at the water around me and felt nothing except for the cold creeping up my hands and along my arms. The mud beneath my feet was slippery rather than deep, a pleasant change after the gloop of the Fens and Somerset Levels. I let myself slide a few feet before dropping in.

I got the immediate sense of being an idiot for having thought I could trust Roger when he said the brackish water here was warm. Of course it was, to a man who swam in a moat opposite his farmhouse every day, but not to someone who'd swum in a wetsuit consistently for the previous two months. I tried to keep going, but after a minute the internal screams grew so loud that I stood up, knee deep and turned back to see Tim shaking his head in disappointment.

'Just you wait, pal,' was my immediate thought as I dropped my shoulders back under and swam the final few feet to dry land.

I handed Tim my gloves and boots and enjoyed the wince on his face as he donned them and made for the water. His traditional hollering and hooting echoed out over the peaceful marsh. Doubtless even the pigs would have paused when they heard his hearty swearing, before taking up their squealing again.

To be fair to Tim, he waded out a lot further than me before sinking under, giving a thumbs up as I shouted warnings about hidden posts beneath the still water. But soon he was back next to me, shivering and struggling to get dry.

This was not the dreamy re-creation I had expected, although the surroundings were beautiful, especially on such a perfect autumn day. But it was handy to remember that despite having tracked Roger all over the country for more than two years, I still hadn't developed his capacity for long, cold-water swims. My stamina was still lacking, and nothing was going to change that now.

The end of my *Waterlog* trip was now well within reach. It had taken me two and a half years to do what Roger had managed in roughly eight months.

But before I could nose my bike up the track to Walnut Tree Farm from Mellis Common and slip quietly into my predecessor's hallowed moat for the final swim of this long journey, I needed to go west. Far west, through the English borderlands and to the Rhinnog mountains of North Wales.

This rather gaping miss from my itinerary had hung over me all summer. Those vertiginous cwms and burbling streams were only ever going to be welcoming to naked skin on the sticky afternoons of June, July and August, and I had merrily spent that time skipping around

Dartmoor, criss-crossing the West Country and pottering around Yorkshire on Roger's trail. Whenever I had remembered the need to bathe in those Welsh waters I had suppressed guilty thoughts of failing to make time for them. Usually these came when I was floating on my back in a cool river or ploughing out lengths on an early-morning swim in Brockwell Lido.

Now, though, autumn was fast becoming winter, and if I left it any longer I'd either be breaking ice or waiting another six months for a modicum of warmth, my journey edging into a fourth year.

Getting to the Rhinnogs was going to be a challenge, its lower reaches miles from the nearest town of Harlech. Beyond that, the weather was going to make a long camping trip like Roger's, an unappealing schlep, one which I didn't much fancy undertaking.

Instead, I alighted on a plan to swim in Llyn Cwm Bychan, the largest of the lakes Roger visited. I started researching plans for a long solo train trip, a six-hour mission followed by the need to track down local taxis and traipse into the hills with camping and swimming kit strapped to my back.

I was in the pub one evening with Joe, Tom and James and mentioned this significant undertaking. James put his pint down, sucked the foam from his upper lip and piped up.

'I'll take you if you like.'

This was taking the rides I'd been given by friends and family to a whole other level. Usually I would take the train to a station close to the destination where they would pick me up and ferry me to my chosen swimming spot. This time, though, James, who made it abundantly clear he would not be getting in with me, was willing to drive over 200 miles for my benefit. Once again, the journey was reminding me how good my friends were to me. James was soon leaving London to move to New York, and I knew this would be a great chance for us to hang out properly before he headed off.

It was a grey day as we drove north out of London. The forecast was appalling, with showers due to sweep in from the Irish Sea. We spent the night in Chester, ready for an early-morning assault on a country my predecessor said was 'stiff with magic'.

It certainly felt mystical the next morning as we crossed the border, a thick fog clinging to the hills, low trees rearing up over the road. The occasional glow of fog lamps was the only reminder of other human life close by. Not coming here at the height of summer was beginning to look like a bigger mistake with every mile we covered.

Out west, though, on Barmouth Sands, we watched as the sun slipped through the low clouds, burning off the mist and opening out huge views to sea. We dashed up the coast towards Llanbedr, where we turned off and followed the crashing Afon Artro upstream. The river tumbled beneath old stone bridges and over huge boulders. I thought back to the rushing waters of the West Dart and began to grow itchy for water, for its cold sting on my skin.

The road narrowed, grass and gravel scattered across its high crown, turning hard away from the river before swinging high over a final hill, Llyn Cwm Bychan, below us. I could see Afon Artro sliding from its western end, skittering away to where we had just driven and on to the sea. White-tipped crests dotted its lower reaches, the wind creating unrepeatable patterns across its surface. Rain fell lightly on the windscreen.

'You're actually going to swim in that?' said James, as he stopped the car so we could take a better look.

Any excitement about getting in as we'd passed the gushing river had evaporated, quickly replaced by fear. Roger swam here on a golden summer morning, sliding in from a sheep-mown peninsula and pushing out into the depths, limbs loosening after a night under canvas. My version was going to be very different, and having been driven here all the way from London, I couldn't just baulk and turn back.

The lake appeared to shallow as we reached the campsite at its eastern shores, reeds sticking up just above its surface. It wasn't whipped up into quite the same frenzy here, the shelter of Carreg-y-saeth affording me some slight protection from being slapped about the face by angry Welsh water.

I changed into wetsuit, boots, hat and gloves in a mossy wood, the rain now tumbling fast as I threw my leg over a stone wall and lowered myself into the lake, James wrapped up in a waterproof coat and watching from beneath a red and white golf umbrella. The cold gripped at my ankles and sent a shiver through my body. It made the marshes at Blythburgh feel tropical by comparison.

I waded out, the lake's bed grassy and springy beneath my feet. I walked 200 metres towards its centre before I realised that it wasn't going to get any deeper and splashed into the fresh, freezing water. My hands were numb, but I swam on in a long line, the slopes of Carreg-y-saeth glowering up ahead.

The passages in *Waterlog* about the Rhinnogs are full of joy and energy, of bounding between one swimming hole and another, skin by turns seething and tingling. This felt very different. It was a battle to stay warm, let alone look up and enjoy the beauty and isolation of the place. I forced myself to stay in for longer, lying on my back and sinking the crown of my head until the water lapped around my ears.

Yes, there was magic here. I could feel it, as if I had been pulled to this place rather than followed a road to its shores. I imagined the water falling from the sky dropping into the narrow streams which fell fast down from the Rhinnogs, before slipping quietly into Llyn Cwm Bychan. Rather than me going in search of it, I felt it flowing towards me.

As ever, thoughts of Roger were never far away, as if he were scampering between stream and cwm away up in the hills, always in search of the next swim. I had followed him to the very edges of Britain and found his swimming holes to be largely untouched, but offering wholly different experiences to those he had encountered. No water was ever the same in any one place; everywhere was being renewed and reborn all the time.

I felt those differences keenly in Llyn Cwm Bychan, the weather throwing everything into sharp relief. I swam and waded back towards the woods cold and high, a burning sense of satisfaction that I had come to Wales at a different, less welcoming time of year, but still found water that was magical to sink into.

CHAPTER ELEVEN

April

~

Walnut Tree Farm, Suffolk

It was the kind of day that seemed inconceivable in darkest January. Hazy clouds bled at the edges of a huge sky, rising to a deep, reassuring blue. The temperature read 18.5°C on the car's dashboard. Dad and I were driving across Suffolk on the warmest day of the year so far, the first yellow sunbursts of rapeseed flecking the fields as we drew ever closer to Mellis, the moat and the final swim of this long journey.

In the nights before this trip, I had dreamt about the moat. It was long and stretched for a kilometre or more, reed beds lining its banks and a boardwalk meandering across its narrow point. Swimmers pushed themselves in wayward strokes in all directions. I stood on, watching, ready to dive in, when I rolled over and woke up.

And now we were nearly there at last. It was almost ninety minutes from my parents' home in Essex, our ride soundtracked by the squabbling of politicians on the general election trail. As we turned off the main road and trundled across Mellis Common, I had a keen sense of this being the culmination of a far longer ride, one which had started with those first tentative swims across London from Tooting Bec Lido to Highgate men's pond and gone onwards to the River Lark, across

Jura, down through Fladbury, west to Dartmoor, Cornwall and Scilly, and north to Wales and the Rhinnogs.

I had first laid plans to swim in the moat a year into the journey, but my trussed-up wrist ensured it didn't happen. It wasn't until over a year later that I once again spoke with Jasmin, who bought Walnut Tree Farm from Rufus, Roger's son and her school friend, the year after Roger passed away. We settled on a November date, but the hefty slap of a wet winter left us aiming for spring and better weather. I had passed the colder months happily, writing up earlier swims, revelling in memories of those dips, the encounters I had had, the relationships that were now bound closer thanks to my undertaking of this long journey, even the wrist break on the way to a swimming pool that had inadvertently set me on a path to finding a healthier, more rounded cure for my anxiety by seeing Mark. What had begun as a trip with a narrow focus had become something much more holistic. I had learnt that there were many ways to fix myself and keep my mind at peace. Swimming, therapy and time with friends were all of equal importance.

Now, as the temperature clicked over to 20°C and we turned up the narrow, unsealed track towards the farm, I couldn't have been happier at how things had turned out. Not only would my journey finish where Roger's had started, I'd also get to enjoy my first outdoor swim of the year in nascent summer weather. Dad was excited too. I'd spent many evenings over winter telling him about my journey and felt bad that he hadn't come on more swims with me. We'd only managed a few dips in Lyme Regis together the previous summer, even though he'd been a real help in Jaywick. When he offered to drive me to Walnut Tree Farm and swim with me, I was delighted.

I did warn him, however, that the water was not going to be warm. A couple of days before heading to Suffolk, Jasmin wrote to me: 'Our first Easter here I went swimming in the moat. It was painfully, panic-inducingly cold. Do you have a wetsuit?'

Of course I did. But this was the last place I could use it, surely. Packing that morning, I shoved the neoprene into my rucksack just in case, and covered it with other essentials: shorts, notepad, my tatty copy of *Waterlog*.

We parked up by the old barn and tumbled out of Dad's hatchback, sweaty and desperate for water. A deep bark emanated from the farmhouse. Branches and kindling were piled high over the chassis of an old baby-blue Alfa Romeo. The steps which ran alongside the outside of the barn creaked and Jasmin appeared, walking down and offering her hand to Dad and me.

'You found it OK, then?' she said, leading us along the side of the house and out onto the lawn. It glowed a verdant green, the remainder of the previous night's dew glistening on its surface where it rolled gently towards the moat.

The bark became louder as we reached the heavy old kitchen door.

'You're OK with dogs, yeah?' said Jasmin, leaving no time for a reply before Hercules, a hulking delight of a Labrador cross bounded out towards us. Jasmin grabbed his collar just in time as Dad and I knelt to ruffle his thick-set neck.

Jasmin brewed tea and collected cups onto a tray as Dad and I looked around, peering at bookshelves and running our hands over exposed, ancient beams. Herc sat on an old sofa, upright, imperious. This was very much Jasmin's home, not Roger's, and that made me happy. She had made what was once his, hers. I realised I had perhaps done something similar with *Waterlog*.

We drank tea outside on a stripped-back bench, looking out over the lawn, the moat just about visible below its banks. Unlike in my dream, it wasn't long, bordered with reeds or blessed with a boardwalk. I had known all of this anyway, but it was reassuring to see that it was every bit as simple and beautiful as Roger had described it.

Jasmin told us how she had come to live here. How she and her husband Titus used to visit as teenagers and sleep in the shepherds' huts which dotted the fields of the farm, swimming in the moat when the mood took them. She explained how they'd decided to leave London and come to this rural corner of Suffolk to bring up their children. They had converted the old barn into a workspace where Jasmin created her art and jewellery.

The loft space above was a bolthole, a bed nestled into the eaves with a view across the moat, blue tits nesting in the high branches of the trees which grew up alongside it.

I loved how Jasmin and Titus had made Walnut Tree Farm their own while staying true to the aesthetic which Roger had created when he rebuilt the place in the 1960s. There was still no central heating, and much of my predecessor's carefully collected junk could be found lying around if you looked carefully. A vintage Citroën was buried beneath a vast growth of brambles. An old bath had been pulled from a hedgerow and used for the new hot outdoor shower which Jasmin had installed under the barn's staircase as a birthday gift to Titus.

When I heard about this particular addition, my ears pricked up. Any plans I had had about slipping into the wetsuit were now shoved to the back of my mind. A hot shower after a cold swim is one of life's great pleasures, and one I was not going to turn down.

While Jasmin and Dad chatted, I stared across the lawn at the water. At the very last, I had managed to find some symmetry in this haphazard retracing of Roger's swimming journey. An idea which had come to my predecessor while working his way through countless lengths of the moat had set him off on a long trip starting here in Mellis. That same idea, which had struck such a chord within me that I had wanted to find my own way into it, was about to come full circle in the place where it had all begun. The sense of connection I had felt earlier as we pulled up the drive pulsed inside me. I stood and declared that I was going swimming.

I walked down to the edge of the moat while Dad went back to the car and returned in a pair of natty blue and white striped swimming shorts, towels under his arm, his belly pasty white. The water looked deep and inviting. There was no breeze.

I struggled out of my trousers and pulled my neoprene gloves and shoes from my bag. Jasmin laughed at these accessories and my firmly held belief that they would stave off the chill. I dipped an ungloved hand into the water and winced.

'It told you it was cold.'

'There's no way I'm putting that on, not here,' I said, pointing to the wetsuit which was poking out from the top of my rucksack.

'Oh, Roger wore wetsuits all the time. Way more than he let on, too.'

This was not the time to learn that all those icy swims of the past few years could have been offset with neoprene. That the guilt I'd felt whenever I'd pulled it on had been unnecessary.

Jasmin plunged her arm into the water and found the top of the old ladder which Roger had submerged when he first started swimming in the moat. I dropped my foot where she pointed and found the first, weed-slicked rung. I sat on the bank and felt the water quickly cool my legs. Its depth dropped to ten feet almost immediately, so there was no time to hang around and get used to it. I began a countdown from three and pushed forward on two, ploughing out a fast breaststroke as the moat lifted me up and away on my final swim.

It was cold, but delicious. I knew I would be happy and high when I scrambled out, skin tingling. I heard a splash and a huff behind me and turned to find Dad following me along the middle of the moat. He flashed me a quick grin, the dark gap of a missing molar the same colour as the water.

As he pulled himself out, having been in for a brief couple of minutes, I pushed on for the far end, where the moat grew silty and shrubs hung low over its surface. My bow wave slapped gently on the grassy bank. I looked across at the house and thought back to that very first dip in Hampstead mixed pond with Keeley, the happy mix of terror and elation as I slid forward and offered myself up to the head waters of the old River Fleet. I remembered the crushing low of not being able to swim after I had broken my wrist and the swells of anxiety and worry that swimming outdoors had helped me to begin combating in the years since I had set out on Roger's trail.

Calm settled over me as I realised that all I needed to focus on was this moment, the full expression of my long kick and the wide sweep of my arms. I turned onto my back and allowed the water to bear me up and floated, the rush of the moat's water in my ears. I smiled at the memory of Mark's words, of remembering to let myself bob along as life floated around me. I thought back to the start of my journey, the anxiety I had dealt with, the way I had worked myself into a state about not living up to the expectations I had set myself. I thought too about the worries I had about this trip ending and how I would feel when it did, and remembered another Kerouac line from *The Dharma Bums*: 'When you get to the top of the mountain, keep climbing.'

I thought back to those months when this journey felt as if it would never end, when more and more swims seemed to reveal themselves, as if Roger were daring me to keep searching his pages for more. I had realised then, for my own good, that I had had no choice but to finish.

This trip had developed into something so much more than going and swimming where my predecessor had. It was the start of a healing process, one I knew now would never end, even once I'd emerged from the water this last time. I felt pride at having come this far and excitement about what was next, whatever it was. There would be more swims, more times with friends and people I loved. There was no end, only beginnings and possibilities.

As I floated on, I thought too of all of the life in the moat. The newts and larvae buried deep beneath me. The kingfisher which Jasmin had told me was an intermittent visitor, hunting on amphibious treats. The birds which wheeled above it. The clacking great tits, whirring goldfinches, the unidentifiable chaos of birdsong which rose in my ears as I allowed my legs to fall, before I spun around and made my way back to the ladder.

But most of all I thought about Roger. How many lengths of the moat would he have had to do, to complete the mile he tried to swim each day? And what would he make of this retracing of his swimming journey? Had I done him justice? I knew that it didn't really matter, but I hoped so nonetheless.

My thoughts continued to wander off along happy tangents as I took a deep breath, closed my eyes and plunged my head under. I emerged cleansed, my hair slick and my mind quiet. I felt for the first rung of the ladder as Dad's hand reached to pull me clear.

ACKNOWLEDGEMENTS

~~~

Travelling for *Floating* was an experience that changed my life. It also reignited old friendships and sparked new ones. My eternal gratitude goes to those who drove me across the UK, often taking time out of busy schedules to indulge my swimming whims.

Thanks to Tom Sutton for his steadfast friendship, encouragement and critical scrutiny of early drafts of the text. Molly Naylor, for her kindness, spectacular driving skills and ability to get me into some less than alluring stretches of water with a swift put-down about wetsuits.

Thanks to everyone who opened up their homes and welcomed me, especially George and the gang at Fladbury, Lucy Moy-Thomas and Jasmin Rowlandson at Walnut Tree Farm.

Much love to James Holland, Joe Svetlik, Tom Bailey, Tim Clare, Joe Dunthorne, Luke Wright, Emily Kindleysides, Yanny Mac, Suz Close, Megan Quinn and Amy Liptrot for joining me in the water when it wasn't always as enticing as I made out it would be.

Thanks to my agents Georgina Capel and Rachel Conway for their good cheer and helpful guidance. To Robert Macfarlane for his encouragement and enthusiasm. To Peter Mayer, Gesche Ipsen and all at Duckworth Overlook for their help bringing the book to fruition.

Special thanks to my uncle, David Parkin. Your enthusiasm for this project's most daunting swims, planning long jaunts through western Scotland and northern England, not to mention your willingness to drop everything at a moment's notice, helped turn this whole thing from a passionate hobby into the book it is today.

To Mum and Dad, for endless love and support. To Gran, for your kindness and ability to make everything seem like a happy, hazy childhood afternoon. To Jess, Matt, Evalyn and Mabel for all of the laughter and joy you bring to my life.

This book is dedicated to the memory of my my granddads, Sonnie Minihane and Geoffrey Parkin, my grandma, Tess Minihane, and my uncle, Michael Minihane. Much loved and much missed.

Finally, and most importantly, to my wife, Keeley. For seeing me out of the door on swimming days with a flask of tea, a world-beating packed lunch and a kiss. For listening to my worries and anxieties without judgement. For making life wonderful from the moment we met.